WAS SHE STILL DEAD IN OCTOBER?

BRENDA MALY
with LAURA DALPIAZ

WAS SHE STILL DEAD IN OCTOBER?

AN ORGANIZED CRIME AND ADOPTION SCANDAL

WAS SHE STILL DEAD IN OCTOBER?
An Organized Crime and Adoption Scandal

Published by Rebel Press
Austin, TX
www.RebelPress.com

Author Photo Credit to Anna Elisabeth Wuebbles

ISBN: 978-1-64339-941-6

Printed in the United States of America

In Loving Memory of

Ksenia Bryan
Grant Corbin
Michael Kintz
Josh Ritter

DEDICATED

To the 1800 Children of Small World Adoption
Foundation of Missouri
To Ryan, Laura, and Alex — For all you gave me
And to Gracie, Emma, Addie, and Sammie —
For making our world so bright

CONTENTS

PART 1

PART 2

PART 3

PART 4

WAS SHE STILL DEAD IN OCTOBER?

PREFACE

I LONGED TO MAKE A lasting difference and make the world a better place, believing in the possibility of playing a part in something truly great. I genuinely wanted to believe, and I became a believer.

Once believing, it was easy for the trust I placed in myself and the others involved in my dream to grow and deepen. I knew in my soul we were working for a greater good. Of course, this was a righteous endeavor because all of the pieces had fallen so easily into place, as if orchestrated from above. I believed and trusted.

There were others who voiced negative thoughts and feelings about my dream-turned-mission, that of saving impoverished and orphaned children, but I refused to listen. I would have defended to the death my dream and the others, who I believed played such heroic roles. My commitment was strong; I believed, trusted, and was loyal.

Then came the day when words were spoken in a hushed voice. Each sentence alone had a simple meaning but strung together in such a fashion they became earth shattering. As I heard the words, my palms began to sweat, and the room seemed to grow fuzzy. The world as I knew it, my dream and my belief in my hero, exploded into a million pieces. I had believed, I had trusted, I had been loyal, and I had been shattered.

The ensuing, intense sadness bored a hole through my heart and into my very soul, creating a cavern into which my whole body began to fall. The top of the cavern began to close, and the darkness began to envelop my being. Would I just fade away or fight my way back into the light? I chose the light.

This is a record of my memories from periods in my life in which I encountered the best and the worst of humanity. It is my story of a broken childhood, an international battle to save my own child, and subsequently my work in intercountry adoption, with the events building upon one another to a shocking conclusion. Along the exigent road, I encountered loyalty and betrayal, intense happiness and heart wrenching disappointment, liars and innocents, crime, federal prosecutors and indictments, honesty and deceit, suspicious deaths, and wondrous new beginnings. This is my story of survival, perseverance, and forgiveness.

Most of the names have been changed to protect confidentiality. All real names were used with permission, some belong to public figures, or the named individual is no longer living.

PART 1

CHAPTER 1

THE BEGINNING

I WAS RAISED IN A small town, a suburb of St. Louis, Missouri, and was the middle of three daughters born into my family. One sister was four years my senior, with the other six years my junior. My father was a pharmacist and my mother was the Director of the St. Louis County Police Department's Records Center. Both of my parents were small in stature and were considered to be quite attractive. They had a lot of friends, frequently went to dances, played cards, and hosted parties in our home. My mother was an incredibly intelligent person who read book after book, never watching the television. My father's pharmaceutical sales job often took him out of town during the week, and when he was home, he was most often in his private office. We were expected to be at the dinner table every night on time.

My mother smoked like a fiend, but my father never allowed her to smoke in the main area of the house. She had been relegated to the three-season room, in which, following dinner, she would sit night after night in the dark, smoking her cigarettes and drinking her beer. In the winter, she sat there in her winter coat.

Conversations between my parents were generally acrimonious in nature. My father's hands frequently shook, and in later years my mother shared that his unsteadiness was the result of an addiction he developed to some of the prescription drugs which he sold.

Our home was the epitome of perfection, not a thing out of place, the beautiful furniture strategically placed to my mother's liking. She had special names for the rooms, such as the library or the music room, preferring to be ostentatious. My mother never left the house unless she was stylishly dressed, and her hair and makeup were perfect. My father took his dress shirts to the cleaners, having them crisply starched, during an era when the majority of the men in our neighborhood were having their shirts ironed by their wives. They drove pretty cars; my mother's a bright yellow convertible. My parents purchased a ski boat in a color which perfectly matched the color of my father's company car.

I learned that appearances were of the utmost importance to my parents, the quintessential perfect suburban couple, and from a distance our family played the roles of the family into which everyone wished they were born.

Father

Although raised in that upper middle-class home, I was not protected from abuse. My father had a wicked temper and an aggressive nature. My mother complained a great deal about my older sister and me to our father; we never quite lived up to her expectations. We lived in the perfect storm, two unhappy parents and three little girls at their mercy.

My mother had run for political office when I was very young, and as part of her campaign, hundreds of cardboard yard signs and slender wooden stakes were delivered to our home. The pointed, unfinished, wooden stakes were about three feet long, one-half inch thick, and about two inches wide. The campaign signs were affixed to the stakes with a staple gun and then the pointed stakes were driven into the ground in the yards of supporters. My mother did not win the election. After the election, the left-over campaign signs were discarded, but my father stored the mammoth bundles of remaining stakes along an interior wall in our garage.

I can still hear the crack of my addicted father's favorite weapon, "the stick," the name eventually given to those stakes stored in our garage. The most disturbing thing about "the stick," other than the pain it elicited, was my father's instruction about it after concluding his verbal reprimand.

When I had perpetrated an offense worthy of "the stick," I was told to go to the garage and get one. I can still hear my father ordering me to go to the garage and bring him a stick. I recall the angst arising within as I carefully examined them to find the one that looked as if it would break the easiest, knowing from experience that as soon as one broke, the beating ended. I can still physically feel the quivering of my body as I made my way to the garage for his "stick." The beating was bad enough; the fetching of "the stick" was torturous and humiliating. Eventually the sticks ran out, and my father turned to wooden hangers from the closet.

I never knew which father would walk in the door each evening. He could come home at the end of his work day and be kind and loving, or he might just as easily beat or kick me after knocking me to the floor. Just a glance at his face would give me the indication of his mood. When it was the angry father walking in the door, I could almost smell and feel his wrath in the air, as one can feel the electricity of an approaching storm. He would become enraged if the house was in disarray, if there were dishes in the sink, or sometimes for no apparent reason at all.

I learned that a tidy home was paramount to peace. One of the hundreds of examples occurred late on a Saturday night, when my parents came home from a party. I was in the 10th grade, and my girlfriend had spent the night and we had enjoyed soda and popcorn while watching movies. Before going upstairs to bed, I placed our two glasses and the bowl from the popcorn in the sink. From a deep sleep, we awakened to my father flipping the light on, yanking the bed clothes from the bed, after which he grabbed me by the leg and dragged me to the top of the stairs. He pitched me down the stairs, screaming at me that I knew better than to leave dishes in the sink. He ordered my girlfriend out of the house. Our stairs were carpeted, and I was physically unhurt, but my pride and dignity were as broken as a piece of crystal. The event also shattered my relationship with my girlfriend. For my whole life, I have required a neat and tidy home in order to feel safe, the result of those childhood experiences such as described here.

Sometimes, for a small perceived affront, he would hurl things at me, such as knives, at the dinner table. But perhaps the worst thing he flung was the unending barrage of words about being worthless. In the third grade, after being told that I was nothing but a parasite, I went to our library to look up the meaning of the word. As I read in that oversized, red, leather covered dictionary I was confused and thought, *That's not me; I am neither a bloodsucker, nor a leach, nor an insect.* As I continued reading the many synonyms of the word, I came to "freeloader." Then I looked up that word. *Could that be what he thought of me?* I was a despondent, little eight-year-old who suddenly felt hollow. That feeling remained with me most of the next twenty years, and it was the birth of my driving, life-long need to feel valuable.

However damaging these incidents were for me, they taught me to always consider the consequences of my actions, to be thorough with work being done, to complete tasks, to be a good time manager, and to strive for success/perfection. These skills became valuable to me in my adult life.

My father was also an odd dichotomy, being the one who gave me affection, and he could be very kind. He came to my swim meets, taught me to ski, and played catch with me in the back yard. He was the one who studied my spelling words with me in elementary school. I craved and gobbled up those segments of my childhood like a starving child. But I always had to be alert for the moment when he would shift without warning from the loving father to the abusive one. I became very good at reading him, which I honed into the skill of successfully, rapidly assessing people in other areas of my life, which was eventually very useful, especially beneficial in business relationships.

For much of my life, I worked to keep the peace in situations in which I found myself, whether it was at cheerleading practice, on the hockey field, or in later years, the board room. I craved peacefulness in my external world since my childhood home was, more often than not, a war zone. I extended kindness to everyone and hated seeing others hurt. For the first half of my life, I desperately needed everyone to like me. It was as essential to me as air is to human life.

Mother

I can still smell the lingering beer on my narcissistic, alcoholic mother's breath at the end of most days. Both of my parents were emotionally absent the majority of the time, with my mother seemingly only interested in herself or my younger sister. My older sister and I held little importance to her. I didn't figure out until I was a teenager that my mother should have protected us, which was her most important job. Instead, she threw my older sister and me under our father's angry bus, which was always on the brink of careening out of control at every opportunity. I believe saving her children would have meant forfeiting the lifestyle to which we had all become accustomed, and she refused to give that up. She lived the life she wanted at the expense of her children, burying herself in a cocktail of alcohol and self-pity. My younger sister eventually enjoyed a career on Broadway, which I sensed gave our mother the greatest fulfillment in her life.

In my senior year of high school, I came to understand the origin of my mother's disdain for me. In one of her drunken episodes, as she angrily pointed her finger at me, my mother screamed, "No wonder you are the way you are, after all, your father named you after his girlfriend.

What more could I expect?" Her cold and hurtful words cut through me like a sword. I had known that my father had had an affair while he was in the military. I also knew that she had let him name me. I imagine that sometime during my early years, most likely during one of the many bitter arguments in their tumultuous relationship, he told her the origin of my name. I believed that was what made her keep me at arm's length, selecting me to be responsible for the misery of her life.

My father moved out of our family home the day before my eighteenth birthday, and my parents subsequently divorced. For the first time in my life, I experienced a life that was free of the ever-present fear under which we had all lived for so many years. However, the cloud of stress which my mother brought down upon our family remained.

Sadly, throughout our childhoods, my mother pitted her three daughters against one another, being sure to share with the appropriate daughter whatever catty tidbit one sister had said about the other to her. She was mean spirited, and I believe she enjoyed making me feel badly by telling me nasty things my sisters said about me. I imagine she returned the favor to them. Our family was so damaged by my mother's alcoholism and my father's abuse that loyalty and trust were in short supply. It was an environment of emotional chaos which made it easy for my mother to undercut any positive connection I could have forged with my sisters.

The Result

We had been five people residing under the same roof, sharing little emotional attachment to one another, and sadly I often felt isolated and lonely within the walls of my home. I spent many years of my life trying to find a place to belong, trying to matter to someone.

We had no aunts or uncles or grandparents to shelter us from the storm. We were terrified of our paternal grandparents, and our maternal grandparents passed away when I was quite young. My parents had siblings, but they had little to do with one another. There was no safe place for us.

I learned from an early age that helping other people gave me an internal fulfillment and helped me to feel valuable and gave me a sense of safety. The acceptance I received from those I helped and the satisfaction of having given that help sustained me when I went home at night. I built external connections that became my own personal life raft. I volunteered at every possible opportunity at school, in organizations to which I belonged, even at Sunday school. I earned love from a family for whom I babysat every Saturday night from age twelve to leaving for college. Fortunately, and probably life saving for me, I developed good interpersonal skills.

After I reached adulthood, my father kicked his drug habit and, after a ten-year long break in our relationship, we formed a more kind and loving connection, albeit a shallow one. He married my step-mother, Donna, who I came to adore. She was the best thing to happen to our family. She is kind and loving, and sincerely cares about me and my children. Her calm demeanor had a way of soothing my father rather than revving him up as my mother had done. My mother had been the lighter fluid to my father's already smoldering internal embers. Donna's kind overtures, along with years of therapy, assisted me in leaving the terror of my childhood locked away in my brain and only permitting the memories of the kind father to enter my consciousness. My father eventually sank into a deep state of dementia, and I remain grateful that at least most days he seems to recognize me.

I ended up caring for my mother before her death, in her state of alcoholic dementia, during which time she was the kindest she had been to me in my life. Her apparent life-long unhappiness and her alcoholism led me to believe she was a tortured soul and I could do nothing but pity what her life had become at the end.

I believe my strong personality and deep inner strength developed because of the abusive home in which I was raised. I inherently knew that any potential, positive self-esteem would be built through my friends and my accomplishments. I never wanted anyone to be mad at me or disappointed in me; I received enough of this at home. Building positive self-esteem in children was never a priority in my home; striving for approval or reward from my parents was as elusive as chasing butterflies. I was often a privately, melancholy little girl who turned to my books and my external relationships for escape. I craved acceptance from my friends and tended to be the compliant friend, doing things like giving away a treasured doll to a playmate that seemed to really like it. I learned that pleasing gave me a path to acceptance which led to my survival.

It was an extreme blessing that I developed the skill to block from my consciousness the tragedy of my home life. I honed to a fine point the skill of compartmentalization of thoughts and feelings, simply putting things on a secret shelf in my brain, in their own little, internal locking file cabinet. Regardless of the horrors within the walls of my home I always put a smile on my face as I stepped over the threshold to freedom. This skill served me well throughout my life and was a primary asset in helping me to survive the many betrayals that lay ahead for me.

Unfortunately, my damaged home life left my soul with scars of self-doubt, inadequacy, and emptiness. But, those same experiences made me tough, turning me into a person with skills of anticipating and avoiding problems, and also the ability to quickly solve the unanticipated ones. I had learned the importance of attention to detail and task completion. My terribly marred childhood made me want to be a person who was so much better than the parents who raised me. Those childhood incidents planted seeds of a fighter, who would spend a lifetime battling injustice.

CHAPTER 2

ESCAPE

Shortly after my high school graduation, I left for college, never to return to the home I desperately needed to escape. By order of the divorce decree, my father had to pay the cost of my tuition and room and board for school, if I lived on the college campus. I paid all my own personal expenses, clothing, college books, meals on the weekends, summertime apartment expenses, and my transportation costs. Money was very tight for me, and I always had at least one job during college, and sometimes two.

I knew that I wanted to work with children and had begun college with the goal of being a physical education teacher and coach. I was very athletic, and my high school coaches had been positive, influential role models for me. However, I suffered a serious knee injury, resulting in extensive surgery after my first year of college, and the orthopedic surgeon recommended that I not pursue a job which would require me to be on my feet all day. I didn't want to be a classroom teacher, or a nurse, and thus began reading the school catalog describing the various majors. I had a roommate at the time who was also considering her future career path, and as we read about Speech Pathology, it sounded like something we would both like to do. My roommate and I decided to pursue the degree together, and I graduated with a degree in Speech Pathology and Psychology.

While in college, I met Jeffrey and we became best friends, eventually growing closer and closer. He was wild and fun and made me laugh, always being the life of every party. I used to tell people he was the best time I ever had. He took me home to meet his family and I fell totally in love with all of them. I married Jeffrey at the end of my junior year of college, perhaps as much because his parents loved me as he did. My in-laws turned out to be one of the greatest gifts of my life. Jim and Lois loved me, supported me, and gave me more "good parenting" in my late teens and early twenties than all of the parenting I received during my childhood. They were always kind and loving toward me and encouraged me to sprout wings and reach for the stars. I had finally found a set of parents to whom I really had value. They were an enormous blessing to me.

We graduated from college and Jeffrey was accepted to dental school in Kansas City, Missouri. Nine months before Jeffrey began dental school, our son, Ryan, was born. When holding him for the first time, I promised Ryan I would give him a life filled with love and devotion, vowing to be nothing like my own mother. After he was born, I cuddled him and watched him sleep, pondering when he would walk or talk, or say mama. He was incredibly beautiful, with eyes bluer than a bright summer sky, and I felt as if I were living in a fairy tale. I simply adored this tiny, now independent being, who had just hours ago been a part of me. But, I still struggled with the fear I could never be good enough for him.

Jeffrey left Ryan and me for six months to attend Officer Basic Training with the army before the beginning of dental school. Those first six months alone with Ryan were extremely difficult, and I was in a constant state of exhaustion, having returned to work when Ryan was only four weeks old. But they were blissful all the same, with Ryan and I developing an unbreakable bond, having only each other upon whom we could rely for comfort.

While Jeffrey was in dental school and when Ryan was two years old, I was diagnosed with a disease which precipitated the removal of my right fallopian tube and ovary and three-fourths of the left ovary. I was given a very small window of time before the disease would overtake that last one-fourth ovary. Wondrously, Laura was conceived, and from the beginning she was a miracle. I felt exceedingly blessed to be given this second gift from God.

Little Laura looked so much like her brother, it was astonishing. I had been filled with fear before her birth that I could never love her as I loved Ryan. But, literally in the blink of an eye, my fear was replaced by total devotion to that tiny wonder. I was totally in love, again, and felt warm as waves of tenderness washed over me.

I vowed that I would love and parent them as I wished I had been, promising myself to treasure them and never speak unkindly or ugly to them. I worked hard to make sure they were adored, and each day I told them how worthy, smart, beautiful, and talented they were, and always how much I loved them. They made the rainy days bright with their sunshiny smiles.

During Jeffrey's trek through dental school, I supported our family by working as a speech pathologist for an elementary school. Each morning, during the school year, I would dress Ryan and Laura in adorable outfits, with bows in Laura's curly blond hair, and deliver them to the babysitter for the day. Often, the best part of the day would be scooping them into my arms when I picked them up at the end of my work day. When possible, I tutored children after school hours to give our income a boost. It was a challenging time with two small children, a lack of money, working two jobs, and Jeffrey in school full-time with little time to assist with the children, but I was happy. I greeted each day with a smile and saw it filled with promise and hope; and of course, adored Ryan and Laura more than life itself. I thought we were the most fortunate family that ever lived. My self-esteem was healthier than it had ever been as I worked hard to be super mom, super wife, and super speech therapist. My emptiness had been replaced by fulfillment and my self-doubt by confidence. I felt the success of having broken the cycle of abuse that had been prevalent in our family for generations.

With the assistance of a therapist, I forgave my parents, an action which was necessary for me to embrace a full and rich life. I was able to purge the bitterness from my heart, realizing that persistent bitterness is an acid that eats away at one's humanity and destroys the soul.

CHAPTER 3

BLINDSIDED

JEFFREY GRADUATED FROM DENTAL SCHOOL and our contented little family moved to the small town where he had been raised. He opened his dental practice, and I looked forward with great anticipation and joy to this new chapter in our lives. Every day, my life felt like Christmas morning for a child.

But, within a year of his graduation from dental school, my world came crashing down around me. Jeffrey shared that he no longer wanted to be married or to parent two small children. Although I heard rumors around town, it didn't really matter. The only thing that I knew was that I hadn't been enough...again. My hard-sought-after emotional gains disappeared like falling snowflakes on a thirty-five-degree day.

Jeffrey insisted that Ryan, Laura, and I return to St. Louis. Being too devastated to stay and fight, I scurried back to my home town, which in no way provided support or comfort for me. My hopes and dreams for my future were dashed, and I was left to start my life over.

In retrospect, we were very young, barely twenty-one when marrying, and from the beginning, our life was stressful. I had been the single bread winner, making too little money, two small children, and the pressure of dental school. Jeffrey wasn't a bad guy, he just desired a fun and carefree life, and ours had been anything but that. We lacked the important tools to navigate our way through the deep waters of a young and stress-filled relationship.

Realizing that it was time to move forward with a new life, I knew it couldn't matter how frightening or daunting it was to me. I had two small children totally depending on me. I chose to embrace this new season of my life.

I was blessed during this time to have the love and support of my marvelous former mother and father-in-law. Daycare expense was my greatest barrier to survival, and they helped by paying for daycare, so I could work. They occasionally took the kids on a weekend, giving me a break, but more importantly they allowed me to retain the close relationship we all enjoyed. During those first few years, I spent many hours with my checkbook, figuring out which bills I could afford to pay each week. I grew thin from skipping meals, fearful there wouldn't be enough money at the end of the month to pay the bills. I struggled as a single mother, with their dad giving little assistance. But, I got tough and learned how to figure things out, how to be on my own, and became very resourceful. I got a therapist who assured me that my children would not perish from a regular diet of hot dogs and macaroni and cheese. I even made some of Laura's dresses and hair bows. I was determined to give Ryan and Laura full lives on the limited resources we had. They played on sports teams and had ballet lessons. I volunteered at their school whenever I could.

I had worked hard with my therapist to come to terms with the abuse of my childhood, and then with the abandonment of Jeffrey. Despite my self-doubt, our lives were normal, happy, and full.

Years later, in a conversation with adult Ryan and Laura, they told me that they had never known that we were "poor" when they had been young. I was filled with gratitude to learn that and it eased a burden I had carried for many years. I realized I hadn't needed a lot of money to give them a good life; I had simply needed all that limitless love I had for them.

CHAPTER 4

HOPE FOR THE FUTURE

THREE YEARS LATER, I MET a sensitive, intelligent, and kind man, Allen. He was a chemist and was as much the opposite of Jeffrey as a person could be. He was serious, responsible, steady, and solid, and he loved me dearly. We went to the symphony and played tennis, and life with him was very calm. Allen and I decided that he should be a permanent part of our lives. He not only loved me, he also truly loved my children, which was extremely important. Plus, I was simply worn out by the hard life we had led for so many years.

We were a happy family of four, and it felt right to want to add another child to our crew. I could no longer bear children, so we decided to adopt. Ryan and Laura were thrilled at the idea of a little brother or sister and so, in 1991, shortly after getting married, we began the process to adopt a baby. This was a pivotal turning point in my life and would lead me down a path I never could have imagined.

It didn't take long to discover we had a lot to learn about adoption; there were countless rules and road blocks to be an adoptive parent. I had been able to be a biological parent twice and hadn't completed a single form except for those relating to insurance or school registrations. To complete a private adoption in the United States, at least in St. Louis, divorce was frowned upon, which was our initial hurdle. It was preferred that the adopting parents were childless; I had two. Many of the adoption agencies had religious affiliations or requirements, and the agencies preferred that applicants share the agency's faith. We would have gotten preferential treatment had we been Lutheran or Catholic, but we were Methodist. There was no adoption agency in St. Louis which was attached to the Methodist faith. Unbelievably, the wait to adopt a child under three years of age through the State of Missouri was reported to be seven years. It was discouraging, and the process seemed to be little more than trying to scale an ice-covered mountain with no shoes—cold, frightening, and impossible.

Our next-door neighbor was out of the country for a few months and had rented his house to a lovely, single woman. Fortuitously, I was in our yard one day, watering my newly planted, spring petunias when she came out to get her mail, and for a reason still unknown to me, I struck up a conversation with her. I learned that her name was Kathy. We began telling each other about ourselves, and I ended up telling this total stranger that we were hoping to adopt a child, but that we were finding it challenging.

She told me about her friend, Debbie, who had adopted internationally. Kathy believed Debbie's process had been relatively painless. She had met Debbie's daughter and sung the little girl's praises. She suggested that I call Debbie and invited me into the house while she wrote down her friend's number for me. I couldn't believe my good fortune at meeting someone who could potentially help us. The already brilliant spring day just got ultra-bright.

I was totally unfamiliar with international adoption, as it hadn't been a consideration for us. But I decided to give it a try and I called Debbie and left a message. I believed that God placed this stranger in my life to give me this direction. A month later, Kathy moved away and was gone from my life forever, never knowing the important role she played in my future.

Debbie called me back later that day and we spoke for more than an hour. I learned about her international adoption experience, and after our conversation, I was eager to speak with her adoption agency. She gave me the name and phone number of the agency director.

I called the director, and she seemed committed to helping Americans adopt children, primarily from Romania, from where her own daughter had been adopted. I failed to request any additional references. The only thing my laser-focused head was hearing was that she could help me, and that was all that mattered. So, with no further investigation into the agency, which was located on the other side of the country, we paid huge sums of money to a lady who promised she could help us adopt a young child in less than a year.

More than a year later, and after disclosing more personal information about our life than would be required to run for president, and filling out a tree's worth of paperwork, we were offered a child from Hungary. The agency director told us about a little boy, who had been born in the Harghita Region of Romania to a Hungarian, Roma (an ethnicity previously known by the slang word gypsy) mother who subsequently placed him in a Hungarian orphan program. She didn't want him to be placed in a Romanian orphanage, where at the time AIDS was rampant and children were dying every day from the disease.

On the day we learned of our son's existence, we were given thirty minutes to decide if we wanted a small child named "Szilard" (Pronounced See-lard). She faxed to us a copy of a fax she had received from Eastern Europe, and the photo in the fax did indeed appear to be a small child. We were provided neither health information nor familial history, but he had a name and he needed a family. Every other consideration paled in comparison to that fact. As soon as we saw that blurry picture, we knew that little Szilard would be ours and we would call him Alex.

We had additional paperwork to do and more fees to be paid after accepting our referral. We were told he would be able to leave Hungary in just a few short weeks. I painted his bedroom and bought him a crib. I bought a soft sculpture made from material in primary colors that was cut in the shape of his name. I bought another soft sculpture of billowy, white clouds to hang on his wall. We bought baby toys and supplies and clothes. In no time at all, an adorable bedroom, decorated in primary colors and perfect for an angel, was ready for little Alex.

We learned that Alex was with a foster family in Szeged (pronounced Seh-ged), Hungary, and a few weeks after receiving the fax, we received pictures and video of him with his foster family. His foster family was a young married couple who appeared to be invested in our little guy. It gave us comfort to see him getting such good care. We watched his little video nearly every day, falling deeper and deeper in love with the little guy on the screen. But our anxiety was building about the length of time it was taking to bring him home.

Months passed, and the director made one excuse after another for why Alex wasn't coming home. He was supposed to be home that fall of 1992, by his first birthday, then Christmas, then Valentine's Day. There were weeks when the agency wouldn't even answer their phone. I often felt that they were being dishonest with us. Initially, the agency would request payment of another fee, so the process could progress, but we stopped sending them money as our trust in them evaporated. With each passing week, I became more and more apprehensive and began to think I was going to need to discern a way to save Alex myself. I launched a one-woman campaign of speaking regularly with the consular officials at the American Embassy in Hungary and with US State Department officials. I felt like I was surrounded by a dark mist through which I kept trying to reach for answers that were untouchable. It wasn't long before I was familiar with who was who in both organizations—their names and their responsibilities. I spent hours on the phone making those long-distance calls, and in the end, we expended over $7,000 on long distance phone calls alone. But, even with all of that, I had not been able to identify the reason for the delay in Alex coming to America.

During the process, our agency director shared information with me about a British man, named John, who was an aide worker in Hungary. He ran the program into which Alex had been placed and was working with our agency. I coerced our agency director to share John's contact information. She had been such a failure as an adoption agency director, I was frequently annoyed. She often didn't know answers, gave inaccurate timelines, and was not forthcoming with information about the children.

I called John and he provided me with more information than any of the other people up to that point, either those from the adoption agency, the US, or foreign governments. After connecting with him, I learned that we were part of a group of twenty-six families who were hoping to adopt twenty-eight Hungarian/Romanian orphans, and he assisted me with locating a few of the other waiting families who resided across the US. It was affirming to learn that we were not alone and all of the families seemed to be trapped in the same nightmare as us, many of them working with our same agency. John agreed to help me, and he began giving me regular updates about Alex, as he had been the one to place Alex with his foster parents and routinely visited the family and Alex. He became the emotional connection to Alex that sustained me, helping me to remain strong.

About a month after my initial conversation with John, he called to tell me that the children, who had previously been in foster homes in Hungary, had been removed from their foster homes and had been placed into two dilapidated, abandoned, state-run pre-schools, which overnight had been turned into makeshift orphanages. He said the "word on the street in Hungary" was that an American woman was stirring up trouble. John said he believed that the American woman was me and my barrage of phone calls, to both the US State Department and to the American Embassies in both Hungary and Romania, were making officials on both sides of the ocean uncomfortable.

The story got worse. He said armed soldiers, members of the Hungarian secret police, had stormed the foster homes in the middle of the night, forcibly taking the children from the arms of their foster parents at gunpoint. John shared that the foster parents had been panic-stricken and hadn't known what to do except to watch the children be taken away by the soldiers. The foster parents were reportedly devastated by the aggressive actions of the Hungarian secret police. But my thoughts turned to the poor babies! I couldn't imagine the trauma of being ripped from the arms of the only caretakers they knew. I imagined a chaotic scene of yelling and arguing, and guns being waved around in front of our innocent children. The ghastly vision brought tears to my eyes. Picturing the events was reminiscent of my own very chaotic childhood, and I became nearly hysterical picturing Alex in that situation. But, all I could do was to wait and continue my freedom campaign from my home. Sometimes the only thing that helped was just holding tightly to Ryan and Laura.

I was continuing to search for the other twenty-six families about whom John had told me, but with whom he had been unable to connect me. One day while in J.C. Penny, selecting items for Alex in the baby department, I shared my story about Alex with the cashier. She suddenly stopped working and said, "Stop, wait right here, one of our buyers is also trying to adopt a child from Hungary!" Surely, God was watching out for me. I couldn't believe it! That day I met Jayne, who would one day soon become my roommate in Hungary. Jayne had already discovered a couple of other families in St. Louis, and I further coerced my adoption agency into providing me with the contact information for the rest of the names. We formed an unofficial alliance of concerned, waiting, adoptive parents.

After I shared the information about the children being moved in the night with the other families, a small group of parents of the children banded together, and we began working collectively to get the children released from Hungary. We began coordinating our efforts and phone calls, and most importantly, we shared information. I believed from the beginning that continuously updated information was going to be critical in this struggle. Our situation had clearly become one of us against them, but we still didn't have a clear picture of who "them" was. We began calling our children *The Szeged 28*. We commenced a battle to win the freedom of the *Szeged 28*, but was it a battle that we had any chance of winning when we couldn't even identify the enemy? We had no clue that within months, the whole world would know who the *Szeged 28* were!

CHAPTER 5

CONGRESSMAN TALENT

For the time being, we had to be satisfied with the pictures the adoption agency sent, and then eventually another video of Alex arrived. Our family would sit around and watch the tapes, those moments instrumental in bolstering us in our mission to bring Alex home. He had a brother and a sister awaiting him.

Early one Wednesday morning, in the spring of 1993, I received a phone call from John. He told me that the Hungarian government was making plans to send all of our children to a Romanian orphanage.

Many of the children had been born in Romania, in Hungarian provinces, and were brought to Hungary to be placed for adoption, just as Alex had been. Some of the others had been born in Hungary, primarily to Hungarian-born Roma women. The birth mothers of nearly every one of our children were considered to be Hungarian Roma, not Romanian, based on the region of Romania from which they came. It seemed there were areas of Hungary and Romania where, over the previous 100 years, lands had moved back and forth between the borders like ping pong balls.

I assumed that the Hungarian government did not want to deal with this group of adoptions, which I had already discovered was creating a hailstorm for the Hungarian government. I believed they were looking for a quick exit out of an ugly adoption mess.

However, there was no way I could stand for the children to be sent to Romania. It would have meant certain death for any number of them, mostly the result of the Romanian dictator Nicolae Ceausescu's disastrous social policies of the previous twenty-five years.

Ceausescu came to power in the late 1960s. The birthrate in the former communist country was low, and he desired a strong army for his country. To create his massive army, he needed more Romanian citizens. To accomplish this, he created social policies which would increase the country's population. Ceausescu outlawed abortion, required every woman to have four or more children, eventually banning condoms and birth control pills in the 1980s. Men and women of child bearing ages were forced to pay a hefty tax for not having children. The cruel dictator made motherhood a state obligation.

The population doubled, but the result was catastrophic for the Romanian people. The economy was bad, jobs were scarce, and poverty was rampant. Thousands of children were left in the care of the state-run orphanages, which had neither the manpower nor the resources to care for the children. Ceausescu had mandated that the orphaned children receive blood transfusions to "make them strong." At some point, the AIDS virus was introduced, and through the repetitive use of unsterilized needles, thousands and thousands of the children in Romanian orphanages were exposed to the terrible disease. In that era, AIDS was barely treatable, and almost always terminal.

However, the Romanian people had endured enough at the hands of Nicolae Ceausescu, and his equally evil wife, and on Christmas Day in 1989, the citizens overthrew the government, tried the Ceausescus in an empty school house, and executed them the very same day.

The damage of the dastardly regime had been done though. By 1993, more than fifty percent of the children in Romanian orphanages were dying from AIDS. This knowledge was my first introduction to the horrors experienced by children living in orphanages and would become a driving force for me. The American media was full of shocking stories and images of the plight of the Romanian children.

I was stunned and nearly frantic at the thought of my precious Alex being sent to Romania. Initially, I was simply paralyzed by the picture of Alex in one of those places, but that quickly passed as I realized something needed to be done quickly. My fear turned to iron-clad resolve.

Remarkably, the following day, Allen learned that a local US Congressman, Jim Talent, was planning to hold a "Town Mall Meeting" in preparation for his upcoming reelection. Allen and I had become a very driven team and were searching for every opportunity to help us get Alex home. We thought that by going to the mall and standing in line, I might be able to enlist Congressman Talent's assistance. I knew he was fairly new to the political scene and that he had young children, and perhaps that made him just the person who might care about our story regarding stranded orphans. Early on a Saturday morning, I stood in line for two hours to get the opportunity to beg for his help. I shuffled back and forth from one foot to another in nervous anticipation of speaking to him, replaying my impending speech over and over in my head, trying to get the words just perfect, hoping my message would be impactful.

But when I finally got to the front of the line all I could say, with tears in my eyes, was, "Congressman Talent, if you don't help me, my son and twenty-seven other babies are going to die." He didn't look at me as if I was a crazy constituent, but he looked alarmed by the possibility of what I had just described. This encounter was the beginning of a friendship which would help change our world.

Congressman Talent kindly took my hand, gently looking into my eyes. He asked me to step to the side and to give his aide my contact information, promising to call me that night. I could only hope this politician would keep his word. I walked out of the mall filled with more hope than I had felt in many months.

That evening, when my phone rang and I answered it, I was astonished to hear Congressman Talent's voice. I wanted more than anything for him to be the key to unlock our children and couldn't help but think that surely now the tides were changing. Unknowingly, this conversation ended up being just a practice run for a much larger speech I would give to a chamber of politicians in the not too distant future!

I had never been in a personal discussion with an elected official. I wasn't sure how to address him or exactly what to say. My stomach was doing flip flops and my hands had begun to shake. I wanted to be thorough, yet cautious in this crucial exchange with Congressman Talent, knowing this might be my only shot to be heard. I explained our adoption situation and then told him everything I had been able to learn from John. I shared the information I had received from John two or three days earlier, that there was an American lobby group intent on blocking the adoptions. I had been told that the agency with which we were working was not a member of a powerful, adoption lobby group, American Center for Adoption, in New York City.

When the lobby group, which had a stronghold on adoptions in Romania, learned that a group of Americans were adopting Romanian born children out of Hungary, without using any of their member organizations, a campaign was waged to stop our adoptions. I explained that one of the other waiting adoptive parents spoke with the director of the lobbyist group, Andy Graves. During that conversation, the adoptive dad was told that if all the adopting parents of the *Szeged 28* would pay the required fees to one of their member agencies and work through one of them, we could get our children out. That conversation planted the thought in my head, *Could this all just be about money?* I told Congressman Talent our group had declined the offer, refusing to be blackmailed.

Another experience which I relayed to the Congressman was that of calling the Romanian Embassy, in Washington DC, to discuss the *Szeged 28*. During that call I was told that if I needed information about the children I should contact the director, Andy Graves, at the American Center for Adoption. This was one of the most baffling directives I received from any of the government officials with whom I had spoken up to that point. I wondered, *Why would a foreign embassy official be directing me to an American lobbyist organization for information relating to children with whom it had no connection or relationship?*

I explained that I had correspondence dated February 3, 1993, that the American Consul General in Hungary was expediting the visas, which would allow the children to come home, having agreed to sign off on the release of the children. What had happened to reverse the forward momentum of February? I shared with Congressman Talent it was my belief someone in Washington was trying to keep our adoptions from being successful, or at the very least they were trying to control them.

I shared that a few weeks previously, a full-page ad had been placed in the New York Times with our story, hoping to garner support from the public to help bring our children home. One of the *Szeged 28* parents had a friend who knew First Lady Hillary Clinton. He had the opportunity to speak directly with Clinton, who told him she couldn't help because she didn't know the adoption laws. Although I didn't share my thoughts with the Congressman, I had them nonetheless. *Wasn't she married to a lawyer, the President of the United States? Wasn't she a lawyer? Didn't they have a dozen lawyers working for them? Yet, she didn't know the laws?* I was becoming an angry and thoroughly frustrated person.

In giving the information to Congressman Talent, I had sought to remain calm but had ended up speaking with more passion than intended. He said he would call me back as soon as possible, needing time to investigate the situation. I was fearful he would find no support for my story and would simply write me off as a paranoid, unbalanced person. But true to his word, Congressman Talent called me back about a week later. I was filled with both surprise and gratitude that he was actually following through, and my heart was racing faster than an Indy 500 car engine, after having paced the floor of our kitchen during our entire conversation.

Congressman Talent said that although he could not confirm with one-hundred percent certainty that the information I had been given was accurate, his sources supported my story. He stated that he was in agreement and something untoward was happening to block our adoptions. Congressman Talent then said he would do everything he could to help us. I was practically jumping up and down in my kitchen and I thanked God for bringing this man into my life. From that point forward, Congressman Talent proved time and again that he could be counted on, and we stayed in regular communication.

I often worried that Ryan and Laura were getting too little attention during this time. I seemed to constantly be on the phone with one official or another. But I still made it to every swim meet or every birthday party, and we seldom missed church. We were truly blessed with two terrific children who were well-adjusted, happy kids who seemed equally committed to our efforts to free Alex. We tried to have as normal a life as possible.

But, I was not able to sit back and wait for things to magically get better. In early May, I enlisted the help of some of the other adopting parents and we began a campaign of reaching out to everyone we knew, along with their friends, not only in St. Louis, but across the country. A fax campaign to the White House was organized, asking for help in getting the babies out of Hungary. I had made friends with several staff at the middle school which Ryan attended, and even the school personnel got on board with our plan. We had consistent verbiage which we distributed to our fax-sending friends and acquaintances. On a preplanned, specific date and time, we inundated the White House fax number with the message, "Break the log jam between Hungary and the US and FREE THE SZEGED 28." Less than an hour after everyone began sending faxes, we received a phone call from the White House asking us to please stop sending the faxes, having totally jammed up the fax machines in the White House! We told them it was too late, people we didn't even know had gotten on board with our campaign and there was no way to stop it.

I only hoped that someone in the White House had heard our message. I don't really know if we accomplished anything with our fax campaign, but we did let Washington know that we weren't going away.

CHAPTER 6

TIED UP!

DURING THE LAST WEEK OF May 1993, I was organizing my closet when my phone rang. I picked up the phone to hear John's far away sounding voice in Hungary. He was clearly distressed as he described what was happening to Alex, who had been in the hospital for a few days with a severe ear infection. John solemnly shared that Alex had been tied up, with one of his legs tethered to a bar in his crib. John said that my precious little boy kept climbing out of his hospital crib to get to the few toys that were in the room. John stated that Alex would retrieve the toys and give them to the other sick children in their own cribs. So, to stop Alex from climbing from his crib, they tied him. I felt as if my chest had been slammed with a gigantic hammer and I collapsed onto the floor, sobbing. Feelings of hopelessness and helplessness were overtaking me as I pictured my sweet little boy tied down and unable to even walk around in his crib. As I cried, John tried to comfort me, telling me that Alex's foster mother was regularly visiting him. However, consoling me was an unachievable task!

He next shared that he had taken pictures of Alex tied to his crib and had placed them in a safety deposit box in a local bank. He expressed his fear that were the photos discovered, they would be confiscated by the Hungarian secret police. He shared that he was being followed everywhere he went and that our adoption efforts seemed to be upsetting the Hungarian government.

Suddenly, my brain kicked into gear and I quickly recovered, knowing immediately what I was going to do. I told John that I would be leaving for Hungary the next day. I told him I would call him after my arrangements were made, and he promised to meet my plane in Budapest. I dried my tears and began making plans. The first thing I did was to contact Congressman Talent to tell him I was leaving for Hungary the next day. He asked me to wait one extra day so that he could make "some arrangements for me." I didn't really know what that meant, but I agreed, and almost exactly 48 hours later, I boarded an American Airlines plane for Budapest, Hungary.

The process to bring Alex home brought out in me a person I didn't know existed. After learning little Alex was tied to his crib, I became that reputed mother lion that protects her cub. This shift in my thinking gave me a new focus, and I grew stronger and more resolute with each passing hour. This event was a pivotal point for me, and the emergence of a young woman who suddenly not only knew she could do anything, but was also willing.

I spent the next two days preparing to depart for Hungary. I hugged and kissed on Ryan and Laura and cried each time I let myself contemplate how much I would miss them. We spent some time playing family games and getting ice cream, trying to grasp every moment together we could. But I had to go; there was no other choice for me. Allen would take good care of the children, and I knew they would all be fine. Alex was the one suffering, and I had to go make them untie him from that crib.

I had never traveled outside of the US before and suddenly found myself heading to a foreign country, completely by myself, to take on a foreign government. In fact, I had been on an airplane less than six times and was terrified to fly so far from my family. After a tearful goodbye at the airport, I got on a plane with as much determination as a human being can muster. I had no idea what I would face when I arrived in Hungary, but I did know one thing—Alex would no longer be tied to a crib. Regardless of anything else, I was unwavering about that.

As my plane took off from the St. Louis airport, tears were streaming down my face. A minister just happened to be sitting next to me and kindly told me God was watching out for me. He handed me his devotional, which I carried with me everywhere I went for the next six weeks.

CHAPTER 7

BUDAPEST, HUNGARY

I ARRIVED IN BUDAPEST, HUNGARY and was met by John, a tall and broad man with an engaging British accent. We hugged each other, and I cried with relief at having arrived, at finally meeting John face to face, and also some tears of fear about what lay ahead of me. After climbing into his small European car, we made our way from the airport to the city.

The beautiful day in late May when I arrived was about eighty-five degrees. One of the first things I noticed as soon as I exited the airport terminal was the air. Because of the lack of emissions' controls safeguarding the air quality, it had a chemical sort of smell mixed with a heavy odor of gasoline. But my simply being in the same country as Alex had me floating on that malodourous air.

I was amazed by the sights I saw and immediately fell in love with the beautiful, old city. The buildings were predominantly made of white/gray limestone, and there were ladies selling flowers on the street corners. Everywhere I looked, I saw old-fashioned street cars connected to electrical power lines above them. Many of the streets were cobblestone, and I imagined that they were hundreds of years old. The buildings had narrow entryways, most with big, heavy, wooden doors. As an American traveling abroad for the first time, I initially viewed Hungary to be a dirty place, but I soon realized that it was actually many hundreds of years old and buildings, streets, and doors that antiquated can't look new and clean, no matter how much paint is applied.

I was told that one hundred years ago, Buda stood on the west side of the Danube with Pest on the east side, being two different cities until the late 1800s. John explained that most Americans don't pronounce the name of the city correctly. Its actual pronunciation is Buda-pesht, with the 'sh' sound inserted.

There were beautiful old bridges about every half-mile or so all along the Danube, separating Buda from Pest. The brown water of the river looked terribly polluted and the river had a large number of boats making their ways both up and down the river. There were people everywhere you looked; it was an incredibly bustling city.

One of the first things John shared with me after we got into the car was that Alex had been released from his crib and had in fact been returned to the makeshift orphanage. John said he heard from his contact at the American Embassy that Congressman Talent had been responsible for making that happen. That made sense, as I believed Congressman Talent didn't want me to have to force the hospital to untie Alex; it wouldn't have been a pretty scene. I was later able to confirm that Congressman Talent had in fact contacted the American Embassy and instructed them to do what they could to get Alex untied and returned to the orphanage before my arrival in Hungary. I believe that was his reason for requesting that I wait an extra day. I was grateful that he interceded on Alex's behalf.

The day after arriving in Budapest, I went to the American embassy to register my presence in the country, as Congressman Talent had asked me to do. It was my first foray into an American Embassy, and I was unnerved before even walking into the building. It sat on the corner of two streets and across from a park-like area. It appeared to be five or six stories tall, and like many of the other buildings, it looked incredibly old. A large American flag flew proudly from a stanchion on an upper floor balcony. From across the street, I had attempted to take a photograph of the Embassy, and an armed American soldier, pointing his automatic weapon directly at my chest, rushed over and told me to put my camera away, informing me that it was illegal to photograph the exterior of an American Embassy. Little did I know that this would be the first of several times I would find myself facing the barrel of a gun over the next fifteen years. There were probably about two dozen armed American soldiers standing guard all around the outside of the Embassy, and they appeared quite serious about the work they were doing. It made me feel safe to be in their presence.

Entering the American Embassy, I was surprised by the starkness of it. It seemed old and tired, with drab colors, antiquated metal furniture and worn out flooring. The bright overhead florescent lights gave the interior a feeling of harshness. Inside the embassy, I was directed to the office of the American Consul General (ACG), to whom I had spoken several times by phone while still in America. My stomach was churning as I walked down the hall toward his office to meet him, silently reminding myself, *You can do anything.* He was tall and thin with a receding hairline. Introducing myself to him, I pleaded for his help. He was as cold in person as he had been on the phone and told me I would likely never get the children out of Hungary, and that it was probable that they would be sent to Romania. His flat refusal to help reminded me of a stern parent speaking to a misbehaving child. Sitting in stunned silence, I tried hard to comprehend the words of this man, whose salary was paid with my tax dollars. I thought perhaps compassion had been omitted from his emotional wheelhouse. We were talking about innocent, orphaned children. I left the American embassy with a new determination, suddenly grateful that I had been forced to be self-reliant and tough as a child. It was clear I was going to need every one of those traits in Hungary.

CHAPTER 8

SZEGED, HUNGARY

AFTER SPENDING THE FIRST TWO nights in the Budapest "Buro Panzio," a lovely, kind of Hungarian Bed and Breakfast, without the breakfast, I boarded a surprisingly modern train for Szeged, Hungary, the small town in which Alex and the rest of the children were being held. This was the first of nearly a dozen two-hour rides each direction I would take while in Hungary.

I arrived in Szeged and went to the Forrás hotel (pronounced For-ăj). John said it was the nicest hotel in town, but it was very much a communist era hotel. It was plain and simple, with no frills, having wide stairways and high ceilings. It was clean but lacked air conditioning, which was challenging as the temperatures were climbing every day, some days more than ninety degrees. Perhaps the warm weather was foreshadowing the heated events that would be occurring in Hungary in the coming weeks. The guest rooms were clean and simple, with pale blond laminate furniture and brightly colored curtains. The hotel favored many shades of reds and oranges. The bathroom was unlike anything I had ever seen before. The faucet for the sink was also utilized for the shower. It slid up and down on a metal rod and rotated toward either the shower or the sink. The bathroom floor got totally wet each time one showered. My room had a small balcony on which I would stand each night, watching the stars. I liked imagining my children at home, watching those same stars.

The initial morning after my arrival in Szeged, I took my first of nearly a hundred taxi rides to and from the orphanage, Pósz Jenö Utca (pronounced pos-yanos-utza), often making two and sometimes three trips a day. Like most other buildings in the small town, it was in a sad state of disrepair. It was overgrown with bushes, looking as if it had not been tended to in a long time. A black iron fence with spikes along the top, with a huge creaky gate, surrounded the orphanage. The building itself was made of concrete blocks that were chipped and the paint was peeling. I will never forget knocking on the big, old, solid, wooden door of the locked and antiquated preschool-turned-orphanage in which most of our children were being kept. One large room contained several rows of cribs on one side and a large pen, into which the children were placed, on the other side of the room. The medical exam room looked much as I imagined a doctor's office of the 1940s would look. The windows, like most of the windows throughout Eastern Europe, were covered with thin, nearly translucent lacey curtains.

It brings tears to my eyes when I play the memory of the first time I saw my precious Alex, playing outside in a barren little play yard which was mostly dirt with small patches of green weeds. The sun was shining brightly that day, and I remember hoping it was an omen of good things to come. My heart was filled with such love as I stood in the doorway, watching him. He was sitting atop a small, riding toy which he could push forward with his feet. He was wearing a little sun suit. He looked so beautiful, so angelic. He was very, very thin and small for his age, with huge dark brown eyes, weighing only seventeen pounds at eighteen months of age. But, boy did he talk up a storm. Of course, I couldn't understand anything he said.

One of the nurses picked him up and carried him into the building so that I could meet him. I remember the minute when she explained to him that I was his mama and she placed him in my arms as I sobbed. I couldn't believe I was finally holding this little boy about whom I had dreamed on so many nights. He was squirmy at first, being unsure of who I was, and then suddenly began to study my face intently. His big, beautiful, brown eyes were twinkling, and he had a mischievous grin. After a few seconds, he struggled to get down, wanting to return to his riding toy. It's hard to describe my feelings that first time I met my child, who was already a walking and talking human being as opposed to a newborn infant. I was filled with wonder at how smart, coordinated, and precious he seemed to be. The experience was nothing short of magical, and I could not imagine loving him anymore had I given birth to him.

I moved around in a constant state of disbelief at what was happening to me, grappling with being a naïve, thirty-six-year-old woman in a non-English speaking country, preparing to wage war against an unknown enemy, and the melting icing on the cake was that I was always so incredibly hot. I spent the next weeks fighting my own internal demons of self-doubt.

Within a few short days, each time I appeared at the orphanage, Alex would run into my arms and I would hold and hug him. He began calling me mama almost from the beginning, evoking such tenderness within me. His adoration toward me was like sewing warm patches over my cold feelings of fear and anxiety.

Over the next weeks, for a few hours each morning and then again each afternoon, I visited the facilities in which our children were held. Most of the children were in the same preschool/orphanage as Alex, but a smaller number of them were a few miles away, in another facility. Most days, I arrived to find the children in that large, wooden pen off to the side of the room. Once upon a time, I think the spindles had been painted bright red and blue and yellow. But by the time our children arrived, only traces of faded color remained. Every day, I held, rocked, and sang American lullabies to each one of the children, traveling between the two facilities daily. I sang "Old McDonald Had a Farm" at least twelve million times! I took turns with the caretakers feeding the children at lunch time. They allowed me to assist with caring for the children, but their solicitous monitoring sometimes made me uncomfortable, even though I completely understood their unease about this strange American in their midst. I was falling in love with not only Alex, but each of the *Szeged 28*. I cherished each one of them, wishing for more arms with which to hold them.

I was amazingly busy from the minute my plane landed in Budapest that first day. During my time in Hungary, I was followed by the, so called, Hungarian secret police. One time, the police were following me and a companion in their tiny unmarked car through a busy market area. They were so close, I suppose in fear of losing us, that they almost ran us over. It was often the same few men following me, and I grew to recognize some of them. Sometimes, I would exit my hotel in the morning to catch a taxi to the orphanage, and one or two of them would be leaning against the wall of a building across the street from the hotel. I would sometimes smile and wave as they became flustered and turned away. A piece of me actually enjoyed watching their discomfort.

On one of my first visits to the orphanage, I met a brilliant, Hungarian doctor, who expressed how pleased she was to meet me, after having heard the townspeople discussing me. With the help of a translator, I learned from the doctor that everyone in Szeged was talking about the American who had arrived to adopt a group of orphans. She said the story of my strange appearance had been on the local news. I was stunned to learn, after less than a week in Hungary, my presence was garnering local media coverage. I was a little frightened by the notion of media coverage, knowing that it could just as easily work against me as work for me. I suspected my presence was having an impact on our situation, although I was not yet sure if it was a positive one. The doctor told me there was great concern among the townspeople that I was going to steal the children. I listened to this, trying to imagine how I was going to smuggle 28 children out of the country. Under my shirt? Or was I going to load them on a bus after storming the orphanage in the middle of the night and make a run for the border as Ross Perot's commandos supposedly did in 1978 when trying to rescue his American employees held in Iran?

The doctor also explained to me that Alex suffered from continual ear infections and needed to have tubes inserted into his ears as soon as possible. She described his enormous, double inguinal hernias which needed repair as well. The hernias were large, and she taught me the process of tucking Alex's little intestines back into his body through the gaping hole in his abdomen. His little intestines seemed to escape from his body from exertions such as intense crying. So, the kindly caretakers were careful to help Alex remain calm and to keep him satisfied so he wouldn't cry much.

From John, the man working for the adoption agency, I learned about the terrible things that had been done to Alex as an infant. He shared that Alex had suffered from terrible ear infections, which had gone unattended, and that his ears had become so infected the infection had invaded his mastoid bone, behind both ears. Surgery had been required to open up the infected areas and scrape the bone and clean out the area. Little Alex had big scars behind each ear. The most awful aspect was the result of Alex's orphan status. I was told it was common practice that little pain relief was given because some doctors felt it was wasteful to use the precious medications, of which there were few, on an orphan. The knowledge of Alex's suffering gave me an incredibly heavy heart. John then shared that Alex had already had surgery for one of the inguinal hernias, but it was obvious it had not been successful. I asked John if pain medication had been withheld after that surgery too, and John just sadly nodded. Silent tears coursed down my cheeks, my despair over Alex's suffering like a knife through my heart.

There was nothing I could do to change the perception of the townspeople, regarding my presence in Szeged, so I continued to visit the children and lobby for their release. Every day, my heart broke for these young orphans who seemed to be more like hostages than innocent children. The lack of physical contact some of the children had experienced was painfully evident, some physically recoiling when being attended to. One of them bit me rather badly on the arm when I tried to pick him up. I had a perfect full-mouth imprint of his teeth on my forearm which remained nearly a week. I had been trying to get him to warm up to me, but he always kept his distance. He was one of the oldest and seemed to have gotten the least attention. I just wanted to hug and kiss him and tell him a better life awaited him.

With time, the children seemed to warm to my English-speaking presence and they began to look forward to my visits. One of the nurses reported that sometimes she would hear the older children singing "E-I-E-I-O" after I left.

Alex was the "go baby," as the caretakers called him, because he was always on the move and was frequently on one of the riding toys when I arrived. He seemed to bond quickly with me and while I was learning Hungarian phrases, he was rapidly absorbing English ones from me. After leaving the orphanages, the rest of my day was usually spent on the phone or in meetings, trying to win the freedom of our children. Daily, I had to keep at bay the panic that could have so easily taken over in my head. I tried to live minute by minute, without looking very far into the future, because that view was far too frightening.

At the beginning of my stay in Szeged, each morning I would ask the hotel desk clerk to summon a taxi which would take me to the orphanage. By day three, a taxi was always waiting for me, and when I got into the car, I didn't even have to tell the driver where to go. I had the same experience at the end of the day when leaving the orphanage to return to the hotel. I didn't seem to have the same taxi driver every day, yet they all still knew my destinations. I no longer had to wait for taxis; one was always waiting for me. It was an odd sensation to be flitting around this small city and everyone seemed to know who I was and the nature of my business.

John and I met when he was in town, from Budapest, and helped me to plan my next moves. But, much of the time I was lonely, feeling almost as if I were in some form of exile. I ate many of my meals alone and would sometimes stroll the streets around the hotel, taking in the sights and sounds of the town. The buildings were small, and the streets narrow. I discovered a favorite little restaurant in the basement of a building near the hotel. There was a small market across from the hotel where I would frequently buy water, bread, and cheese for my meals. Generally, the townspeople were nice to me. Although, everywhere I went I felt the intensity of their constant stares.

The Hungarian government, still reeling from years of an oppressive communist regime, was clearly not happy to have a thirty-six-year-old American woman in their country, stirring up international relations. I was obviously bringing pressure upon the American Consul General, based on the way he had behaved toward me. I was speaking with every official into whose office I could gain entrance. Although the care givers and doctors at the orphanage in Szeged were warm and genuinely kind, most of the government officials maintained a very detached manner.

A week or so into my stay in Hungary, the ACG summoned me to his office in Budapest. Back to the train station I went for my two-hour train ride. With the greatest anticipation imaginable, I sat trying to discern the purpose of this summons; perhaps our children were going to be released. I could hardly sit still on the train, and every few minutes would get up and stroll to the front of the car. I was nervous, but nearly giddy with excitement, as I convinced myself good news would be forthcoming.

That was not the case. Entering the ACG's office, I was invited to take a seat. He calmly told me that he had an offer for me. If I would leave the country, I could take Alex and let the case rest. Standing up, completely in shock, I responded, "No thank you, they are all going home to America." I stormed out of his office, got back on the train, and returned to Szeged. I had not been in his office even five minutes that day. On that solitary return to Szeged, I tried to manage the anger I had for what I viewed as attempted bribery. There had been no possibility I would leave one member of the *Szeged 28* in that country. Clearly a more aggressive approach of some sort would be needed, but I had no idea what that might be. I later learned that another father in our group had also received the same offer months earlier when he had flown to Hungary to spend a few days with the daughter he hoped to adopt. Like me, he too had refused the offer.

CHAPTER 9

ANOTHER SUMMONS FROM BUDAPEST

B<small>ACK IN</small> S<small>ZEGED</small>, I <small>SHARED</small> with the other adoptive families, who were all still in America, what was happening in Hungary and I gave them information about their children, who I continued to visit daily. I told the families I could see the impact my presence was having on the country. I shared with them stories about the cute things their children were doing. And I continued my daily routine of visiting them.

Less than a week after my first summons from the ACG, I received another call requesting my presence in Budapest, as soon as possible. I contemplated the chances of another extortion offer coming my way. I let Congressman Talent know I was going to the Embassy in Budapest, and the next day I hopped on the train to hear what would be said to me this time. I did not have the hopeful, anticipatory feelings I had experienced on my last trip. I was becoming jaded or angry, or both.

After I arrived at the American Embassy, and after the barest of pleasantries, our conversation began with the Consul General telling me that the birth mothers had not legally relinquished the children for adoption. Then he continued, advising me that some of the birth mothers couldn't be found and there was no way to get relinquishment documents signed. He next said that it would be better if the children were returned to Romania, and they could be adopted from that county. Something suddenly became crystal clear to me. Our prospective adoptions were creating an enormous amount of work for this man and he was eager to pawn this whole mess off on the Romanian government and the American Embassy in Romania. Also, I knew that the birth mothers had legally relinquished the children, having seen copies of the paperwork at my first meeting with John. It appeared to me that someone, somewhere, had begun working even harder to stop our adoptions and this man was listening to them.

At precisely that moment, the phone on the desk of the ACG rang. He picked it up and suddenly sat a little taller in his chair. I couldn't hear the other side of the conversation and had no idea to whom he was speaking. I was only privy to his "yes sirs." The Consul General looked at me and said, "Congressman Talent would like to speak with you." The look on his face and the condescending tone of his voice sent me a message that said, "Ha, you are in trouble now." I smiled to myself at his interpretation of the Congressman's request to speak with me.

I took the phone and after exchanging cordial greetings, Congressman Talent said to me, "What is this I hear about you planning a major demonstration in the streets of Budapest?" I laughed out loud, assuring Congressman Talent I had no idea to what he was referring and that there was certainly no plan to hold a demonstration of any kind.

I thought, *I am a solitary, English speaking, mid-western woman in Hungary, how on earth could I make anything like that happen?* But suddenly I knew for sure that I was having an impact on the situation in Hungary! People in the American government were afraid I was going to create an international scene! I viewed this as a very hopeful development. Congressman Talent asked me to keep in touch with him and to keep him informed of my travels. We agreed that we would talk soon. He asked to speak with the ACG again. I sat quietly while they concluded the call. I much later learned that during that conversation, Congressman Talent told the Consul General he needed to continue taking steps to ensure that nothing happened to me while I was in Hungary. So, I am not really sure if the secret police followed me to keep track of me for their government or for my own.

After hanging up the phone with Congressman Talent, I could clearly see the ACG was fuming. I believe he was shocked that an American Congressman was calling me and that we obviously had a friendly relationship. I desperately didn't want to engage in an acrimonious conversation with this man, I needed his help. But, I noticed that he was staring at a tall stack of manila file folders sitting on the side of his desk. I realized they were the files belonging to our twenty-eight children. At the time, I believed that one of the only things keeping our children in Hungary was the lack of this man's signature on the forms, which would allow the children to leave. All he had to do was sign his name! Why was he refusing? He was obviously getting orders from higher up, but from whom and for what reason? Could the lobbyist group be that powerful?

These were innocent babies with loving families awaiting them, and they shouldn't have been pawns in some lobbyist's game. Looking at the files, my gaze moved to the Consul General. He looked at me and flatly stated, "You will never get these children out of this country." The tension in the room was so incredibly thick it was practically suffocating me. He picked up the files, walked to a filing cabinet, opened the top drawer, dropped them in, slammed the cabinet closed, and pushed in the lock. He turned around, looked at me and said, "You can go now." Little did he know that each time I left his office, I was stronger and more determined to free our children.

I realized after our encounter that I needed reinforcements, and as soon as I could get to a phone, I contacted three other American women, also waiting for their children, and asked them to join me in Hungary. It was obvious that more American women would be necessary to increase the pressure on the American Consul General!

CHAPTER 10

A NIGHTTIME VISITOR

AN INCREDIBLE YOUNG AMERICAN WOMAN, Abby, was working for me as my translator. She was living in Hungary and had been working for John. Were it not for Abby, I probably would have lost my mind. Her positive spirit was like an antidote for me, helping me to hold my internal desperation at bay. She became my companion when possible, my translator, my advocate, and my friend. Abby was frequently in my hotel room with me in the evenings as we strategized our next move in our battle to win the release of the children. Many of the other waiting families were busy working on the release of the children back in the United States. We regularly shared documents and had many, many phone calls in the evening hours.

One night, about ten days after arriving in Hungary and before my three American friends arrived, while reviewing a group of faxes we had received that day from the US, someone began pounding on my hotel room door. Abby went to the door and there stood a young man in a police uniform. They began a rapid, obviously combative and brusque conversation. I fearfully listened to the exchange, able to tell that the subject matter was intensely personal for Abby and our visitor. After a few minutes, he left. She returned to the table and said, "Wow, we are making a difference. That was my friend Zandor, and he wants me to stop helping you. He said your phone is tapped and the Hungarian secret police are listening to all your calls. He thinks I might be in danger and wants me to stop helping you." Abby assured me that she was as committed to the children as I and she had no intention of abandoning me. I was so grateful to her. We already knew we were being followed everywhere we went. But, it was unnerving to have it confirmed in this way.

Suddenly, Congressman Talent's comment regarding my impending protest plans made sense! I had early on, shortly after arriving in Hungary, made a joke on the phone to my husband that perhaps I would end up marching in the street to get the kids out. I had completely forgotten that simple, silly comment. From my exchange with Congressman Talent regarding my impending demonstration, combined with this new information from Zandor, I knew that what Abby had just said was true. Someone was listening to all of my calls, but were we really in any kind of danger? The reason explaining why this was happening was still misty, but perhaps we needed to just find a way around the mist rather than through it. My resolve to get the *Szeged 28* out of Hungary only strengthened.

CHAPTER 11

MAKING AN IMPRESSION

THERE WAS ANOTHER INCIDENT CONFIRMING that I was a topic of conversation in Hungary. At the end of each day and upon returning to the hotel, I would go to the bar in the lobby area to get a soda, always begging for an extra ice cube. Eastern Europe wasn't enamored with the American custom of iced drinks, preferring them at room temperature. I had the distinct feeling that not many Americans had ever been to this small, former-communist, Hungarian town. With no air conditioning at either the orphanages or in the hotel, by the end of the day, all I could think about was a Diet Coke with ice! So, each afternoon I walked into the bar to get my Diet Coke with three little ice cubes, never ever more than the allotted three. As with the people I encountered everywhere I went, the people in the bar always seemed to be quite interested in me.

One evening, I walked into the bar and on the TV behind the bar—there I was! I stood there feeling disoriented, watching myself on TV. It took me a minute to reconcile what I was seeing on the screen with the fact that a newscaster was speaking in Hungarian and I had been filmed leaving the orphanage. The local news was covering the story and filming me without my knowledge! As I stood staring at the television, I realized that everyone else in the little bar was staring at me. All I could do was smile and make a quick exit. This was proof that my presence in the country was having some kind of effect!

My three friends, Jayne, Denise, and Becca arrived a few days later, and I traveled to Budapest to meet them. I was so excited to see them, I could hardly sit still on the train. I couldn't wait to have someone to speak English with every day and knew their presence would create further angst for both the Hungarian and the American governments! I had even received a phone call from the American Consul General, who demanded to know if it were true that I was bringing three more American women to Hungary. He asked me how many more I was planning to bring, and I responded, "Well there are twenty-six sets of parents awaiting the release of the Szeged 28, so I guess I will be bringing twenty-two more mothers to Hungary." He was quite displeased with my response and quickly hung up the phone.

Now there would be four determined, American women who wanted to get all the children out of Hungary. When they arrived, I couldn't recall ever having been as happy to see anyone in my life.

We stayed overnight at the Buro Panzio, and the next morning decided to explore Budapest for a few hours before catching the train to Szeged. We were walking around the city and suddenly found that we were lost. We were trying to look at a map of Budapest but were wholly unsuccessful. We happened upon a telephone booth on the side of the street. I said, "Oh great, we will just look up the number for the Buro Panzio and get directions back." I had the Hungarian coins for the phone booth.

A huge telephone directory was hanging on a chain in the phone booth. I stepped up to the booth, opened the book, and began to laugh at myself. The book was of course in Hungarian, and I couldn't read a word of it. I glanced up at my American friends, and they were thoroughly enjoying my gaffe and one of them snapped my picture. When they had finished laughing at me, we finally made our way back to the bed and breakfast, without the breakfast, to collect our luggage and we headed for the train station.

After arriving at our hotel in Szeged, Jayne, who became my roommate for the rest of our time in Hungary, opened her suitcase and out poured a small cache of food! Oh, happy American day! She even brought a canned ham after my having told them that the food was not what I was used to and was too spicy for me.

CHAPTER 12

ADDRESSING THE HUNGARIAN PARLIAMENT

INITIALLY, BACK IN THE US, I had been led to believe that the American Consul General just needed to sign off on the paperwork and the children could leave. Then while still at home, I was told by John that an American lobby group was responsible for convincing the American, Romanian, and Hungarian governments to withhold help. It seemed that no one could help, and I didn't really know who to trust. John explained that he felt our best chance of success was convincing the Hungarian government to let the children go, in essence sidestepping the Americans.

So, about three weeks into the battle, John arranged for me to have the opportunity to speak to a group of Hungarian Parliament members. On June 22, 1993, I got back on the train and returned to Budapest. John met my train and we headed for the Hungarian Parliament building. Standing on the other side of the Danube and looking magnificent was the enormous, one-hundred-year-old Parliament building, and the sight was overwhelming for me. It was a massive structure with hundreds of spires and columns and arches, and reputed to have nearly 700 rooms. John shared that it was one of the two or three largest parliament buildings worldwide. It was truly spectacular looking and appeared to be a quarter mile wide. I found the view breathtaking.

We crossed the bridge, entered the building, went through security, and I found myself standing in the most cavernous and lavish room I had ever seen. The ornate columns, the intricately painted walls and ceilings, the marble everywhere I looked, the red carpets – all of it was just stunning. Two huge staircases on either side of the giant entry hall led to an upper level, where I was to meet with the Parliament members.

I will never forget walking up that tremendous staircase, wide enough to easily handle twelve people walking abreast of one another, taking in the breathtaking beauty, and anxiously anticipating what I was about to do. I was profoundly aware that much was riding on the message I would be delivering. I met with Mr. Gabor Fodor, the Chairman of the Committee on Human Rights, and other Parliament members.

That day, through a translator, I told our story and begged for the Parliament members' help to get our children out of Hungary. Telling the members how twenty-six sets of parents had been looking at photographs and video and falling in love with twenty-eight Hungarian/Romanian orphans over the past year, I described how broken-hearted we were that we hadn't been able to take the children home. I painted a picture of the lives the children would have; good health care, education, they would have brothers and sisters, and they would be monumentally loved. I promised that the parents would always make sure the children knew from where they came, and we would teach them to be proud of their birth countries. I spoke in a clear and impassioned way and was able to keep from sobbing. At the end of my speech, I couldn't help that a single tear escaped down my cheek. Damn, I had been so determined not to cry.

The parliament members had been attentive, and I felt as if they had truly heard me. Mr. Fodor asked to meet with me after I spoke to the group, and I hoped he had been so moved he would do what he could to help.

He shared truly outrageous information! He told me that he had already spoken with Mr. Thomas, the US Ambassador to Hungary, and offered his help to resolve the situation regarding the orphans, but that Mr. Thomas had declined the offer of help! Reportedly, Mr. Thomas told Mr. Fodor that the American government had the situation under control. I was shocked to hear this. Alarms were screaming inside my head; clearly, the US did not have this under control.

Mr. Fodor further explained to me that the Hungarian government had been willing to allow the children to leave Hungary several months ago, but the brakes had been put on by someone in Washington. He said someone from the United States had cited the wording in an antiquated and outdated treaty between Hungary and Romania stating that Hungarians could not adopt Romanian children and vise-versa. Both Hungary and Romania had been advised that considering the implications of that treaty, the waiting parents should not be allowed to adopt the children! However, we were a group of *Americans* hoping to adopt babies who had been born in both countries. I believed that treaty had nothing to do with our situation. Nothing was making sense to me; my head was spinning. Mr. Fodor next explained that his government was just waiting for an official request from the US, directed to the Hungarian government, to release the children. Mr. Fodor shared that once that document was received, the children could leave Hungary. I was humiliated. I had begged a group of politicians for something they had, unbeknown to me, already offered.

I finally understood that what John had conveyed about the lobby group had been correct. The group had successfully halted any cooperation between the three countries by convincing them about that ridiculous treaty. Again, I questioned myself, "Had this only been about money being paid to the right agency?" I couldn't believe I was now hearing that the Hungarian government would allow the children to leave – if only they were officially asked. I stood in stunned silence. I needed to get back to my hotel room and sort through all of this new information as well as my increasingly out-of-control emotions.

I departed the Parliament building feeling hopeful, but incredibly angry, now with tears streaming down my face because I felt like I had gotten to the truth. I knew exactly who the enemy was: it had been confirmed for me – it was my own government, but that government had been persuaded by a powerful lobby group!

As I rode the train back to Szeged, my brain couldn't process the information from so many different people during the past month. I wished there was a mute button that could switch off their voices and give me some quiet time inside my head. I wanted to ride that train in peace, but my mind was zooming faster than the train. After getting back to the hotel, I shared the new information with the parents who were waiting back home and asked them to brainstorm from their side of the ocean. My brain was exhausted. I called Congressman Talent and tearfully told him what had happened. I learned that Senators Jeff Bingaman from New Mexico and Jesse Helms from North Carolina, as well as Representatives Christopher Markey from Massachusetts, Jim Talent from Missouri, and Tom Lantos from Maryland, all wrote letters to the Hungarian government requesting the release of the children. But, I was told that an official request directly from the White House was needed. I had no idea how to make that happen.

A few days later, we learned that a group of Hungarian officials was going to visit the main orphanage office in Szeged. I was hopeful that this visit by government officials would in some way be tied to my impassioned plea to the Parliament. I remained hopeful that the Hungarian government would decide to let the children go even without the official White House request.

Jayne and I made plans to go to the main orphanage office and wait there to see what was going to happen, to see who the visitors were, and to try to find out if they were there to help us. We waited hour after hour in a dark hallway for their arrival, which thankfully was air conditioned! To lighten our mood, I removed my shoe and began talking to it in the spirit of the bumbling spy Maxwell Smart from the old TV show, Get Smart. We laughed and laughed. It was a well-needed release from the constant stress we were under. However, our hope to gain information was without reward that day. We learned nothing. We never saw any officials arrive, and it appeared that our initial intelligence was flawed.

The four of us were all from St. Louis, and our hometown newspaper was covering our efforts to get the children out. The newspaper had kept in touch with us, and already a couple of stories had appeared in the paper. We had not known each other before this adoption disaster, but Becca, Denise, Jayne, and I formed a forever bond working together to get our children out of Hungary. We were four anxious mothers visiting the children every day and, unknown to us, making headlines around the world. I was thrilled to have my friends join me in Hungary, but my heart still ached for my two precious children and my husband back in St. Louis.

CHAPTER 13

LAURA'S 10ᵀᴴ BIRTHDAY AND THE NEW YORK TIMES

My LONGING FOR MY FAMILY intensified almost daily. I had been in Hungary for nearly five weeks and was hot, tired, emotionally and physically exhausted. Laura's tenth birthday was on a nearly one-hundred-degree day at the end of June. My sadness was overwhelming, and feelings of defeat were beginning to eke their way into my soul. I was developing a quiet desperation. In my hotel room, I called her to wish her happy birthday and began to cry. I missed my family more than words could describe and told Laura that I was considering giving up and returning home, which was uncharacteristic for me. My precious Laura, ever the pillar of strength, reprimanded me with, "Mom, why are you crying, you are there with Alex. You can't come home without my little brother. *He* is my birthday present." We both cried. I was extraordinarily moved by her incredible strength and bravery. We were close, and I knew her little ten-year-old heart was breaking as she tried to be so strong on the phone.

After our chat, I strolled down to the lobby of the hotel and out into what was the most forlorn, little courtyard I had ever seen. There was no grass, just dirt, a lone tree under which stood a little stone bench, and of course that blazing hot, one-hundred-degree sun. I sat on the bench and sobbed, missing home so much. I began to pray to God, asking Him why this was happening to me; I hadn't asked to be thrust into an international hailstorm. I told Him that one day I could only hope to understand His plan. I just wanted to bring this little boy into our lives to love. Those old childhood feelings of failure were sneaking up on me. Suddenly, the most remarkable calm came over me and I knew we were going to take all the children home. In that instant, on June 29, 1993, I sat there in the hot, hot sun and my tears of fear turned to tears of joy. But I still hoped to one day understand why this had all happened.

The next day, I received a call from the *New York Times*. I was thrilled that a reporter, Judith Ingram, and her film crew was coming to Szeged and wanted to interview me and tell our story! My head was spinning with all the pleas I wanted to make to the reporter. My belief that the kids would get out was further strengthened. I had no idea our story was so impactful that the *New York Times* was following it. I knew if the *Times* was covering our story though, we were big, big news back home. I later learned that our story was also being covered throughout Europe as well.

My three American friends and I spent the third of July 1993 with a reporter and film crew from the *New York Times*. The experience was like being in a dream. They interviewed us and took pictures of the children in the orphanage, telling us the story would be on the front page the following day, America's Independence Day. I hoped this could do nothing but help us. A front-page article about winning the freedom of orphaned children on the day America was celebrating its own freedom! I knew there would now be international pressure placed upon the Hungarian government to let this small band of American women take their children home. I tried to envision an end to this nightmare, trying to imagine finally going home, and after speaking to the reporter, I stood on our little balcony and wept.

CHAPTER 14

UNDERSTANDING THE ISSUES

Dᴜʀɪɴɢ ᴛʜᴇ ᴡᴇᴇᴋs I'ᴅ ʙᴇᴇɴ in Hungary, so much of the new information I'd learned had made me so angry all my senses had simply shut down. I felt incapacitated by my fury over what was transpiring and by my utter lack of control and total inability to impart change. There were times I just wanted to scream like the star of a horror movie but feared once I began I would be unable to stop. My feelings of frustration begat feelings of helplessness, which begat hopelessness – but I refused to concede to that! So, I chose anger to keep me on the other side of the precipice of despair.

Because I was in Hungary and receiving in-depth details from John, and getting updated information from home every day, along with my conversation with Mr. Fodor, I had been able to paint an absolutely discouraging picture of what was happening. I now fully understood what was keeping our children held prisoners in Szeged.

I learned that the director for the lobby group, American Center for Adoption, Andy Graves, had admitted in a newspaper article that he had in fact advised both the Hungarian and the American governments that the children should not be allowed to be adopted. He further encouraged the Hungarian government to return the children to Romania. He admitted that he had been the one who cited the antiquated, bilateral treaty between Hungary and Romania as the basis for his interference. Once the treaty issue had been introduced, all three governments became nervous and our adoptions, which should have been finalized months before, had been halted.

It was confirmed through sources back in the US that the Hungarian government was willing to let the children go if the American government would just make an official request. But a powerful source in Washington was keeping that request from being made. Instead, again, the offer had been made to us that if the children were transferred to Romania, we could adopt them *if* we utilized a member agency of American Center for Adoption. I simply could not understand our government's refusal to make the formal request for release of the children and instead support the lobby group. It had become clear to me that the Hungarian citizens, with whom I was in contact, were total champions of our efforts to win the release of the *Szeged 28*. I had won over the Hungarian government and verified that our only remaining nemesis appeared to be our own government.

I fully believed then, and continue to, that the entire issue centered on our not utilizing the right adoption agency for our adoptions. After I returned home, I learned that the American Center for Adoption received a fee for every adoption facilitated by their member organizations. The lobby group, however, did not have an official agreement with Hungary as it had with Romania. Clearly the fear of the organization was that if children were allowed to be adopted from Hungary, their organization would be cut out of the Romanian adoption pipeline and it wouldn't be receiving a cut of every adoption. I was too angry for words! I needed a miracle.

CHAPTER 15

GOING HOME!

Late in the evening on July 3rd, I got a phone call from the American Consul General in Budapest, who told me all of the children were being released and that I would be the first one to leave with Alex. I held the phone in my shaking hand, asking him if he were sure. I yelled thank you into the phone, slammed it down, and went screaming down the hall to find Jayne, Denise, and Becca! They were in Denise and Becca's room, into which I flew screaming and crying, and suddenly we were all screaming and crying and hugging and jumping up and down as if on pogo sticks. Our prayers had been answered. Perhaps, just the threat of that *New York Times* coverage had really been the catalyst to get our government moving! Judith Ingram's article did appear on the front page of the *New York Times* on July 4, 1993.

I immediately returned to my room and called to confirm this information with Congressman Talent. He excitedly greeted me on the phone and said, yes it was true, and I just kept thanking him repeatedly. I learned that the White House had finally issued a formal request that the children be permitted to leave Hungary for humanitarian purposes.

We were all going home, nearly six weeks after arriving in Hungary. Next, I called home to share the news with my joyful family and then I contacted the airline to get reservations for Alex and me on the first flight out of Budapest which would take us home to America. That night I enjoyed the first truly peaceful sleep since leaving home. I had been given the job to fight an international battle and, with the help of many others, we achieved our goal and we were all going home.

Three short days later, I was packed and found myself bidding farewell to my American friends, who would all be following me within a day or two. I left the hotel in the familiar taxi and made my way to the orphanage to retrieve Alex. I hugged and cried with the orphanage caretakers, who had been so kind to me and who had played such an important role in my life during the past weeks. I was eternally grateful to these angels who had cared for and loved all the children before our arrival. I felt blessed that I had been able to learn enough of the Hungarian language that I was able to express my love and gratitude to the caretakers in their own language. I was excited to be going home, but it was a bittersweet farewell. This group of loving women had earned a "forever" place in my heart. I hugged each of the children goodbye, praying to someday see them all again, but fearing I would not. The one child who remained beyond the reach of my hug was the child who had bitten me. Little did I know that this little boy, who would be called Michael, would over the next twenty years teach me incredible lessons about love, compassion, and resiliency.

I took one last look around the dilapidated couple of rooms in which Alex and most of the rest of the children had been forced to live for months, and gleefully we went out of that heavy, wooden front door for the last time. There were people all around and reporters were snapping pictures. We got into a waiting taxi for our final trip to the train station.

Alex and I boarded our train for the trip to Budapest. It was a challenge for me to manage a nineteen-month-old baby, an enormous suitcase, and a make shift diaper bag I had acquired at a shop in Szeged.

But, I was so determined, there was no way a little cumbersome luggage was going to slow me down. That two-hour train ride seemed to last for six. I simply couldn't believe that I was finally taking my precious Alex home to meet the rest of his family. My heart was singing with joy, finding it hard to fathom this would be my final journey on this train. Wanting to enjoy the countryside of Hungary on that final ride, the farmland, small train depots, and dirt roads we passed, I took pictures through the train window. It wasn't uncommon to see a horse drawn wagon loaded with hay alongside the road. Someday these pictures of the countryside would be shared with Alex.

After arriving in Budapest, we went directly to the Hungarian Immigration office to retrieve the paperwork so that Alex and I could fly out of Budapest on the afternoon of July 6, 1993. At the Hungarian Immigration office, I was told I had to wait. Feeling that something was amiss, I moved away from the desk to sit on a cool vinyl chair and studied this plain room, which looked like so many of the other offices I had visited in Hungary. It was stark and sparsely furnished with well used but clean items. I tried to divert my attention, but we had a plane to catch in just a few hours, and I was slowly becoming uneasy.

Suddenly, the American Consul General (ACG) came rushing into the Immigration office. Oh no, this man who had only wanted to stand in our way had shown up. I couldn't fathom the reason for his arrival, which confirmed for me that something was wrong. I held Alex even tighter to my chest, secretly repeating I would never give him back, trying to push back the panic that was rising up inside of me. I suddenly feared I might vomit.

After heated exchanges with Hungarian Immigration officials, the ACG came over to me and said that one of Alex's medical documents was not included in the official document packet, and it was needed to allow him to leave the country. I was speechless; we were so close to freedom – less than two hours away! I knew our plane would be boarding soon and I became frantic.

The ACG scurried back over to a desk and feverishly began making telephone calls. After several minutes on the phone, he advised me that the Hungarian authorities had agreed to accept a faxed copy of Alex's medical record. He said this was the first time this had ever been allowed and that original documents were required by law. Once again, as I had so many times in the past few days, I began to cry tears of joy, thanking God for his help. But our time was continuing to run out. The ACG called the airport and asked them to hold the plane, buying us a few extra minutes.

I almost laughed at how obvious it was to me that this man could not wait to get me out of his hair. He was actually perspiring in his frenzied efforts to help me. The American Counsel General was being nice to me and actually acting like he cared, which was diametrically opposed to the way he had been behaving for many months toward me. The interactions between us were strained and uneasy for both of us. I began to think that had pressure from Washington not been placed on him to be uncooperative regarding our adoptions, he might very well have been helpful to us.

The fax arrived from Szeged, the Immigration officials stamped it, the ACG signed off, and we were free to go. By this point, I wasn't even thinking. I was on autopilot and was just doing what I was told. The ACG had ordered up his official embassy limousine and it was waiting in front of the building to transport Alex and me to the airport. We didn't have enough time for a regular taxi. The ACG ushered us out of the office and into the limo, warning me we would be cutting it close and that the plane could not be held for long. I thanked him and jumped into the car, the assistant throwing my suitcase into the trunk. The big, black limo into which we climbed had two American flags flying on each of the front fenders of the car. As I looked at those flags, for some reason I thought to myself how interesting it was that they were perfectly spaced! I couldn't totally comprehend everything that was happening so fast. I had viewed a scene like this in a movie once. The

American Consul General's aide drove like a maniac through the streets of Budapest! He was honking for people to get out of his way, other people were honking at him, and Alex and I were being thrown back and forth inside the cabin of the car like tennis balls in a big match. It occurred to me that we could be killed in a car accident after everything we had just been through. But, in a matter of minutes, we made it to the airport. We all ran in, the aide threw my bag on the conveyer belt, I rushed through check in, and amidst nasty stares from airline officials, I finally made my way onto the airplane.

As I watched Budapest disappear beneath us, I quietly sobbed and hugged little Alex to me. With tremendous joy and gratefulness, I whispered to Alex, "We won."

CHAPTER 16

LAYOVER IN ZURICH

OUR FLIGHT SCHEDULE REQUIRED THAT we overnight in Zurich. I had wanted to get out of Budapest as quickly as possible, and this flight was the first one available on such short notice. As we were landing in Zurich, the flight attendant made an announcement over the intercom instructing me to see the gate agent after landing. Although curious about the announcement, I was not overly concerned. Certainly, I had been through the worst weeks of my life, and anything else going forward would be a cake walk. After deplaning, I met an airline official and was escorted to an Immigration holding area, where I was told that I could be allowed to leave the airport, but "Szilard" could not. With a sinking feeling in my chest, I listened as they explained that Alex was traveling with a Romanian passport and Romanians had to have entrance visas to enter Switzerland. That meant Alex would not be allowed to leave the airport!

I was far from hysterical after what I had just been through and began to consider a way out of this new mess in which we found ourselves. I asked to use the phone and I called Congressman Talent to request his help. The thought of spending the night at an airport with a nineteen-month-old baby was not appealing. Congressman Talent said he would see what he could do to help us and promised to get back to me shortly. We were instructed to remain in the holding area. Several police were guarding the area everywhere I looked, all carrying the Uzi weapons to which I had unfortunately become accustomed. While sitting there waiting, I kept speculating on why Alex and I had come to the attention of the Swiss officials before even landing.

A brief time later, a Swiss Immigration official told me that Congressman Talent had reached an agreement with the Swiss government allowing both of us to leave the airport and go to a hotel. I was told that we would, however, need to surrender our passports to Swiss authorities. I was instructed when and where to retrieve them the following day for our flight. I was uncomfortable being parted from my passport. But, the exhaustion of the past many weeks weighed more heavily on me than my discomfort over my passport.

We took a taxi to the nearest hotel and collapsed in bed, both of us sleeping through the night in a lovely air-conditioned room. I was thoroughly exhausted, failing to take the time to marvel at the beauty of Zurich and the mountains surrounding the city. Unfortunately, I can hardly recall our time in the beautiful country of Switzerland and have no memory of even eating dinner that night.

The next morning, according to the instructions given to me the night before, we returned to the airport to retrieve our passports. Finally, we were once again on an airplane and we were headed home. I was ecstatic at the prospect of returning to America and couldn't wait to see my family. The plane was backing away from the jetway, when the brakes were engaged. The plane stopped and then began to move forward, returning to the loading area. Inside my head, a voice was screaming that this was about us and it could not be good. Before the plane had fully stopped, my legs had already begun to shake.

The plane stopped, the doors were opened, and sure enough, three Swiss soldiers, all holding Uzis, got onto the plane and walked directly to me. One of them demanded my paperwork for "Szilard." I was terrified to allow it to be taken from me. I had been told by the American Consul General that the sealed envelope must be delivered intact and unopened to the US Immigration officials upon my arrival in the United States. For the second time in 24 hours, I was asked to surrender my passport, and this time I *was* nearly hysterical. As the armed solider and I stared each other down, I realized there was no choice and with a quivering hand, I surrendered both of our passports, Alex's immigration paperwork, and all of our travel documents. Two of the soldiers remained on the plane, seemingly to "guard me" while the other left the plane. I wasn't sure why I was being guarded; it wasn't as if there was an alternate, convenient way off the plane!

The plane was deathly silent as everyone sat staring at me, then slowly everyone began whispering to one another. I imagined them asking each other if I could possibly be some kind of criminal. I was glad they had not asked me to stand, being unsure I would have been able to do so because I was trembling so badly. I sat quietly on the plane, gently rocking Alex back and forth, trying not to think about what this could mean. After about ten of the longest minutes of my life, the Swiss soldier returned, dropped the documents and passports in my lap, and told the flight attendant the plane could depart. To this day, I have no idea what happened while we sat trapped on that plane.

Alex was the star on the plane from Zurich to Chicago! As word spread that he was the first of the *Szeged 28* to leave Hungary, many people on the plane, having already read about us, wanted to meet him and talk with me. I was stunned that so many people had heard of us! But, I also thought that perhaps people were just relieved I was not a dangerous criminal.

Little Alex ran from one person to the next, entertaining the entire cabin. The airline pilots invited us to come up into the flight area! The pilots and the flight attendants gave us a gift before exiting the plane. They had asked Alex and me to come to the cockpit, and standing together, they gave me the original flight-path map from the cockpit, with each having signed it, leaving inspirational and meaningful messages. They told me they wanted to properly welcome Alex to the United States. As I hugged each one of them, I again wept, overcome by their thoughtfulness and kindness.

That framed map would hang next to the puffy clouds on Alex's American bedroom wall.

CHAPTER 17

CHICAGO!

As the plane was descending into the Chicago O'Hare airport, the flight attendant made an announcement on the intercom, again! I was instructed to meet an American Airlines gate agent upon exiting the aircraft. By this time, I was exhausted and numb to whatever else they would throw at me. But now, for me it just wouldn't matter. I was an American back in America, and I was not letting go of my child. Plus, I was buoyed by the amazing gift the flight crew had just given to us.

Awaiting me was a lovely young woman from American Airlines with one of those little motorized transports, who explained that Congressman Talent had arranged for me to be personally escorted through Immigration and then to the American Airlines lounge to await our flight home. After everything we had been through, this kindness made me cry, again. Alex and I waited in the American Airlines lounge, enjoying a diet Coke that was more ice than soda, thank heavens! As promised, at the appropriate time, Alex and I were summoned by the airline official and escorted to our next flight. We took off from Chicago without incident.

When we landed in St. Louis, as I exited the gate, there were hundreds of people waiting and cheering everywhere I looked. Ryan, Laura, and Alex's new daddy all rushed forward to hold and kiss him as we flew into the arms of our waiting family. Alex was the only one not crying but looking all around at the balloons and flashing cameras, with everyone seeming to talk at once. Ryan stuck a small baseball cap on Alex's head and Laura thrust a white teddy bear into his arms. Both Ryan and Laura looked as if they had grown a foot. I was shocked to see that even my mother, who had not been supportive of my going to Hungary, had shown up.

I was overwhelmed by the love and support of our many, many friends who came to welcome us home. Surprisingly, I didn't cry. The news media was even there! After lots of hugs and pictures, our now complete family was finally united, and we were heading home.

I was particularly thankful because I recognized I was just an ordinary American who had been given an extraordinary opportunity. I was grateful for the gifts the Hungarian experience had given me; it was life changing. My lingering feelings of inadequacy had been replaced by feelings of empowerment. I had developed a belief in my own abilities and learned that I was tough and resilient. Against formidable odds, I had returned to St. Louis with my son. And I was so grateful to God for giving me the strength to fight the battle.

Along with a few other parents in our adoption group, I was contacted by federal authorities about our adoption agency a few weeks after our return to the US. We later learned that due to the questionable actions of the agency, the Director was prosecuted by the State of Washington and was barred from working in any field relating to adoption for the rest of her life.

CHAPTER 18

HOME

WE HAD WAGED WAR WITH our own government officials, with foreign officials, and with forces unknown to us. But in the end, we won and were able to obtain the freedom on July 3, 1993, of not only my son, but the entire *Szeged 28* group of orphans who had been trapped in the loneliest and most desolate place imaginable, an Eastern European orphanage. Our story was front-page news in the industrialized world. I had learned from some of the families who were just arriving in Hungary as I was leaving that newspapers in the airports throughout Europe featured the headlines "*Szeged 28* Released," "*Szeged 28* Win Freedom," and on and on and on. When setting out on this adoption path, I would never in a million years have pictured this kind of ending to our story!

Those first few days after getting home were spent in utter bliss. I felt such deep happiness at being reunited with my family and sheer joy having Alex with us. But I was also adjusting to not being afraid or feeling stressed and desperate all the time. I slept a great deal the first two weeks I was home. My time in Hungary had taken a physical and emotional toll on me.

On a Sunday afternoon about a month after returning home, we had a big reception to welcome Alex to our family and give our friends a chance to meet him. At church that morning, Alex had been christened. He had looked precious in his little white outfit; I envisioned a whole world just waiting for him to conquer.

The streets of our neighborhood were filled with the cars of our friends. I had a banner printed which read, "He wasn't expected, he was selected!" and it was prominently displayed in our front yard. Jayne, Denise, and Becca, with their husbands and their newly adopted children, joined us, and it was a special celebration for us four women. We wept as our four little ones were once more back together, but this time in darling little outfits, each of them having already gained weight and with glowing smiles on their faces. It was surreal that such a short time ago these precious little ones had been living in a desolate place and had now won the lottery. They had families who loved them.

We invited Congressman Talent, and unbelievably he had agreed to join us! We had a second big banner in our front yard saying, "Thank You Congressman Talent." When he arrived, it was tremendous to see him again in person, to introduce him to Alex, and to express my deep, deep gratitude to him for his help. Of course, I cried. I never knew what went on behind the scenes, but I knew that Congressman Talent had worked hard to help our little boy and the other twenty-seven orphans come home to their families.

Bringing Alex to America had been both a traumatic and exhilarating experience. I had participated in an event I never imagined. But, the reward was also something I never dreamed possible. I couldn't believe how much little Alex changed our world; I loved him so much it was almost painful.

Having biological children had been astronomically easier than Alex's adoption, making our relationship even more special. He was a tiny, little guy for his age, but he was bright and busy and made us laugh all the time. By the time he was two years old, he was singing the whole

Simon and Garfunkel song, Cecilia, with headphones on. His musical talent was off the charts, and he remembered the words to songs with the mastery of someone three times his age. Alex brought us incredible joy, and our whole family was thankful to have him in our lives. We knew we had been truly blessed.

But I continued to ponder the reason all the barriers had been placed in the way of adopting Alex. I needed to understand how the experience was supposed to influence my life.

I believe the process of adopting Alex planted in me the seeds of a hunger, of which I was unaware at the time, to really be impactful in the lives of children. I had spent days in a depressing and gloomy Hungarian orphanage setting. I had vivid, wretched pictures and institutional odors in my head which I couldn't erase. Unbeknownst to me, the experience of bringing Alex to America would be the catalyst to set me on a path which would enable me to help rescue 1800 more orphans, but also turn me into the primary witness in a Federal, criminal investigation some fifteen years later, and subsequently place my life in danger.

PART 2

CHAPTER 19

MEETING SLAVA AND SVETLANA FOR THE FIRST TIME

ALTHOUGH TERRIBLY BUSY AFTER OUR arrival home, my mind continued to wander back to Hungary and the orphanages.

About eight weeks after returning home, I was volunteering as a timer at Ryan's swim meet and was partnered with a Russian gentleman named Oleg, whose son swam on the same team. During a break in the meet, Laura came down to the swim deck for a visit and brought Alex with her. I visited with them for a few minutes, hugged them both, they returned to the stands, and the meet resumed. After the next race, Oleg turned to me and exclaimed he realized why he recognized me, inquiring if I was the woman in the news who had helped to gain the release of a group of orphans from Hungary.

With my reply of yes, he questioned me about the experience, and I offered the briefest of explanations regarding the *Szeged 28*. He asked what I did for a living and I described being a fundraising consultant for non-profit organizations. He then told me about a friend of his who was hoping to facilitate adoptions of Russian orphans but was running into obstacles because he wasn't familiar with international adoption processes. I agreed that it was a challenging system. He asked me if I would be willing to speak with his friend and share what I knew about international adoption. Expressing delight about the opportunity to speak with his friend, I hoped that by sharing what I had learned through my own adoption nightmare other orphaned children could be helped.

About a month later and having forgotten about the conversation, just after getting the big kids off to school, I received a phone call from a man with a thick accent. He explained he got my number from his friend, Oleg, with whom I had spoken at Ryan's swim meet. He described how he and his wife had been pediatricians in Russia and had worked extensively with Russian orphans. He said he had become an anesthesiologist and his wife an emergency room pediatrician in St. Louis, and they had a deep desire to help orphans like those with whom they had worked in Russia. He stated that he had followed my story in the local newspaper and, then when his friend told him about meeting me, he said he felt compelled to contact me. His accent was thick, and it was a struggle to fully understand him. He asked if I would meet with him and his wife for lunch at a nearby restaurant.

I had nothing to lose and hoped information about my experience could help them save more orphans. I had learned a great deal about the process of international adoption during the past eighteen months and was happy to be able to share this knowledge with someone who wanted to save children. I was actually excited to have the opportunity to help in this way. It seemed natural for me to assist this couple and we set up a date to meet.

I couldn't stop thinking about the impending meeting and what it could mean for Russian orphans if I were able to provide some guidance to the Russian doctors. I knew nothing about international adoption from any place but Hungary but had an excellent grasp on the American immigration system and the process for gathering documents. Perhaps

I would have something to offer them, and I was excited to meet with the two doctors, eagerly awaiting the date of our meeting.

Walking into the restaurant to meet Slava and Svetlana, I experienced a crowd of emotions running around inside of me, being nervous, excited, curious, and a little intimidated. I was meeting two successful physicians who had come to me for help and I didn't want my internal sentiments to show. I don't know how they felt about me, but Slava and Svetlana made a strong impression on me. In person it was easier to understand Slava's English. He was short, about my height, with beautiful Mediterranean coloring, and had black, curly hair. He was a bit on the roundish side, but he was a nice-looking man with an engaging smile. When he spoke, I was pulled into his bright, sparkling, brown eyes and captivated by his fascinating accent. Slava again explained that he was an anesthesiologist, having originally been a pediatrician in Russia, giving me snippets about his experiences in Russia. Slava explained that his real name in Russian was Viacheslav (pronounced Vi'-che-slav), but everyone called him Slava. I noticed that Svetlana called him "Slavitchka." He seemed to be intelligent, friendly, and open. The best word to describe Slava was charismatic. I sensed that when he entered a room, he was most likely in command.

His wife, Svetlana, was petite, with brownish hair and a pretty face. She spoke little English during that first meeting, speaking primarily in Russian directed only to Slava when she did speak. Although unsure, because she spoke so little, I felt that her English skills were far weaker than his. I remember wondering how effectively she could interact with patients in an American emergency room. She was not as warm as Slava and at times seemed disinterested in the conversation. But perhaps that was due to her inability to fully follow the English conversation. Slava appeared to be deeply invested in the prospect of helping Russian orphans find loving homes; Svetlana's position regarding Slava's vision remained a mystery.

I learned much about them during that first meeting. Slava shared that he and Svetlana had both gone to medical school in St. Petersburg, Russia. He was from St. Petersburg, but Svetlana had been born in the small country of Belarus. They had both immigrated to the United States, and at the time they immigrated they had been married to other people. They met while training in New York City and ultimately ended up together. Slava described his process of immigrating to the United States for religious reasons, his mother had been Jewish, and his father had been an ethnic Roma. This knowledge created an even stronger internal bond for me with Slava, as my Alex is also Roma. His story was fascinating.

Slava said they had ended up sharing a tiny apartment in New York City with Svetlana's two daughters. While preparing to take the medical boards, which would allow them to practice medicine in the United States, Slava drove a taxi and he claimed that Svetlana knitted one sweater every day to help pay the bills. After passing the American medical boards, they moved to St. Louis, where Slava had been accepted into an anesthesiology residency at Washington University. I was in awe of this man who had given up everything to come to America and seemed to have made a successful new life. With each new fact he shared about his life, I found him to be more impressive.

Slava described how much their lives had improved since leaving Russia, but they found themselves continually thinking about the Russian orphans. I was able to totally relate to this after my experience in Hungary.

He asked about my experience with the Hungarian adoptions and seemed genuinely interested in my story. I relayed the saga of freeing the *Szeged 28* with great emotion and got teary eyed, even though I tried hard to hold my tears at bay. After a couple hours of conversation, Slava surprisingly told me I was just the person for whom he had been searching. He asked if I would be interested in creating an adoption program, if I would be willing to partner with Svetlana and him to unite Russian orphans with American families. He explained that he had already incorporated the company, having named it Small World Adoption Foundation because the "It's a Small World" ride at Disney World was his young daughter's favorite ride. I thought that was incredibly sweet and I immediately began to like Slava very much. I can still hear him saying to me in his thick Russian accent, "Russia has so many babies, but they have no mamas." That statement pulled with atomic power at my heart strings. All I could think about was how closely our *Szeged 28* had come to being babies with no mamas.

Slava explained that he had identified a woman named Maria in St. Petersburg who would be the coordinator in Russia. He said he desperately needed someone with whom he could partner to create and coordinate an adoption program from within the United States. He explained that we would all work together.

I expressed interest in helping him but shared that I needed to think through his offer, having been totally unprepared for that kind of conversation. I told him I was not exactly sure how to run an adoption agency, but because of my own dreadful adoption experience, I felt I knew what not to do, which made him laugh.

He said there was no money to pay me yet and that he had begun the company with his own funds. Slava told me that he and Svetlana were not planning to draw a salary from the organization, but he hoped to begin paying me once the program was self-sufficient and there were available funds. I realized if I were going to create this program for him, it would be primarily on my own and initially for free. But I could already see a future for me in Slava's vision; there were many Americans desperately hoping to adopt children. Since returning from Hungary, and after the media coverage, I had been inundated by around fifty phone calls from people around the country who wanted to know if I could help them. I understood their pain because recently I had been one of those Americans. We agreed to speak by phone within a few days and I left the restaurant.

Driving home, I kept questioning myself, *Is this what I was supposed to do?* I thought again about the story I had just shared with Slava and his wife, of that afternoon in a hot courtyard in Szeged, the day of Laura's 10th birthday, and how I questioned God about the reason for my heartache. While thinking about the meeting with Slava and recalling the many stories he told me about the Russian orphans, I also recalled the day when my neighbor, who had been in my life so briefly, set me on my path to international adoption. It seemed there had been many unrelated threads that had come together to weave this new tapestry in my life.

As I drove home following my meeting, waves of emotion washed over me. I wondered if this opportunity, just placed in my path, was the reason I had experienced so many obstacles during our adoption of little Alex. Through my adoption experience, I had learned to navigate the US Immigration system. I had come to understand the nuances of foreign country documentation, the importance of perfection in notarizations and certifications of documents, and the necessity to persevere. I had become a champion for orphaned children. I felt perhaps God had just sent the answer to my question of just a few short months ago. I felt that I finally understood why adopting Alex had been one of the greatest trials of my life. Perhaps that challenge and experience was to empower me to contribute even more to the world of international adoption.

Was it possible this proposal was supposed to be my life's new mission? With so many thoughts buzzing like bees around in my head, I couldn't help but stop to make a connection. I truly believed that my painful childhood had given me the strength and tenacity to face down government forces, enabling me to help get the *Szeged 28* out of Hungary. Now that experience seemed to be opening a whole new world for me. I believed that everything in life truly does happen for a reason.

CHAPTER 20

I'LL DO IT

I DISCUSSED SLAVA'S PROPOSITION WITH my family, who were excited and offered me strong support. My husband and I had to evaluate the financial implications, since I would be taking a pay cut if I shifted my fundraising business to part-time. The day before the children had been released by the Hungarian government, the division for which Allen worked at Monsanto announced that his department was relocating to another region of the country. He had chosen to reject the relocation offers and had decided to start his own consulting firm. With his severance and after studying the numbers, we agreed it was feasible for me to make this enormous leap. However, I would need to keep my fundraising business going and we would need to become frugal spenders. I was hesitant and nervous because just before meeting Slava, our lives had finally calmed down. I couldn't help but be concerned about the changes this would bring to our peaceful life.

A few days later, in October of 1993, I contacted Slava and told him that I would be interested in helping him, preferring to only work part-time if possible, at least for a year or two. I told him I didn't want to give up my fundraising business which I had worked hard to create. Plus, although I didn't share this fact this Slava, I needed the paycheck my fundraising business provided. I explained that it was also important to me to have quality time with Alex because had never experienced the security, love, and nurturing of a family, and my devotion and attention would be essential for him.

I was grateful to have Alex in my life and I was unwilling to give up too much of our early time together. I was enjoying my time and relished the opportunity to share so many first experiences with him. I loved putting him on the back of my bicycle in a carrier and riding through the neighborhood with him. I loved reading to him and pushing him in the baby swing. His joyful laughter rang through the house and his antics made his siblings laugh with glee. I hoped that Slava would understand just how much Alex meant to us.

He said he did, thankfully, and it was acceptable to him if I worked part-time from home if that worked for me. I was extremely excited at this new prospect of helping more children and being able to do it in my time frame. I liked that I would have some control over the process and its timing.

I began to create a business model which I felt would work not only for me and my family, but also for my prospective clients. Over the next three months, I worked creating informational brochures and contract packets. I researched the laws for Russian adoption, the requirements of the Russian immigration system, the rules for becoming a licensed agency in Missouri, as well as the exact specifications of the Russian foreign country dossier (the "tree's worth" paperwork required by the foreign country) which the prospective adoptive parents would need to gather.

I developed a detailed program description of the services that would be provided to clients. I was determined that my families would have fond memories of their adoption experience and it would not be akin to the nightmare I had encountered. I made a secret vow to respond to phone messages within 24 hours and to create honest and open relationships with clients. These pledges were important to me because of the bad experiences we had with our own adoption agency.

I understood that this would be a real business. But for me, from the beginning I believed it was my mission, and one into which I poured my heart and soul.

I thought about a quote that I had heard years ago, "save a child, save the world" and thought about my previous careers. Helping children to learn to articulate correctly had been a wonderful career. Helping non-profit organizations to raise funds to benefit the children served by the organizations was also important work. But being able to save a child from the horrors of growing up in an Eastern European orphanage was, for me, the ultimate in "saving the world." I had been given an important role to play in freeing the *Szeged 28* and I relished this opportunity to make an even greater impact in our world.

About three months into the building of our new agency, I began working on the requirements necessary for Small World to become a "Non-profit Licensed Child Placing Agency" in Missouri. This was going to be necessary to attract clients, and my Russian research indicated this was going to be a Russian requirement in the near future. As physicians, Slava and Svetlana had been able to legally facilitate adoptions, but that was likely to change. Initially, Slava had incorporated Small World as a non-profit entity, which had been good, but it still needed to be licensed to help it become more than a mom and pop adoption organization. That meant a mountain of information to master and I dreaded failure. But when I would feel overwhelmed, I would picture our *Szeged 28* and imagine hundreds and hundreds more children just like them, and I would be fully reenergized and become laser focused on Small World's objective – saving Russian orphans.

CHAPTER 21

WHAT HAVE I DONE?

To LEARN AS MUCH AS I could about operating an adoption agency, I went to California and spent a week with a director from another agency. I spent several long days picking Gina's brain, listening to her philosophy, learning about the adoption paperwork and about what made an agency successful. I learned an enormous amount, but one of the most important lessons was the need to retain and demonstrate deep compassion for all of the clients. I never lost sight of that lesson, regardless of occasional challenges with clients. I was deeply grateful for the important start she gave me.

To help me understand more about the Russian adoption system, Slava provided me with the name of a local couple, Craig and Carol, who had already completed an adoption with his help. They had agreed to be his test case after he first decided he wanted to pursue facilitation of Russian adoptions. The couple ultimately finalized their adoption but admitted having a taxing experience; primarily because Slava lacked the knowledge or tools to adequately assist the couple. After his first experience, Slava recognized the need for someone who had the experience, knowledge, and the desire to carry out his plan; that person was me. I felt both privileged and blessed to have been given this opportunity. My involvement was critical for Slava because he of course already had a full-time career.

I met with Carol for several hours and learned as much from her as I could about their experience, what worked, what didn't, and getting a feel for the emotional roller coaster of international adoption from Russia. Carol and Craig, as well as Gina, were instrumental in enabling me to spend the next fifteen years finding loving families for 1800 children.

The further I progressed with building the agency, the more it consumed me. Learning how complicated Russian adoptions could be, at times I was frightened that I would never be able to create a program, of which I could be proud, that would provide a great experience for clients while assuring orphaned children got loving families. I had created a tall order for myself and for what I wanted to become an iconic adoption agency. Having the sense of being engulfed in a murky world of complicated paperwork, adoption processes, and business development, at times I felt as if I was drowning. But I would continuously pull myself back together with that vision of the *Szeged 28*. I continuously reminded myself of where those 28 babies would be had someone not stepped up to fight for them. I had become committed to fighting for the orphans in Russia.

As I learned more about international adoption, I realized that there were four things that seemed to set our new agency apart from the other agencies to which I had either spoken or read about. First, all of the children being made available for adoption would be identified by Svetlana, a pediatrician who would be reading their medical records in Russia and speaking directly to the Russian doctors about the children. She would be able to personally verify the health of the orphans, although not doing a complete American style physical examination of the children. An action such as that would have been insulting to the physicians caring for the orphans. I already knew that most Americans only wanted to adopt the healthiest babies possible, and I was convinced the involvement of pediatricians in the selection of the available children would be incredibly meaningful to prospective clients. Second, Slava was setting up programs in areas where he had personal connections, and according to him, that was the preferred way to do business in Russia. He shared that Russians don't do business with strangers. Third, neither Slava nor Svetlana were planning to draw salaries, and I believed this fact would convey to prospective clients that this was a truly humanitarian enterprise on their parts. Lastly, the organization was being run by me, someone who had lived through a very challenging adoption experience, learned a lot, and had made it my personal quest to save orphans while helping adopting parents to have positive experiences. I completely understood adoption from the perspective of the adopting family who was frightened and anxious. Small World looked like a terrific package deal, and it came to be that I would rarely speak with a potential client who would not in the end apply to become a Small World prospective parent.

Within five months, I was no longer operating my fund-raising business, having become totally devoted to my Russian project. I was not providing good service to my fundraising clients and felt guilty about that. So, I passed all my accounts back to my fundraising mentor. I realized that there was no way being a director of Small World would ever be a "part-time" job after all and was beginning to question my belief that I would have control. I looked in the mirror and thought, *"Brenda, what have you done?"*

CHAPTER 22

THE EARLY DAYS

I SET ABOUT CREATING A comfortable and welcoming office in the basement of my home. Office equipment and phone numbers were acquired, and I developed a business plan that could be sustainable for the long term. I fully understood that I was going to have an important role in an endeavor we all hoped would be significant to orphaned children. I trained my ten-year-old Laura to assemble the information packets that would be sent to prospective clients.

Meeting with Slava at his home, we worked together to form a solid business. Slava was an anesthesiologist during the day, so our meetings were nearly always in the evening. I was proud of the work we were doing, the direction we were taking, and eventually with each child we brought to America; my heart grew a little bit bigger.

By January of 1994, we were ready to roll with preparations complete to begin taking clients. I don't really recall how all the initial clients found our organization, most were people who contacted me after having read about the *Szeged 28* in a newspaper and wanted to know if I could help. A few had been referred to us by Carol and Craig. But regardless of the means by which they found us, I was receiving daily phone calls from prospective clients. I was proud and pleased to be helping these people, knowing exactly how they felt.

My clients came to me from many different life paths; they all had stories to share. There were young couples who had been trying for several years to have a baby, there were blended families looking for this child to be the bond of the joined families' love, single women, couples who had lost children to illness, those for whom the actual act of carrying a child could be dangerous for the mother, couples married for the second time, and those for whom surgical procedures prohibited having a child, etc. There seemed to be no end to the sad stories. My heart ached for each client and I became more and more determined to help every family.

I met with each new, local family in my home office and interviewed them. I wanted to be able to help them the best way possible and felt that getting to know a little of their personal journey would be valuable. Almost all of the meetings were pleasant and productive. Nearly every new client left my house with paperwork in hand and they would be on their way toward their goal of being adoptive parents.

One unusual meeting was with a business man and his wife, and it did not turn out quite so well. It was my first, and one of the few times our agency would reject a prospective client. The couple had a young biological daughter but had explained on the phone that they could have no more biological children. They were considering adoption to expand their family. After they arrived, the couple sat down at the table and their little girl, of perhaps two and one-half years of age, just wandered around the room. They had brought no toys for the little girl with which to occupy her time while we spoke together. As she began inappropriately getting into things, I retrieved some of Alex's toys to occupy her. As I sat talking with the couple, the mother's hands shook so terribly that she was unable to sign her name. The father explained that his wife was on a lot of psychiatric, psychotropic medications.

I immediately knew this would be problematic, having already learned that Russia would not accept prospective adoptive parents suffering from significant medical, psychological, or emotional issues. The more alarming thing for me was that the entire time the couple was in my office, the mother never had a single interaction with her daughter. The father was slightly more engaged with her. The mother behaved as if there was not even a child in the room, never once glancing at her. This was a tremendous red flag for me. My goal was to protect children and place them in loving homes. I did not view this family as capable of providing that for an orphaned baby. I told the family that I was sorry they would not be able to adopt with our agency. I explained that the orphanages with which we worked in Russia required that the adopting parents be healthy by the Russian interpretation of the word. The many medications being taken by the mother would preclude her from a successful Russian adoption.

The father jumped up, got red in the face, and began saying harsh and nasty things to me about my unwillingness to help them. I calmly tried to help him understand that this was not my decision; it was the law in Russia. The father grabbed his daughter and stormed out with the mother silently following. I was not even sure she had understood what had just transpired.

I felt terrible for the family and called Slava immediately, needing to verify with him that I had taken the right action. He assured me that I had and that most assuredly a judge would have denied an adoption for them.

Many months later, I received an ugly voicemail message from the father. He told me he had found a better agency and that he and his wife were leaving for Russia to adopt a child. He exclaimed that he would be sure to let other people know how they had been treated by me. I could only be sad for the child that would be brought into this odd family and wondered about the ethics of the agency that had allowed it to happen.

Not only was I learning how best to work with clients in America, in those early months I was also learning about the relationships Slava maintained in Russia which enabled him to facilitate the adoptions. In the beginning, we worked with three orphanages in St. Petersburg where Slava was well acquainted with the directors. Slava said that he had gotten to know them during the time he was a pediatrician in St. Petersburg, and the orphanage directors sincerely cared about the children, wanting them to have loving families. Fortunately, he stated, the orphanage directors were committed to the orphans and genuinely interested in their well-being.

Slava explained that adoption in Russia was not socially acceptable, as it was in most industrialized nations of the world, and few Russian citizens adopted children from the orphanages. There were literally millions of orphans in Russia and the rest of the former communist countries of Eastern Europe, primarily the result of the destitute economic state of that area of the world. According to Slava, Communism had taken a huge toll on that part of the world, creating immense poverty across the lands.

Slava further elaborated, explaining that it was socially acceptable for indigent families to deposit their children at orphanages during the harsh winter months, so they could receive better care. The caveat was that a family member had to visit the child every six months. If the child was not visited by a family member during that time, the child could be made available for adoption. Many children were left at the orphanage doorstep with no subsequent visitors, or the parents out-and-out relinquished their rights when leaving the children at the facility. My heart broke for biological families when Slava described how an impoverished family with two children might be placed on the brink of despair if a third child came into the family, so the newest baby would end up at the orphanage. I was determined to find homes for as many of these children as possible. Daily I thought of my three amazing children and how blessed all of us were; these thoughts being a catalyst to push me to work harder and faster.

CHAPTER 23

BUILDING RELATIONSHIPS

THOSE FIRST MONTHS WERE CHALLENGING for me as I tried to manage my new business. Slava was generally kind to me during this difficult time and I clearly felt his commitment to orphaned children. He seemed as committed as I to make our small agency a success. I could tell that Slava didn't take on a project unless he was fairly certain he could be successful. He clearly liked to be in control, he had high expectations of those around him, and he could be impatient. Over the next few months, we developed a rhythm that worked for us. He was demanding, and I was eager to please. Being a "pleaser" was sure to keep him from getting angry with me! The relationship blossomed. I developed a deep belief in and an incredible respect for Slava.

After about the first eighteen months or so, I finally began getting paid, and that was the end of my knowledge of the business finances. Slava and his son initially took care of the finances and we ultimately went through several accountants after his son left the business. I didn't have a deep knowledge of the accounting systems being used, how money was tracked, how bills were paid, or even what the company expenses actually were. I only signed checks when Slava was unavailable. I was not uncomfortable with the little bit of financial information that was shared with me during the first eleven or so years the company was in business. I didn't feel that Slava was withholding anything, but more that he felt the financial responsibility was not included in my job description. I was super busy, and I welcomed not having to learn anything else! This would become one of my greatest regrets.

During those early months, I had little contact with Svetlana. If she were present for a meeting, she primarily spoke Russian with Slava and he would translate her communications for me. I felt that their continued practice of speaking Russian in front of me and excluding me from conversations was a markedly rude behavior. In spite of the downfalls of my parents, I had learned to have excellent manners and social skills and found this continued conduct offensive. I thought this habit was probably the result of poor parenting, a culturally accepted norm, or perhaps Svetlana's poor grasp of the English language. In retrospect, was that really the reason behind this rude behavior, or were they filtering the information to which I was privy?

I frequently visited their home, often two or three times a week in the evening. It was a beautiful, minimalist home with a contemporary design. Although I found Slava to be very welcoming and a genuinely warm person, when I visited their home, I found their home to be cold, sterile, and stark. It was often full of Russian speaking people, housekeepers, other family members, and a lot of interesting, unfamiliar food. I had the opportunity to fully experience the Russian culture. At times, I would chuckle to myself about the differences between Americans and Russians, at least these Russians, who seemed always to be drinking vodka and to be such a happy group of people.

Not long after getting to know them, Slava told me how miserable Svetlana had been when they first moved into their beautiful home. He said they had always lived in tiny apartments and in the beginning, she cried all the time, wanting to move back into the city to their small apartment. In her broken English, Svetlana explained to me that it took a long time for her to feel safe in so much space. I felt sorry for her, imagining how frightening that must have been when she came to the United States and left everything with which she was familiar in Russia. I wondered about the impact these same losses were having on our children. The children were losing everything that was familiar to them, the food, the smells, the sights and sounds, but they did not have the ability to understand why their world was suddenly changing so dramatically.

Slava and Svetlana had interesting artwork on their walls, comprised primarily of original, post-impressionist paintings brought with them from Russia. They were incredibly bold in color, lots of reds and oranges, and I had not experienced art work like it before.

I discovered that Slava was an incredible host, regardless of where we were meeting, a restaurant or his home. He was generous and always wanted to provide his guests with something to eat and/or drink. The vodka flowed freely, always served directly from the freezer and in small, crystal shot glasses. I had never experienced straight vodka! But eventually, I became quite good at downing a shot without feeling like I had to be sick! But the achievement was not easily attained and took years of practice.

At the gatherings at Slava's home, he exuded an aura of energy just waiting to erupt. He was always busy and engaged in many different endeavors. He was frequently on the phone when I arrived at their home and often took calls during our meetings. Nearly all his phone communications were in Russian and I found the language to be intriguing. When Slava would translate conversations for me, the speaker might seem to be verbose and long-winded, but when he translated the message, it would be a brief comment. The composition of the Russian language seemed to be much more complex than English, although at times I felt that he was abbreviating the speaker's message.

During those first two years, I was getting to know Slava and Svetlana. Slava had a boat and jet skis he kept on the Missouri river and he would invite my family to join him on Sunday afternoons in the summer. We had such fun times and my children were absolutely falling in love with Slava. He was kind and funny, and always generous with them. We would bring picnic baskets of food and drinks. Slava, of course, always had the proverbial vodka handy. I had not yet mastered straight shots of vodka and, in the beginning, often declined his offers.

Those beautiful days together helped to form a tight bond between our families. I was meeting many new people from the Russian community, as frequently Slava would also invite other friends along. It was always loud and fun and crazy. Sometimes people with us were friends who had come from Russia to visit Slava. It was such an amazing time for me; a whole new world was opening up and I was excited to be a part of it.

Our relationship was always evolving, and we would at times butt heads over decisions that needed to be made. Slava had ordered letterhead for Small World after he had incorporated and prior to my meeting him. In building the business, I needed business stationary, business cards, etc. The logo that had been designed for Slava was pleasant looking, a silhouette of a family standing in front of a sun and its sunbeams. However, he had selected an embossed gold letterhead which, as it turned out, nearly doubled the cost of the items. I expressed my concern to Slava that this was a waste of money and the color wasn't all that attractive. I told him this kind of waste would likely be noticed by our clients and I thought we should pick another color. He grew angry at my words and wouldn't discuss it. However, as would be his habit in years to come, after having time to consider the issue, he later called and apologized for being ugly, admitting that perhaps I was correct and I should go ahead and choose a color I liked.

Slava was at times explosive and unpredictable. As the agency grew, when my staff would run for cover during his outbursts, I was usually able to calm the situation and talk him down out of his rage. My staff could never understand not only my willingness, but also my ability to do this. I was willing because I had a fervent belief in the mission. I was able because of the skills I gleaned growing up with an explosive, unpredictable, and abusive father and an alcoholic mother. Although it never felt good when Slava treated me disrespectfully, said cruel things, or berated me, sadly it wasn't actually all that uncomfortable.

About eighteen months into our relationship, Slava called me while I was in my car, having just dropped Alex at the preschool he attended three mornings per week. I have no recollection of the issue about which he was furious, but I can still feel the all-encompassing pain of hearing him scream mercilessly at me over the phone. We had engaged in heated discussions before but never anything reaching this level of inappropriate meanness. Initially, as he was screaming at me I began to sob, then suddenly got very angry. I couldn't stand being attacked in that way and told him he could never scream at me again like that and I hung up the phone on him! I couldn't believe I had done that – to Slava! Either his rants did in fact lessen over the years, I just got stronger or gained confidence, and his explosions had less impact on me. The first eighteen months simply flew by.

This became the ebb and flow of our relationship the entire time we worked together. Many years later, a staff member would say we were like an old married couple, the way we bickered about things. But we always had each other's backs.

When Alex was around two and one-half years of age, I needed to find a nanny for him. Slava told me not to worry and arranged for Olga, the beautiful wife of Slava's son, to take the position. She was kind and sweet and Alex loved her. If there was a problem, Slava seemed always to find a solution.

By the time Alex was three, he was demonstrating recognizable trauma induced behaviors; he had difficulty sleeping, following directions, broke his toys, and couldn't sustain his attention toward one activity for more than just a minute or two. He needed to be constantly moving. By the time he was four, he was displaying a rage that at times could be difficult to manage. Olga was kind and consistent with him and we appreciated her. By the time Alex was five, we had enlisted the assistance of psychological professionals as we began what would be a life-long process of seeking the right therapy and medication for Alex. Alex's trauma induced behaviors was one area in which Slava had nothing to offer.

Also, during those years, Allen would go over to Slava's house to tutor Slava's and Svetlana's daughter in chemistry. Slava's and my family became more and more interconnected with each passing year.

CHAPTER 24

CONNECTIONS

Although I was focused on assisting with Russian adoptions, I never wanted to forget where it had all begun. I didn't want to lose that connection that had been the catalyst for my involvement in Small World. In July of 1994, one year, almost to the day, after the release of the *Szeged 28*, we held the first reunion of *Szeged 28* families, which I helped organize. The weekend was something I would never, ever forget, and as I looked around at the beautiful children of Szeged, I felt God's presence in our lives. I was so thrilled to have little Alex home, recognizing what an important role he was playing in every aspect of our world.

Nearly every family attended the weekend-long gathering in St. Louis. Our group met at a hotel and enjoyed two days of fun and fellowship. I can still see the families and their children as they arrived in the hotel lobby. I cried the entire first evening. One year ago, I had been holding these children as orphans, and suddenly I was hugging them as full-fledged American citizens with wonderful lives ahead of them. It was a dream come true to see that amazing group of children wrapped in the loving arms of their devoted parents.

Alex had not been well, and I had been in Hungary a long time, so I was the first one to leave. I was only able to meet a few of the families, as most of them didn't arrive until after our departure. Once I received permission to take Alex out of Hungary, I was on the first available plane out.

Many of the families had the opportunity to spend time together in Hungary, so they knew each other. I only knew my fellow St. Louis moms, but I knew all the children. I can be a little shy, so I stood back and watched a lot of reunions between families. Mostly I watched the children, the majority of them between twenty months and three years of age. Of course, they didn't remember each other, but I believe almost from that first reunion, the children felt the bond they all shared.

Each subsequent year for about ten years, the group traveled to a different city, with the families taking turns as the hosts for the event. On Friday nights when we all first gathered back together, there was always incredible hugging and the children were always ecstatic to see one another. The host families planned fun events for the children, from carnivals to rodeos to swimming with the dolphins. We began thinking of ourselves as family, the children calling one another "cousin." Each year, we took a group picture and had matching t-shirts made for all the family members, allowing us to document the glorious events.

Three of the Szeged 28 families subsequently adopted a child through my Small World program. Those children were always considered part of the Szeged group and we celebrated them along with all the other children. A couple of families went on to have biological children, and they too just became part of the Szeged group. I simply could not believe my good fortune in finding such a stellar group of people to become my extended family. Having such limited to no contact with so many members of my biological family, I drank in the joy at the reunions like water.

A few families dropped out of the reunions each subsequent year.

By the time most of the children were ten, the reunions fell apart. The children had sporting obligations in the summers and lives seemed to change with people drifting apart. But many of the families stayed in close contact and by their later teen years, most of the children formed relationships with their cousins via e-mail, Facebook, texting, and phone calls. They still call one another "cousin," even now in their twenties.

I was especially blessed to have local families to whom I could cling, but lives got busy and we too drifted apart. However, there was one particular family with whom we formed a life-long and deeply bonded relationship – Michael's family. Michael and his sister, Tana, call me Aunt Brenda, our families vacation together, and we spend Thanksgivings and New Year's Eve together. Alex had been the first blessing; the Szeged families had been unexpected gifts.

We were kindred spirits who had been total strangers, but we indeed became family. After the Szeged 28 reunion, I was excitedly anticipating the upcoming first Small World reunion, held just three weeks later.

At the end of July 1994, we celebrated our first thirteen adoptions with a big party/picnic at Slava's house. His beautiful home had an abundance of room to accommodate our growing Small World family. There was even a lovely pool in his backyard. We invited all of our clients, from families who had finalized adoptions, to those who had recently applied. We thoroughly enjoyed meeting with clients, some of whom we had only spoken with by phone.

We had around seventy-five people at that first picnic. My son Ryan worked in the summer as a lifeguard and volunteered to guard the pool, Slava did the barbequing, and the side dishes were catered. It was a huge celebration with lots of great food and drink, accompanied by boisterous laughing and hugging. At the end of the evening, Slava gave the first vodka shot toast to our families with many more following in subsequent years. It was a tradition that would be honored at each picnic until the last one. Standing on Slava's balcony overlooking the pool below and watching all the families gave me a feeling of satisfaction that was unlike any I had felt before. As I looked at the newly adopted children, already so Americanized, it was difficult to believe such a short time ago they had been orphans with no future in Russia. The children running around Slava's house had been rescued. But, many of the parents would disagree, telling me that their child had rescued them. I guess they rescued each other and their love for one another was almost tangible.

I had learned from Slava that nearly all the children who eventually aged out of the Russian orphanages had terribly unsuccessful lives. It was the norm for the girls leaving the orphanages at fifteen or sixteen years of age to turn to prostitution to support themselves. The boys left the orphanages and turned to crime for survival. Plus, Slava had shared with me the terrific abuse that was perpetrated on the children in the orphanages. The children then in turn became perpetrators on the younger children in the orphanage. It was a vicious cycle from which there was no escape. The best hope any of these children had was that of international adoption.

Fortunately, the orphanage system separated the younger children from the older ones. Generally, the children under the age of six lived in substantially more protected environments. The younger ones were the ones for whom we were working hard to find families, the children who would hopefully one day attend Small World picnics.

At the first picnic, a prospective family from Chicago, Ken and Kelly, joined the fun. They had selected a darling little five-year-old girl from a video and we were expecting them to travel within a few weeks. During the party, Kelly happened to ask about a little boy who had been on the same videotape as their prospective daughter. (Sometimes when Slava and Svetlana videotaped children, there were other children milling around in the video who were not yet available for adoption. The available children were clearly identified for the prospective parents.) Kelly, Ken, and I went in search of Slava to ask him about the little boy. Slava went right to his office and phoned the orphanage director. She shared with him that the little boy had been cleared for international adoption just that week. Ken and Kelly were ecstatic. They had been enamored with the little boy from the first moment they saw him. Now that they were both approved for adoption, Little Anna and Dennis would be Ken and Kelly's children and would be coming to America in just a few short weeks! Ken and Kelly eventually went on to adopt a third child, Leeza, from Belarus. It was an amazing experience to play a role in the building of this loving family, and one that would be repeated for me hundreds of times in the coming years. Ken and Kelly became cherished friends and incidentally, Anna now has two small children of her own!

Slava was the consummate host for the picnics, being friendly and gracious. I loved watching him in that environment, so happy and seemingly so fulfilled by the work we were doing.

CHAPTER 25

MARCIA

Having my work cut out for me, I doggedly began pursuit of licensure for Small World. One of the requirements for licensure in Missouri was employing a person with a "Master of Social Work," or an MSW, for the agency. So, in December of 1994, I placed an ad in the newspaper for an MSW for our budding non-profit. I received several resumes, conducted three interviews, and selected a competent person. She even lived fairly close to my home, where for the time being the official office was housed. I quickly sent a letter to the State authorities notifying them that the agency had identified a new MSW.

During that time, I was very busy setting up the company as well as trying to meet the needs of our little Alex, who had been with us such a short time. From the beginning, Alex had difficulty sleeping and required a lot of extra reassurance to fall asleep. I wondered sometimes if he were too frightened to sleep, fearing that when he awoke his family would not be there. We wanted so much to just love the fear and anxiety he seemed to have right out of him. I had read to Ryan and Laura from the time they were a few weeks old, but Alex would never hold still long enough to get through more than just a few pages. He was an active, high energy little boy, and required constant monitoring. Some days, I tried to devote time solely to him, which on one occasion created a setback of my normal, timely business responses.

A week or so after I hired the new MSW, late one afternoon she called my office phone and left a message. I listened to the message that night and since it was not an emergency, just a general question, I thought I could return the call the next day. But the next day came and went, having spent most of the day with Alex, and I didn't make the intended call.

I called our new MSW back first thing the following morning, not even thirty-five hours after her call to me. At that time, she informed me that she would not be able to work with someone so disrespectful that they could not return a phone call! She further advised me that she had already notified the State licensing authority, advising them I had been unresponsive, and she was not going to work with my agency! My stomach began churning as I thought, *Oh no, Small World didn't even have a license yet and I was terrified it was going to lose it!* I was nearly hysterical trying to imagine how I would explain to the State authorities why I had kept an employee for less than a week. I couldn't imagine what they would think of me and prayed this would not preclude my getting us licensed.

I immediately placed another ad in the newspaper and received more resumes. One stood out above all the rest and I decided to contact the applicant for an interview. After calling the applicant, Marcia, we met, had a terrific interview, and I ultimately offered her the job. Marcia would primarily work from home, as her job would be meeting with the prospective parents to provide them with home studies for their adoption and to develop and present pre-parent training for the clients. A few days later, she and I had the opportunity to have lunch with Slava and Svetlana. It seemed that our personalities complemented one another, and I believed the four of us would make a strong team.

Marcia had a wealth of experience in domestic adoption. She was tall, about five feet, ten inches, with dark, almost black hair, big, dark brown eyes, and a quick wit. She was incredibly bright and intuitive. Being honest to a fault, our office staff would eventually coin the nickname "goddess of purity" for her. Marcia always stood up for what she believed in and was good at defending her position. We had discussions about the adoption business itself, and from early on Marcia was always slightly skeptical of Slava and Svetlana and their motives. But I steadfastly defended them to her for the next fifteen years. Marcia eventually became my close confidant, my second in command, and at times, my therapist! She was invaluable not only to the organization, but to everyone who worked there. To this day, she is one of my best friends.

About a month after Marcia began working with me, we went to a seminar together. I offered to drive that day, picking her up at her house. On our way back from the seminar, as I was pulling onto her street to drop her off, she asked me to come in for a Coke, saying she needed to talk to me. Inside my head, I was screaming, *OH NO!* I immediately feared she was going to quit. I began wracking my brain to figure out what I had done to make this MSW quit too. I knew I had immediately returned all of her phone calls, thinking promptly returned phone calls might be some "social worker thing." I tried to imagine the impending doom of having to report to the state that I had lost yet another social worker. My mind was quickly moving through things I might say to persuade her to stay. I liked her very much; she was professional, knowledgeable and fun. I exited the car and dragged myself into her living room.

I dejectedly sat on her comfortable sofa, noticing the warm and welcoming living room in which I sat while making small talk, waiting for her to resign. She went into her kitchen and brought back a couple of glasses of Diet Coke, with more than three ice cubes. Marcia next said, "Well, there is something I should tell you... I am a lesbian."

As relief flooded over me, I literally jumped up off of the couch and said, "Oh great! I thought you were going to quit!" We both burst out laughing recognizing that this was probably the first time this kind of declaration had received such a response. It was the beginning of our open, fun-loving, and life-long relationship. Marcia never knew how much it meant to me that she confided in me and was so totally honest. I had not encountered that with other adoption professionals. I knew I had hired the perfect person.

CHAPTER 26

MORE HELP TO THE RESUCE

My LITTLE OFFICE IN THE basement got very busy, very quickly. Although the basement was beautifully finished and furnished, it was still a basement with no windows in the office area. I spent long days in the basement never knowing if the sun was out or if it were raining or snowing. And the clients kept coming. I gave each of them my personal attention, hoping to make them feel special and wanting them to walk away with happy hearts and fond memories of their adoption experience.

Marcia's and my relationship continued to develop, and I began reaching out to her more frequently for input regarding client dilemmas or crises. I came to rely on her insight into client behavior.

At home, I was falling into a rhythm that wasn't altogether good for me or my family. I became consumed with my "mission." In the evening, if I heard the phone in my office ring or heard a fax being delivered, I was compelled to race to the office. I had a hard time walking away at the end of the day.

One afternoon, a close friend of ours came by our house for something about 2:00 PM, and I hadn't ever gotten dressed that day. I was still wearing my bathrobe! I had gotten right out of bed, gotten the kids off to school, the nanny had arrived to care for Alex, and I quickly buried myself in my office without even getting dressed. My friend suggested putting a little distance between the business and my family life.

By the time I reached the eighteen-month mark with Small World, I was working sixty to seventy hours a week, and Slava began to pay me a per family stipend. I was happy to finally be receiving a paycheck as we were drawing to the end of Allen's severance pay.

In the early years of Small World, it seemed that many of my clients were people of substance, being demanding and impatient. That was one of the biggest obstacles I faced – helping people who had never had to wait for much, had never been told no, or who, for the first time ever were learning that their vast amounts of money could not fix everything. They truly struggled with being forced to wait for the American and Russian governments to follow their processes. Their money or connections weren't going to do them any good, something to which they were totally unaccustomed. These people sometimes challenged my patience, but I tried to be understanding with them.

Handling all of the client issues alone, along with the huge amount of paperwork, was creating constant anxiety in me. I was feeling more and more overwhelmed. Laura was still my only help, and she was only eleven years old. I agreed with my friend that never getting dressed unless someone was coming to my office was probably not a suitable way to live. I realized I alone could not handle all of the phone calls, meetings, and paperwork. I began thinking about hiring help.

In the spring of 1995, while meeting with a client, Ann, who had quickly become a friend, I shared my thoughts about adding staff. I had already determined the type of person I wanted to hire. I wanted to find a caring and gentle person, someone kind and patient, calm, and most importantly for me, a mother. But she also had to be super organized, have computer skills, and be task oriented. I hoped such a person existed. Ann told me about someone who had worked in her office, a woman named Maureen, who had just been laid off because of company reorganization. Ann told me all about Maureen, who sounded perfect.

Ann gave me Maureen's phone number and I quickly called and interviewed her over the phone. If she was as good as she sounded on the phone, I was home free. The next day, she came to my basement office and we talked for quite a while. Maureen is tall, with light brown, wavy hair, has a twinkle in her eyes, and her whole face lights up when she smiles. She has the kind of personality that makes it easy to talk with her, a trait I felt would be an asset for a client contact position. She met Alex and we talked about our children, as well as the job. I had instinctively known that Marcia was perfect for the job, and now felt the same way about Maureen. I felt she would be a great addition to our little team. However, at that point I just needed someone part time. Maureen was happy to work part time and spend afternoons with her little boy, Danny, who had just begun kindergarten. It sounded too good to be true. So, I looked at Maureen and asked, "Do you think you can work in my basement?" As Maureen smiled and responded affirmatively, we both laughed, and Maureen began the next week. Marcia and Maureen were with me until the final day at Small World, when we all sadly walked out together fourteen years later. We remain dear friends.

Laura remained an important member of our team, having been tasked with assembly of information packets. Of course, I did pay her a little, but she would have done it anyway. Even at her tender age, Laura had developed a true commitment to my efforts. Ryan would sometimes help with the packets when he could. Laura, my little drama queen, would occasionally tell clients that she made the packets and would laughingly add that I sometimes refused to feed her until her work was complete. It was not true, but it was the beginning of my clients' falling in love with this little blond-haired beauty that would one day play such a significant role in the company. Small World was becoming as much a part of my family's life as it was mine.

My son's swimming activity soon played a second major role in the agency, having already been the catalyst for connecting me to Slava. Ryan was a USS swimmer, which means he swam for a licensed, private swim club. The swim club had an office and a couple of secretaries. One of them, Tanya, worked part-time, and I had visited with her many times while taking care of swim club business. We had "swimming sons" in common, shared world beliefs, and we had become fast friends. Tanya had joined me in my frustration with the enormous efforts needed to free the *Szeged 28*. She had witnessed the process to adopt Alex, even participated in the massive fax campaign, and was interested in my new business.

Since I had gotten to know Tanya well, it stood to reason that a few months after Maureen joined the team, and it became evident that I needed more assistance, she might be a great solution. So, I stopped by the swim office to test the water, so to speak. Tanya was thrilled at the opportunity to join in the work of our team. Tanya wanted to continue to only work part-time, as did Maureen, and it was a natural transition for her to join our team. Tanya was a petite woman with dark hair and an ability to grasp the complexities of foreign adoption at a record speed. Maureen and Tanya shared the position and we developed a smooth process for management of clients.

We worked in my little home office, interviewed clients, and made copies of videotapes in the lower level family room – Small World had taken over my house and my life.

Although consumed by Small World, I still participated in normal family events as well. Ryan was a talented swimmer and as a freshman in high school, his times were fast enough that he had qualified to compete at the State Conference Meet held at the end of the swim season. As busy as I was with Small World, during Ryan's high school swimming career, I never missed a single swim meet.

One afternoon, the doorbell rang, and I was holding Alex when I went to answer the door. Standing there on the porch was Ryan, with a completely shaved head! The swim team had shaved their heads in preparation for going to the State meet. I was speechless. Alex, however, was not. His nickname for Ryan was Buddy, and looking at Ryan's head, Alex said, "It's okay Buddy, I'll share my hair with you." My heart just melted at Alex's sweet innocence.

Another time, Alex came to the dinner table after having gotten into Ryan's swim bag, donning Ryan's goggles and swim cap. Of course, Ryan had Alex swimming early in Alex's young life. They were good buddies, and at swim meets, Ryan and the other swimmers would cart Alex around on their shoulders. The teenaged boys gave Alex the nickname of "chick magnet." He was adorable, and the girls would flock around the boys to interact with Alex.

Life seemed nearly perfect. I had my wonderful husband and three children, my *Szeged 28* family, and Slava's and my family were melding nicely.

CHAPTER 27

THE PROCESS

THE PROCESS FOR CLIENTS TO complete an adoption was complicated, unpredictable, lengthy, and frustrating, and we tried to make sure clients had sufficient warning of the challenges they could face. I created an information booklet that was originally about ten pages long, including pictures of children who had recently been adopted. Little did I know that the information packet would eventually become a fifty-page book! But whatever written information was lacking in the beginning was made up for by the exclusive attention we could give every client.

When first speaking with a client on the phone, we gave a basic overview of the adoption process. Before going into the multitude of specifics, to avoid wasting the time of the prospective client or us, we would inquire about criminal records, significant health issues, the client's age, and number of marriages of both prospective parents. Russian law and our own internal policy required that prospective adoptive parents had background checks free of criminal activity, were free of any diseases listed on the Russian disqualifying illnesses list, had to be over twenty-one years of age, and not married more than three times. I personally discouraged people who already had several children from adopting. It had become clear to me in the short time we had Alex, and from the few families that were already home with their adopted children, that they needed a lot of individual attention from their parents, and responding to that need could be challenging for families with many children.

If the client met the basic, minimal requirements, the process was explained and a written information packet, including the official application to work with the agency, was mailed to them. Local St. Louis area clients usually met with me at the office and received the information at that meeting. We explained the first step was to complete the application process. After approval of the application, clients received a contract packet. After the signed and notarized contract packet was returned to Small World, in depth instructions for the adoption process were provided to the clients.

The process for the completion of an adoption from Russia began with obtaining a home study. Marcia provided the home studies for nearly all our St. Louis area clients. A home study was the process whereby a social worker, or someone with similar training such as psychology, visited with the client in their home, gathered considerable documentation on the prospective adoptive person(s) regarding their finances, criminal background clearances, familial backgrounds, employment history, a description of their home, as well as an extensive interview about their life in general. From information provided by the family, Marcia created a full picture, in written form, of the prospective parent(s). The process was lengthy and considered by many to be intrusive. An approved home study was the basis for, and the most important document, in the adoption dossier.

During the home study process, prospective adoptive parents completed in-person workshops and online trainings (in later years, when they became available) regarding parenting, attachment institutionalization, discipline, and trauma. Marcia had created an excellent parent preparation course.

The adoptive families were also assisted with the completion of the foreign country "dossier." Samples of many of the documents the client had to create or obtain were provided. If the family lived in the St. Louis area, they visited the office to review the documentation requirements in person. I taught a "paperwork seminar" every two weeks. Families outside of the St. Louis area received their instructions via the phone with their Small World case manager, either Tanya or Maureen. The foreign country dossier needed to receive special seals, affixed by the State Department, of the state of the document's origin. Once completed, the entire foreign country dossier would need to be translated into Russian. This was the part of my own adoption process which I described as requiring a tree's worth of paper. An adoption dossier could easily consist of forty to sixty pages.

Simultaneously, the clients were assisted with the process of obtaining immigration approval from the Immigration and Citizenship Services (ICE), thereby allowing them to bring their newly adopted child into the US. Clients were also assisted with acquisition of their passports if necessary. As with the home study, a great deal of personal information had to be provided for the dossier.

During the time prospective clients were completing the paperwork processes, they had the opportunity to view videotapes of orphaned children available for adoption. The videos were acquired by Slava and Svetlana on visits to Russia. When visiting the orphanages, they personally met each child, obtained available health information, and then videotaped each child separately, whenever possible. Although Svetlana was not able to do an American-style physical examination on the children, she observed them from a pediatrician's perspective and was able to read through the health information in the file. During the first seven years, I traveled with Slava and Svetlana at least one time, occasionally two or more, annually to assist with this process.

After each of their trips to Russia, Slava would give me the small videotape, initially a VHS-c and later an eight-millimeter tape, and I would make a full-sized VHS copy of every child on the original video. Before making the individual tapes, I sat with Svetlana and reviewed the original one. I would type up the information, which would later be shared with prospective parents. I established a literal VHS library of available children, each tape marked with the name, age, and sex of the child. Waiting clients received a single video tape onto which I would copy three or four available children for them to review. The clients would receive a written history of each child in the order in which they appeared on the tape I made for them. I became a videotape making and copying maven, spending hundreds of hours each year making and preparing video tapes for clients.

Based on the age and sex of the children, if there was a preference voiced by the prospective parents, the clients would view the tapes, receive the meager information available, and select a child. Many clients were not judgmental and quickly fell in love with a child. Over the fifteen years, hundreds of times I had the pleasure and joy of watching families fall in love with a child they were seeing on video tape. It was the most special thing in the world and I loved being a part of the process, especially having experienced it myself. Sometimes a family would be watching videos of several children and a child would simply jump off the screen and cry out to them that they were the child the parents were supposed to adopt. This process often brought me intense fulfillment.

Often, people had a reason for selecting a specific child. Some of the reasons were the way the child interacted with others in the video, a sweet smile or laugh, the child resembled another of their children, had the name they dreamed their Russian child would have, or any number of other innocuous reasons. Sometimes people would believe they had been given a "sign" that a child was supposed to be their child because the baby, for instance, had the adopting mother's grandfather's birthday, or a little girl had brown eyes like the couple's biological son, etc. People always found a special connection to the children they selected.

But, there were a few people who demanded the "perfect" child, as young as they could possibly adopt, and they wanted that child the next week. These people wouldn't consider a child they viewed as thin, or one that didn't smile enough on the video tape, or one that cried during filming. These types of adoptive parents frequently viewed many tapes of children as if they were shopping. This disturbed me, but it was the way Slava had envisioned the process and I tried not to let the "shoppers" bother me. However, it was always hard to watch people view children as merchandise.

The clients eventually figured out that I kept a running list of people waiting to "select" a child. People were placed on the list in the order their initial application to adopt was received and approved. After each trip, when Slava and Svetlana returned to the US with new videotapes, clients wanted to know what position they held on the waiting list, and the number of children that would be available for "viewing." Initially, some clients passed on viewing tapes because they felt they were not "high enough on the list" when compared to the number of available children. Once a prospective adoptive parent told me that if they weren't high up on the list, they feared they would only get to see the "left-over children." I was angry at this statement, thinking, *There is no such thing as left-over children!* Another offensive comment I heard came from a woman who, while reviewing video tape of children, told me, "Oh, I could never love a child with red hair." Another woman once told me she could never love a "brown-eyed child!" After hearing these kinds of comments, I was sad to my very core that such superficial traits were that important to some people. These types of comments always caused me great anguish, and I didn't want those people to have any of "my kids!" But it was out of my control, and I had to put up with the ugly behavior.

Once a family selected a child, it was necessary that they wait for the processing of their paperwork. One time, the process was not moving rapidly enough to suit one of our ultra-wealthy clients. He called me to demand that he and his wife be allowed to travel to Russia immediately. However, Russia had not yet finished the approval of their paperwork and the couple had not yet been invited by the courts to complete the adoption. I tried explaining this to my agitated client. But through gritted teeth, he said to me, "You have no idea who you are dealing with!" He had spoken so menacingly to me that I was internally shaken, and my palms were sweating by the time I hung up the phone. He could not accept that he could not control the process.

But, I was also discovering just how selfless and giving other Americans could be, Americans who would adopt children with special needs or older children. I loved the invincible American spirit. The "Ugly Americans" were by far outnumbered by those who just wanted to give an orphaned child a home.

For some clients, the paperwork would be completed and approved before the client was able to select a child, based on the frequency of trips Slava and Svetlana were able to make to Russia. They both had full time jobs, yet they tried to travel to Russia every three or four months. Sometimes they could see the same child a second time, because either the child had not been fully approved for a US adoption or the adopting parents had not received all of their required approvals. Each time Slava and Svetlana returned to the US with updated video of "selected" children, the waiting parents were always excited to see the changes in their prospective child. I also loved getting to see how the children had changed and grown and I sometimes felt like I knew them before I ever met them.

Eventually, all paperwork processing was completed, and the parents received an invitation from the foreign country to travel to adopt their child. The foreign country coordinators were incredibly important because they kept client's documents moving through the foreign country process, worked directly with the local adoption officials, and they were invariably superb problem solvers. They also worked with the clients after they arrived in Russia. Once the client received permission to travel, we would assist the family with exactly what they needed to take, especially for those who had never traveled out of the US. I recalled how frightened I had been on that scary trip to Hungary and wanted Small World clients to be as prepared as possible to alleviate trepidation about their trip. I loved that all three of my employees, Marcia, Maureen, and Tanya, understood the fragility and fear of some of our clients, and they always treated them with loving support. The four of us became like family, and eventually many of our clients also became the same.

To facilitate the adoptions in Russia, we needed a coordinator, a driver, and a translator serving each of the foreign cities in which we had programs. Frequently, the foreign country coordination and the translation services were provided by the same person. Through the years, I got to know most of our coordinators well. I believed they shared my passion to save the orphans of Russia.

Once clients arrived in Russia, the process usually went relatively quickly. The Small World foreign country staff met them at the airport and took them to their apartments or hotels. Over the next couple of days, the adopting parent(s) visited their child(ren) in the orphanage, received available health information on the child, and then appeared in court, where hopefully a judge would grant the adoption. All adoptions were finalized in the foreign county. The Russian documents were officially translated into English, after which the family could return to the US. In the early days of the program, our clients were in the foreign countries approximately a week, and sometimes as few as four days. Once again, I found it entertaining how spoiled a few Americans were. Some complained that it was too much disruption in their lives to take a week off to adopt their child! They complained of missing social obligations or their job. Yet, I knew that these same people readily had time for exclusive vacations. Such was the message being sent through their behaviors and sometimes even their ugly words. Some did nothing but complain about their trip, despite its brevity, and they easily forgot that they were going to a formerly communist area of the world, which was decades behind America in many, many ways. Parts of Russia were little better than a third-world country. The six weeks I spent in Hungary when adopting Alex tended to make me inwardly less sympathetic to this complaint.

After the families returned to the US, we assisted them in obtaining citizenship for their child(ren) and any other processes that may be required by the state in which they lived. Most states recognized a foreign adoption as legally binding, but some states required that the family readopt their child(ren) in accordance to the requirements of the individual states.

When our first adoptive family returned to St. Louis, my family and I went to the airport to meet the flight. It was exciting to watch my first family arrive and to see their extended family share the joy. I felt honored to have played a role in the adoption of their child and of course, I cried.

We continued meeting flights for several years, and eventually I stopped crying. On rare occasions, Slava would join us for the festivities of meeting the clients. Maureen and Tanya likewise joined in the jubilant homecomings when possible. These were joyous events, and we always felt gratified to be a part of the family's miracle. This was prior to the September eleventh tragedy and when people could meet incoming flights at the arrival gate.

Since the agency was in St. Louis and I didn't do any advertising, in the early years, the majority of our clients were from the local area. Eventually we had clients in other cities, and I always felt I was missing something because the distance prohibited me from meeting their flights or getting to know them throughout their process. As more and more clients returned to St. Louis weekly, and sometimes two or three times a week, we continued to meet every flight. Frequently flights originating from Europe arrived late in the afternoon, near the end of a normal workday. I was incredibly busy and was often rushing to get to the airport. I always took little Alex with me. He went to the airport so many times that anytime we left the house, he wanted to know if we were going to the airport.

Most of the time, I believed I had the most fantastic job on earth, knowing that every day when I got out of bed, I was going to make a difference in the life of a child. However, my personal life was dwindling into non-existence. If I was at home, I was working. Clients were coming and going to and from our home during all hours of the day and evening, including the weekends. I was losing my grasp on the normal family life I had fought to maintain. I was tired, and my family wanted their privacy returned.

CHAPTER 28

CLIENT STORIES

A s we got busier, Tanya and Maureen were working more and frequently; often the three of us were crowded into our small office space together. A favorite story from this time centered on our client I will call Sally. Sally and her husband did not live in St. Louis, so we had never met them, but spent many hours on the phone with Sally. Without a doubt in my mind, Sally wins the award for talking more than any other human being with whom I have ever spoken. This is really saying something, because Laura could talk a person into a coma. But Sally had Laura beat hands down. Tanya, Maureen, and I would try to take turns talking with her because the conversations were nearly always an hour in length, minimum. Much of the time the only words we would speak in a conversation were "hmmm," "really," or "oh my." We had caller ID and when Sally's number came up, there would be a rapid intake of breath by each of us. Sometimes we would paper, rock, scissors to see who would speak with Sally that day. The three of us knew everything there was to know about Sally, her entire family, every friend, every job, every heart break, every operation, and every pet she had ever had. But, she was so likable, often making us laugh at her stories, that we all sincerely loved her. Speaking with her was just a huge time commitment.

One time, when it was Maureen's turn to talk with Sally, having lost at paper, rock, scissors, she had to use the restroom, but could simply not get a break in the normal, one-sided conversation to ask Sally to hold on. Maureen shrugged her shoulders and set the phone down, stood up, went to the restroom, returned a few minutes later, picked up the phone, said "hummm," with Sally continuing to speak never knowing Maureen had stepped away from the phone. This gave us a great idea. From that day forward, we simply put Sally on speaker phone, pushed the mute button, and went about our business, with one of us occasionally unmuting the phone to throw in a word. Sally and her husband had a successful adoption experience and we got to meet them at the next summer reunion. Of course, in person, she was no different, but even more lovable than she had been on the phone.

One afternoon, I was in the office and answered the phone, and a lovely lady said she was calling to get information, having learned about our organization from another local agency. We began talking and ended up sharing information about our lives. She talked about their struggles with infertility and I told her about my own adoption experience. Suddenly, she said, "I think you live down the street from me! Last summer, did you have some signs in your yard after you adopted?" I replied yes, that was us, and we then both walked outside and met each other in the middle of the street. She indeed lived down the street and over the years we became friends, they adopted two children with Small World, and eventually her husband became a board member. We always laughed about our chance encounter and what a truly small world it was in which we lived.

Around this time, Slava began pressuring me to find homes for the "older" children and those with "special needs." He said that the orphanage directors were insisting that we help the older children as well. To encourage people to adopt older and special needs children, after much persuasion from me, Slava agreed to a reduced fee scale. Slava and I had many, many conversations about this. I was concerned about exactly what "type" of special needs he was considering. I did not want to offer children with psychological or emotional special needs, but agreed to place children with special physical needs. I knew that naturally, by virtue of being in an orphanage, the children would need special love and attention to deal with the trauma and deprivation of orphanage life. If there was paperwork in a child's file that gave a diagnosis of a mental health problem, I felt that the child was probably too severely ill for us to place with one of our families. I believed that, most likely, only the most severely disturbed children received an actual diagnosis of mental illness. Plus, after having visited the orphanages, it was clear to me that they had neither the means nor the personnel for providing accurate mental health diagnoses. The only barometer for orphanage doctors would have been the exhibition of severe behavioral issues. So, we agreed to limit "special needs" to mean a physical need. Over the years, we helped families to adopt children with cleft palates, clubbed feet, reparable heart issues, crossed or lazy eyes, missing or mildly deformed limbs, etc.

Sometimes Slava and Svetlana would have learned about a special needs child on one of their trips, or sometimes they had to identify a child specifically for a family requesting an older or special needs child. One of our families who chose to adopt a special needs child lived in a rural area of St. Louis. It just so happened that we had in our videotape files a video of a little boy who had been named "Forrest." They named him this because as a two-year-old, he had been found simply wandering in the birch forest and had no name. There was no information on little Forrest's background; there wasn't even a birthday. The orphanage had simply made one up. He had rickets and his little legs were terribly bowed. But he seemed to be the sweetest little guy you could imagine. The family fell in love with him as they watched his video tape. This little guy, named Forrest by the Russians, would be coming to America! Events like these made me adore my job.

We worked hard to keep clients informed about what was happening in the agency and in the foreign country. I advised the clients when Slava and Svetlana were traveling and when they would return. Sometimes a client would be so anxious they couldn't help themselves and called my home phone, though most understood that in the evenings I tried not to answer the work phone. One time, however, a client, who had already selected a child and knew that Slava and Svetlana were going to return with updated video of their son, began calling around dinner time.

The client had called me at home several times, and I made the mistake of complaining about her to Slava. He insisted on calling her to tell her to stop calling my home phone in the evening, after which she did stop. I felt badly about it, knowing that he was probably not very understanding in his communication with her. I realized since my office was in my home and clients knew this, some felt they had the right to call my home telephone line. It really was time to put some distance between my personal and professional life and obtain an official office.

The urgency of separate office space was made very clear to me when, several months later, this same lady traveled to the foreign country to finalize her adoption. I again received a call from her on my home phone, but this time it was in the middle of the night. She was screaming at me that our translator, who had been escorting her on a train ride to her city of adoption, was a rapist! He had had the audacity and rudeness to remove his sweater while they were alone together in a cabin on the train. She was hysterical, yelling at me that she was a married woman and no man should be removing pieces of his clothing in front of her. I asked if he was wearing a shirt beneath his sweater. She answered yes, but regardless, his action terrified her, and she wanted a different translator. Waking up to this kind of hysteria was just one of the hundreds of "middle of the night" calls I received. I called Slava the next morning and shared the nighttime conversation with him. He angrily responded that our client was being dramatic, and he was not finding another translator. He said Victor, the translator, was as proper and well-mannered as a man could be. He then told me that the temperatures on the trains in Eastern Europe were not well-regulated and the interior of the cabins could reach one-hundred degrees, especially in the winter, which at that time it was. I was learning to take client comments with a grain of salt.

I did subsequently get the opportunity to meet our translator, Victor, who was indeed an absolute gentleman. Victor was short, lean, and had blond hair and blue eyes. He was soft spoken, sweet, and kind, and it was always a joy to spend time with him and his lovely wife over the next several years.

The end result of having my office in my home was that I worked all the time, clients were coming to my house, often without notice, calling my home phone, and I quite simply missed having a normal life with my family.

Fortunately for me, about this same time I was finishing up the process to officially license Small World, and a legal and official business office was one of the requirements. As physicians, even though Slava and Svetlana could legally place children for adoption, being a licensed agency had finally become a requirement in Russia. There were now two excellent reasons to get me moving. So, not quite two years into my mission, I went in search of official office space. We ended up purchasing a little house about five blocks from my home. We updated it, made some structural changes, enlarged the parking area, and moved in. We were happy as clams in a newly remodeled shell, looking forward to summer in our new office.

CHAPTER 29

THE HIGHIGHTS OF EVERY YEAR

IN THAT SUMMER OF 1995, we held our second annual summer picnic at Slava's house. We hosted around 150 people for an event like the one the year before. However, with the increased number of guests, we realized Slava could not single handedly make enough barbecue. So, we had the food catered, and of course Ryan again guarded the pool. Watching the kids playing in the pool and seeing the happiness on so many faces was a joy that is almost indescribable. I was proud and humbled to play a part in such a beautiful thing. I was grateful God had given me this mission.

Our summer picnics would continue until we left the agency. Eventually, the picnic would grow to nearly 1000 people, and to accommodate everyone we had to rent an enormous arena type building in one of the biggest parks in St. Louis. I felt that the summer picnics were the highlight of every year. The weekends began on Friday night with a pool party for all the families from out-of-town. We invited the out-of-town guests to a private event so that we could enjoy extra time with them. Some of them traveled great distances every year to participate in the event.

The Saturday picnics got so big, so fast, that sometimes the Friday night event would be the only time Small World staff would have to visit with the out-of-town clients. We hadn't met most of them personally and had only forged "telephone relationships." So, we relished getting to meet them at the picnics. We loved the opportunity to watch the children grow up over the years, and the weekend was always an affirming time for us. Year after year, many of the same families came and everyone truly did begin to feel like extended family.

The foreign country coordinators, invited to the US for the picnics, also seemed truly moved to see how well the children were doing. The clients seemed to love having the opportunity to reconnect with the people who had assisted them with their adoption processes in the foreign countries as well as the domestic Small World staff. The Small World picnics served as reminders that the demanding work we were doing at Small World was having a positive impact on the world. It was a very affirming time for me.

Each year, the *Szeged 28* reunions occurred about two weeks before the Small World picnics. July was a joyous month for me, filled with reconnecting with people about whom I really cared. With each passing year, the Szeged picnics became more and more valuable for me, supporting one another, sharing stories, laughter, and love.

Another highlight each year became our "Breakfast with Santa" event each December. It began in the fall of 1996, when one of our new adoptive mothers wanted to organize an event for the children who had been adopted in the St. Louis area. She was an event planner for a hotel and offered to organize a "Breakfast with Santa" affair to be held a couple of weeks prior to Christmas. She gathered together a group of volunteers and they worked throughout the fall to organize the first event. They coordinated the food, had crafts for the children, and had recruited Maureen's husband, Dave, to be Santa. However, on the day of the event, Dave was sick, and Dave's father, Fred, stepped in to play

Santa. Every year thereafter, Fred donned the Santa suit and happily held child after child on his lap.

Eventually, the event grew so large that several hundred families attended, and the breakfast was catered by an outside company. There were clowns and games and happy children running around everywhere. Staff began to look forward to Breakfast with Santa almost as much as the summer picnics. It was a treat, and brought even deeper meaning to the Christmas season, hundreds of happy children now in loving families.

CHAPTER 30

DEALING WITH CHANGE

AFTER MOVING TO OUR NEW office, slowly Maureen and Tanya began working more and more hours until they were both working nearly full time. Their increased help was giving me time to work on program development, not just helping clients with paperwork, which became the primary roles for Tanya and Maureen. I also became what I would remain until the end of our tenure with the agency, the official fireman putting out one fire or another almost every day.

I tried to help prospective adoptive families identify funding sources for their adoptions. For many of the clients, the expense of the adoption was not problematic. But for some of our families, it was a matter of taking a second mortgage on their homes, borrowing from their retirement accounts, their families, or in some cases actual bank loans. My heart always hurt when it seemed that building a family was such a financial burden for some people. I wished that the process was not so expensive and frequently asked Slava if there was a way to reduce costs. He was always steadfast – there were no exceptions or allowances for people. He had recently agreed to reduced fees for people adopting children aged five and older and for children with special needs. After all, he would say, "Doing business in Russia is very expensive, there are a lot of worker bees in Russia that need to be paid, and we have to financially support the orphanages in which the children reside." I believed every word he ever told me, and I was comforted by the knowledge that perhaps these funds were being used to make the miserable lives of the orphans left behind a little better.

Slava's outbursts seemed to be almost cyclical. When he was in what I called his "moody cycle," I seemed to frequently be the recipient of his wrath for things occurring in his life which were in no way related to Small World. I had begun to try to read his moods and had become adept at avoiding touchy topics when he was in one of his unpleasant moods.

I remember one day that spring when Slava came to the office in a bad mood. As a licensed agency now, we were required to undergo a full audit. Slava had just come from his accountant's office. The accountant, who was a friend of his, was doing both Small World taxes and its audit. She had just told him he needed to personally purchase the boat and the jet skis from Small World because they could not remain in the company's name. He was furious about this. I didn't understand how or why Small World had owned them to begin with, but I knew Slava had taken visiting guests to the river and out on the jet skis. I imagine that was Slava's justification. However, until that moment, I hadn't known that the jet skis and boat hadn't been owned by Slava. I remember thinking that Slava was going to have to learn that operating a business in the US was different than operating one in Russia, as he clearly never saw any problem with using agency funding to purchase a boat and jet skis. I should have paid more attention to his way of thinking at the time. But, like so many other events or conversations, I was exceedingly busy and didn't pay enough attention to Slava's behaviors. Plus, because of his unpredictable moods, I tended to avoid challenging him about issues.

The adoption laws in Russia were constantly changing. In the beginning, single women had been able to adopt from Russia, but less than a year later, only married couples could adopt, and there were all kinds of new rules around that. As such, we were constantly being forced to change documents and forms. We had become so busy that some days it was almost too much for us to simply keep up with the phone calls, much less the forms. Both Tanya and Maureen became skilled at smoothing out ruffled feathers of clients when they were informed of changing procedures or additionally required paperwork.

As things got busier and the stress increased on Slava, he began the habit of calling me in the middle of the night. Because of the time change, frequently Slava would speak with foreign country officials during the daytime hours in the foreign countries, which were of course our night time hours. If there were procedural changes, he usually waited until the next day to share those with me. However, if the issue involved his perceived notion that I, or one of my staff, had done something wrong, I would awaken to, "Brenditchka, (Slava's nickname for me) what is going on, why did you let that client change her mind," or "why did you let that client give the orphanage director such a stupid gift," or "didn't you warn him there could be a delay?" Of course, clients were warned about delays, and many of the things that upset him were things over which I had no control. There were hundreds of things that occurred which made him mad. Then he would yell, and I would try to calm him down, and of course there was never anything I could do in the middle of the night. For several years, I allowed Slava to call me and rage at me in the middle of the night. However, eventually I had to yell back and tell him it was crazy for him to wake me in the middle of the night when there was nothing I could do to resolve the issue. He did stop calling me nearly so much in the middle of the night, waiting until the next day to yell at me. I discovered that he was never as mad or ugly the next day as he had been during those middle of the night phone calls, thank heavens.

Unfortunately, he also developed the habit of calling Maureen and Tanya and yelling at them whenever he was displeased about something.

I tried to insulate them from those berating conversations with Slava but wasn't always totally successful. All of us were a little bit afraid of him, not in the physical sense, but his tirades were something we all wanted to avoid.

Our little office staff grew closer and closer. Right before Christmas that year, 1995, I got Laura a new kitten because we had lost her cat about six months before. The kitten was to be a surprise, so I brought it to the office until Christmas, which had been just a couple of days away. It makes me laugh each time I think about the first day we had the kitten in the office and how Tanya came into my office complaining that Maureen was "hogging" the kitten. Of course, this was said in a joking fashion, but it was representative of the playful, friendly atmosphere of our office.

Shortly after we moved the office from my home to the "little house," the combination of the increased number of phone calls, the paperwork, and the growing client base made it evident we needed a receptionist. When I posed the idea to Slava, he insisted that I hire his step-daughter, Karena. She was a pregnant young woman who was undeniably pleasant, albeit unskilled in the office world. However, she worked hard and was friendly with the clients. We liked her very much and she fit into our growing family of staff.

Slava's and my family were becoming more and more enmeshed with Small World. Slava's daughter-in-law was Alex's nanny, his step-daughter was the Small World receptionist, and his son was our bookkeeper. Add to that just a few months after Karena joined our staff, she got married and our little Alex was the ring bearer in her wedding.

Around this time, Karena encouraged Tanya, Maureen, and me to take Russian language lessons. Marcia could not be convinced to give them a try. Karena was familiar with a lady teaching Russian language classes one night a week through that fall. I thought this would be helpful for a variety of reasons. First, sometimes when Slava returned from his trips to Russia, he would call me, and he would be having a complete conversation in rapid Russian, having gotten out of the habit of speaking English. When he was finished speaking, I would laugh and say, "Okay, now can you repeat all of that in English?" If I were able to learn more than twenty words of Russian, wouldn't that totally surprise him when I could respond to his soliloquy in Russian! We would also be able to communicate with the Russian children coming to the office after their adoptions, and I would be able to participate in business activities when I traveled to Russia. It sounded like a good plan for us.

Well, at least it sounded good. By the fourth class, Maureen and I were so frustrated, we became night school dropouts! I believe Tanya, bless her heart, stayed that whole first semester. What a trooper she was. My life was so complicated with three children and trying to manage a burgeoning business that I had no time for practicing. Plus, my brain just didn't like the fact that an English R had the "er" sound, but in Cyrillic, the Russian alphabet, the letter which looked like an English R had the English P sound. Here is my favorite example of utter brain confusion. The Russian word "PecTopaH" looks as if it should be pronounced "pec–ta–paw." The word is pronounced "restaurant." My brain just couldn't ever make it past this. Fortunately, I did learn how to recognize enough Russian words over the years that it was helpful when traveling. I also picked up some conversational phrases, at least enough that I could convey simple questions or statements to the people with whom we worked in Russia.

During the Christmas season of 1995, we had our first Small World Christmas party. I hosted everyone at my house, staff brought a side dish, and we enjoyed a lovely Christmas dinner together. Slava and Svetlana always brought the vodka! The spouses joined in the fun and over the years, our families all got to be very good friends, with some of the men playing golf or fishing together. Sometimes we played games after dinner, enjoyed cocktails, and the Small World staff exchanged Christmas presents. Even after our affiliation with Small World ended, several of us continued to enjoy the annual party at my house.

CHAPTER 31

ANN LANDERS AND CNN

SMALL WORLD CONTINUED TO HAPPILY hum along that year. It was late into our second year, 1995, when the client explosion happened. On one of my trips to Russia, I had met a little girl named Valentina who would come to change the course of the agency. Valentina was about three or four years old, a beautiful little blond with bright blue eyes. Her parents had immediately fallen madly in love with her from her videotape and were luckily able to travel quickly to Russia to finalize the adoption. Adoptions from Eastern Europe were still in their infancy at this time, and airline passengers traveling between the US and Europe had not yet grown accustomed to newly adopted children on flights bound for America. Thus, little Valentina attracted a bit of attention on the flight home.

A lovely woman sitting near the family on the plane, witnessing their love and excitement, wanted to give the family a small gift when they landed. Having nothing she felt worthy of offering to little Valentina, the woman gave her a $20 bill to begin her new life in America. In all the commotion of landing, the parents had been unable to get the woman's name and address to thank her.

The parents had been so touched by the generosity and kindness of this stranger that they wrote to Ann Landers. They asked her to publish their story to help them find the kind woman. The article was published and did indeed enable the couple to connect with the generous gift giver. The giver was actually a third-grade teacher who lived in Wiesbaden, Germany. The couple and the lady not only spoke by phone, but they met again in person and the two families stayed in touch for many years.

The nationally publicized Ann Landers article contained Small World's name and phone number. An explosion occurred in our office! For four days after the article was published, we were unable to put the phone down. We had four phone lines and they were all constantly accepting incoming calls. I had to put a message on the phone advising people that because of the article, we couldn't keep up with the phone calls. I explained that we were taking messages and we would return all calls as quickly as possible, but people should expect that it could take a couple of days. Karena spent all her time retrieving the hundreds of messages off our voice mail! Maureen, Tanya, and I spent the days responding to the messages. Marcia even joined in and took on organizing the enormous number of information packets we had to send out. We spent a few weeks responding to all the messages and distributing information packets to interested, prospective parents. Because of this newspaper article, our little agency was shoved into the national spotlight, and over the next year we completed over 200 adoptions from Russia, Ukraine, and Belarus.

Not too many months after the Ann Landers incident, I received a call from a man who was a producer for a major news agency. He and his wife, having also read the article, were hoping to adopt. They ultimately adopted a baby and then subsequently the producer arranged for a CNN special about Russian adoptions.

Years later, the producer and his wife shared with me a picture they had taken on a recent trip back to St. Petersburg. The picture was of their nearly adult child standing next to the same orphanage director who had been in charge at the time of the adoption nearly eighteen years earlier! It was amazing for me to see this picture of not only their grown child, but also Yelena, the orphanage director who I had met many times over the years. I couldn't believe she was still working at the orphanage so many years later. The family included in their message a photograph of their child as a baby being held by this same orphanage director. I will treasure these pictures forever more as proof that miracles did happen.

CHAPTER 32

OPENING BELARUS

IN EARLY 1996, SLAVA INFORMED me we were adding a new program in the country of Belarus. I think he was feeling this necessary because of the huge influx of clients following the Ann Landers article. I was not at all familiar with this country, so I set about doing some research into this small country that had previously been part of the former Soviet Union. Slava explained that we were going to start a program in a small city, Gomel, where the mayor was a childhood friend of Svetlana's. Slava relayed that he had contacts in Minsk who were willing to help him initiate a program in that city as well. Many times, Slava told me that Russian people hesitate to do business with strangers, and I had learned that business relationships in Russia began with personal ones. My own experiences traveling in Russia had taught me that much of doing business in Eastern Europe was about who you knew. Slava once told me that, "Knowing the right people was the only way to make anything happen, along with having enough money to pay them." Slava frequently told me that if something couldn't be fixed with money, it couldn't be fixed. Slava's contacts proved to be invaluable as we successfully completed hundreds of adoptions from Belarus before the country closed its doors to adoption in 2004.

The addition of a second country, which had different requirements for the adopting parents, the paperwork wasn't exactly the same, and the actual adoption itself followed a slightly different process, only served to further complicate an already complicated model for our agency. With Slava relying on me to make sure everything went smoothly with the US paperwork and with preparation of the clients, it was prophetic that I had recently added staff. I would not have been able to do the work without Marcia, Maureen, Karena, and Tanya.

CHAPTER 33

LESSONS LEARNED WHILE
TRAVELING IN RUSSIA

ABOUT TWO YEARS INTO OUR quest to create the best international adoption agency, the gap in my knowledge about Russia was becoming more and more problematic. I was preparing people to travel to a place to which I had never been. I was consistently grilling Slava and Svetlana for details about the culture, the people, the trip, and the orphanages themselves. Additionally, Slava and Svetlana were not providing what I believed to be enough information about the children. It was one of the many cultural differences between the way I viewed information and the way Slava and Svetlana viewed it.

They did not believe the adopting parents needed specific information about the children being adopted. Slava and Svetlana believed that if they personally saw the children and spoke to the orphanage director, that should be adequate for American parents. Svetlana consistently voiced her belief that adopting parents should just trust her. In the beginning, I had to argue and lobby just to get birth weights for the children. Slava and Svetlana did not understand that Americans are a society of people who are information driven. Americans can never have enough information about anything, especially and understandably regarding a child being adopted from a foreign country. Additionally, Americans are apt to want to maintain control over something so significant to their lives. Slava and Svetlana, particularly Svetlana, took it as a personal insult that Americans wanted medical, familial history and developmental information about the children. She felt that as a pediatrician, her word should be sufficient. Svetlana also stated that adoptive parents should only focus on children from the point of their adoption and be less concerned about their lives before coming to America. I believe this was not an uncommon way of viewing child rearing in Russia.

Marcia also tried to help Slava understand the importance of a more comprehensive medical picture of the orphans. Eventually, we convinced Slava to increase and improve the medical information made available to clients by continuously highlighting how our legal risk would be reduced if a more complete medical picture was made available to the adopting parents. Svetlana never really supported providing detailed medical information, always believing that her assessment of the children was adequate. But she went along with what Slava wanted, which was normally the case. I was relieved when they agreed to provide more detailed medical information, knowing it would make our clients feel more secure.

As a result of my never-ending questions, Slava decided that it would be good for me to travel to Russia with him and Svetlana. It was the most exhilarating invitation for me. I would be able to obtain more complete information for the adopting parents, which would enable me to better prepare them for their trips. However, I was also a little panicky about going. I had grown up in the era of the "cold war" with Russia and it was supposed to be a "dark and dangerous" place. Regardless of my apprehension, I eagerly got on a plane to accompany Slava and Svetlana to St. Petersburg, Russia. Marcia, Maureen, and Tanya assured me they could manage the business in my absence, and of course they did.

My children were the ones most concerned about my trip. Ryan and Laura vividly remembered what happened the last time I got on a plane to leave the country – I didn't return for nearly six weeks. I assured them I would only be gone about ten days and I promised to call them every other day. Actually, I believe my whole family likely had a little post-traumatic stress disorder after our harrowing Hungarian adoption experience.

Upon arriving in Russia, I found it to be an intimidating place. Most likely due to all the air pollution, it was gray, and the air felt denser than the air in the Midwest. The mode of dress was predominantly drab and dark. It was amazing to me that many women, of all ages, walked all about town in three-inch spiked heels.

When I had traveled in Hungary, I had occasionally encountered people who could speak English. In Russia, I rarely encountered anyone who spoke my language. The faces of the Russian people were difficult to read; smiles were hard to come by, especially when compared to Americans, who readily smile at strangers. On the crowded streets, Russian citizens ran into us and made no overture to apologize. They appeared to be a tough people. One of the things that frightened me was the large number of soldiers walking around everywhere carrying Uzis. I had never been up close to so many weapons. I had seen a number of guns in Hungary, but somehow this just felt different to me, more menacing. There were Uzi toting police everywhere I looked in the airport, as throughout the city, and this was years before 911. It was just a couple of years after the fall of the Soviet Union and subsequent end of the cold war though, and I believed the mass of weaponry was a remnant of a communist Russia that was still evident everywhere I looked. To me, Russians seemed to maintain an air of distrust of others, never making eye contact with strangers, pushing and shoving in lines with their ever-solemn faces.

The country I encountered was one of great poverty. Independent homes appeared to be little more than shacks with tin roofs. There was mile after mile of high-rise, stark, and run-down looking apartment buildings. The streets were in terrific disrepair, with huge potholes. The yards, common areas for buildings, or boulevards between streets were primarily dirt with a few patches of weeds. There were no manicured grassy areas anywhere to be seen. There were no flower beds to add color to this dreary country. When I looked up at the apartment buildings, most of them had laundry strung across the tiny balconies.

After we arrived, Slava, Svetlana, and I went to an apartment building which housed a flat Slava said Small World had purchased, and it was where our adopting families stayed. Upon entering the building, I saw that most of the light bulbs had been smashed and the aroma of urine was pervasive in the entryway and in the stairwell. It was a shocking introduction to the building, and immediately I thought of how this negative first impression affected our clients. This had to make them uneasy. A single light bulb hanging by a wire, high up on the ceiling, was the only beacon of light in the dark and dank foyer of the apartment building. The elevator did not work, so we carried our luggage up three flights of stairs. Fortunately, our driver assisted us with the bags. As I would discover over the years, nearly every apartment building in Eastern Europe I entered shared these entryway traits.

After climbing several flights of stairs, entering the apartment was an exercise in patience. Slava had a handful of keys for the several different locks on the massive metal door, which was more like a vault door than a door to an apartment. After getting the huge "first" door open, there was another heavy, wooden door which had to be unlocked. Once we finally got into the apartment, it was quite lovely. It was sparsely furnished in a contemporary style, Slava and Svetlana's favorite. The apartment was comprised of two bedrooms, a living room, a big kitchen, and a bathroom. It was clean, comfortable, and had a lot of windows, making it wonderfully bright.

During that first trip, little English was spoken to me. All day long, people were speaking Russian with Slava doing minimal translating for me, and I was rather lonely. One evening, I was too tired to accompany Slava and Svetlana to dinner and opted to spend the evening in the apartment. Truthfully, I just needed a break from the Russian language and needed some quiet time. I turned on the TV and found the movie Die Hard, which had Russian dubbed in over the English. I could hear the English as well and I sat right next to the TV, so I could better hear the English being spoken, hungry to hear my own language.

It was on this trip that I first met our foreign country coordinator for the St. Petersburg area, Maria. Maria was in fact, as I learned a few years later, Slava's sister-in-law. Slava's brother had passed away a few years prior, and Slava and Svetlana were quite close with Maria. Maria was a petite, attractive, older woman who was quiet and reserved. Although we didn't share a spoken language, I felt that we made a connection on that first trip. Maria joined us each evening for dinner.

The first morning after arriving in Russia, our driver, whose name I believe was Victor (a very common Russian name), picked us up to visit the first of three orphanages with which we worked in St. Petersburg. I will never, ever forget that experience. As we drove up to the building, I was stunned by the disrepair of the structure, the crumbling concrete, and the gravel area designated as the "playground" for the children. The paint was peeling from the exterior walls and the building was stark and threatening looking. There were several children outside with a few caretakers. The children were in threadbare clothing and they were quite thin. The few toys with which the children played were obviously many years old, and most were simple, small, metal toys on which the paint had long since worn away.

A little way from the building was an old-fashioned clothes line on which hung a collection of what appeared to be gray rags, but after closer inspection I realized they were clothes for the children. Children who were not yet "potty-trained" did not wear diapers and several were just walking around outside in wet pants. Many of the windows of the building appeared to have been cracked and were essentially held in place with giant pieces of tape which looked similar to clear packing tape. It was one of the first of many shockingly sad and pathetic scenes I would witness on my many trips to Russia.

Upon entering the building, after carefully navigating the cracked and crumbling concrete steps, the first thing to be noticed was the cloying odor of the place. Slava told me it was the children's lunch being prepared. I couldn't even fathom the possibility of eating something that smelled so vile. To conserve energy, the hallways had just enough light to allow us to navigate them. The floors were covered in linoleum, such as I recalled from my grandparents' home when I was a young child. Despite all of this, the orphanage was clean. Things were very old, but the workers certainly made the best with what they had and took excellent care of everything, realizing that replacements would be few and far between. What I was exposed to on that trip, and all subsequent ones, was that Russia was the opposite of the American "disposable" society. Everything was reused again and again, and then after it was completely worn out it was used yet one last time. The frugality of the people was unbelievably impressive.

A caretaker who let us in the locked building escorted us to the office of the orphanage director. The office held an older-looking, large, wooden desk, a couch, and a big piece of furniture against the wall that was partially a book case and partially a storage cabinet. There was a large area rug on the floor. Just as everything else I had seen in the orphanage, objects in the room appeared to be many, many years old and much worn, yet amazingly well cared for. Interestingly, nearly every orphanage director's office I visited through the years was furnished almost the same way. The consistent appearances of the offices made me recall stories in childhood textbooks I had read about the uniformity of communist society. It appeared that even the business offices held little individuality.

Upon greeting the orphanage director, Slava and Svetlana hugged her heartily and introduced me. Her name was Galena, and she was gracious and hospitable to me. The orphanage director, Slava, and Svetlana spoke for a long time. It was rare that Slava would translate a piece of the conversation for me, so I simply sat quietly trying to drink in this remarkable experience.

Even now, when I picture the orphanages in which I spent so much time, a tremendous sadness envelopes me. The buildings used to "house" the orphans always seemed to be worse looking than others around them. It was clear to me that these children had only a minimal value to their society. Slava once told me that the orphanages had to be locked all the time and staff couldn't leave anything outside because the people in the towns would steal anything left outside. Many of the orphanages had huge fences surrounding them. It was hard to process that citizens had no compunction about stealing from orphans. What a heartbreaking picture of Russian society. I felt their actions also captured the intense poverty in which the people lived.

After Slava, Svetlana, and Galena had shared a few shots of vodka, and after being pressured many times to join in, I finally accepted one. I was hungry and still exhausted from our travel and a shot of vodka was all I needed to unplug from the unintelligible conversation going on around me. Also, it was not yet even noon!! I felt myself getting drowsy yet tried hard to stay awake. We had only been in Russia a short time, and the time change was confusing my brain. The shot of vodka sent me into a peaceful slumber. My eyes flew open as Slava gave my arm a rough shaking, telling me to wake up. He was agitated that I had fallen asleep and embarrassed both him and Svetlana. I felt badly about it, but what could I have done?

I learned a valuable lesson on that first trip. For the remainder of that trip and on all other subsequent trips to Russia, anytime I was in a meeting, whether in a governmental office or an orphanage, I positioned myself close to a potted plant. Thus, began my years-long practice of emptying my vodka laden shot glass into a plant, always when no one was watching. It was an effective way of dealing with having to accept vodka while still experiencing jet lag. I was quite fortunate that indoor plants were prevalent in nearly every home, school, and office building I visited. I often wonder how many potted plants were actually assassinated by me, as sometimes a plant received several shots in a single visit!

After waking, I followed Slava and Svetlana on a tour of the orphanage with the director. The four of us visited several of the children's rooms that day. Some sights are burned forever in people's brains, and that was how that day was for me. There were very, very sick children with severe hydrocephalus, their heads so large it was painful to see. There were children with incredibly disfiguring cleft palates and cleft lips. They were all incredibly sweet children who were happy to just be picked up. When we entered the rooms from where Slava and Svetlana were supposed to select children, the children looked unbelievably different. They were all dressed up in bright colors, new clothes, with big bows in their hair. In this room, there were many new looking toys. These children were obviously on display for the videotaping process for the prospective parents. The showcased children made me sad but I understood that the orphanage director felt it necessary to make the children look well cared for and happy. I sat on the floor and played with the children while Slava took videotape and Svetlana looked at the medical records.

During this trip, I experienced just about the worst inside restroom facility to which I had ever been exposed (up to that time!). When it became necessary for me, one of the caretakers in the orphanage was instructed to escort me to the restroom. Traveling back down one of the dimly lit corridors, I was led to a tiny, fowl smelling restroom. She pushed a button on the wall to make the single naked bulb in the high ceiling come to life. Directly in front of me was a hole in the floor on a little raised platform. On each side of the hole was what I can only describe as "gripper pads." The little "pads" were about six inches wide and about twelve inches long and looked to be made of concrete that was rippled, for lack of a better term, apparently to provide traction. The closet-sized room appeared to be clean. The young girl turned and pulled the door closed, leaving me in this awful room. This experience gave new meaning to the "hover" method of using a toilet. And of course, there was no paper in sight. Lesson number two on that day – always travel with packets of tissues.

I experienced similar restroom facilities in a Belarus airport a few years later. But being a public facility, it was 100 times worse! The floors were wet and filthy, the sinks had no hot water, there was no soap, and the smell in that public restroom was nauseating.

One day, after videotaping children who were available for adoption, we went to a restaurant for dinner. It was reminiscent of an old-fashioned discotheque with lots of flashing lights and exceedingly loud music. As became the process when traveling with Slava and Svetlana, Slava would assist me in finding something on the menu I might like. He would translate the menu for me and try to explain the dishes. However, I quickly learned that frequently when Russian is translated into English – a lot can be lost – especially when related to spices, food, and its preparation. What Slava described to me from the menu often had little relationship to the food that was presented to me for dinner.

Before leaving the restaurant that night, I had another interesting restroom encounter. After receiving directions to the restroom, I found myself, once more, in a dimly lit hallway that did not appear to actually be connected to the restaurant. It was as if I had exited the restaurant and was heading down a public hallway to the restroom. It was a little frightening, and my assumption was that the restaurant did not have its own restroom, which is very uncommon in the US.

I entered a dimly lit room which had several stalls. Standing there, as if guarding the facility, was a large Russian woman with a basket over her arm, holding a roll of toilet paper. I am sure the look of consternation on my face alerted her to the fact that I was a foreigner. The meaning of her presence became clear as she pointed to the basket that was full of coins. Although the basket contained almost entirely Russian coins, I glanced a few dimes in the mix. I opened my purse, withdrew a dime and handed it to her. She awarded me with a single sheet of toilet paper. Ok, now clearly, I had to do something differently to accommodate my need. I opened my purse and gave her two single dollar bills and she reeled off a considerable amount of paper from her roll and handed it to me. I noticed that she put the bills into the pocket of her smock, not into the basket. It was worth the two dollars to have toilet paper, a toilet upon which I could sit, and one that actually flushed! This was confirmation of the importance of that second rule I had learned earlier that day. The third new rule was to be sure to carry single dollar bills or a lot of dimes!

After dinner, Slava, Svetlana, and I were crammed into the backseat of a very small, very typical of the time, Russian vehicle. It was a charming evening, warm and pleasant, with bright stars overhead. Our driver and another man, with whom I was unfamiliar, were in the front seat. Suddenly there were flashing lights behind us, and I realized we were being pulled over by the police. There were not many cars on the road, as it was late in the evening. At first, I was not overly concerned. Then, Slava sharply told me to "Keep your mouth shut." He didn't want the police to know I was an American. We were asked to exit the car and instructed to stand in front of an old, stone wall. I was unequivocally, officially terrified.

There were three police officers, one guarding us with the proverbial Uzi pointed right at us and the other two engaged in conversation with our driver standing next to the car. The driver came over to us and said we were stopped for having too many people in the car. I started to object but Slava's very angry glare immediately silenced me. The driver informed us that the police were requiring a fine of $50 to allow us to continue. I recall thinking, *What, no ticket, we pay here on the street? People just pay the police right there on the street?!* I was so naïve. Everyone began opening their wallets and I quietly whispered to Slava that I had some hundreds. He looked at me incredulously, and in that heavy Russian accent, I can still hear his voice ringing in my head, "What, you think they give change?" Okay, yet another lesson learned to add to my growing list of things to remember, but perhaps not one I would share with our adopting families. When being shaken down by Russian police, one cannot expect to receive change.

We were able to put together enough small bills to come up with our $50 fine, aka shake down fee. It was far from my first experience which I perceived to be another cultural difference between Russia and America and would be far from the last. I had to agree with Slava's assessment that Russia was similar to the American Wild West, as he had told me on numerous occasions.

We repeated the same routine for five or six days, minus the shake down by the Russian police. Each night, we would return to the fortress that was our apartment. Slava's explanation for the many locks on the doors and the "shakedown" police was that Russia was a dangerous place. I was therefore frightened most of the rest of the time I was there. I ultimately would learn sometime later that it had never been necessary for me to be frightened. Slava disclosed to me that he never traveled in Russia without fully armed drivers and that usually there were other people around, whom I may or may not see, who were assuring our safety. Slava told me that the other man in the car with us the night of the "shakedown" was an armed body guard. He said he always had at least one while traveling in Russia.

Slava informed me that our clients, the adopting families, would be safe in Russia, but he wasn't. He said people knew he had immigrated to the US and many people knew he was now a wealthy doctor. This was surprising as the city was very large, and it seemed odd that there would be anyone paying attention to him. He said that the officials working in the Customs Control would call their friends outside the airport when someone of interest was entering the country. I was never sure how the Customs officials identified "persons of interest." I should probably have begun to ask more questions and learn more about Slava and his Russian relationships then.

The most haunting orphanage experience I had during this trip was when a group of thin, five and six-year-old children, all wearing faded, worn, and holey clothing, crowded around me, pulling on me, and all talking at the same time. I asked Svetlana what they were saying. Svetlana said they were all begging me to find them mamas and papas. They were promising to cook and clean for them if only I would find them parents. Svetlana explained that they believed if they could "sell themselves" well enough, they might get the chance to be adopted. The sadness on their faces and the earnestness in their eyes made me want to weep. But, I could not let these small children see me cry; I had to be strong. I knew that this experience was just another of God's messages to me that this was my purpose, now literally given to me from the mouths of babes.

I believe it was during my first trip to Russia that I received my first introduction to what Slava frequently called chinks in my innocence. I learned that the orphanage directors expected to be paid a fee for each child being taken from their orphanage. Slava said they had a lot of work to do to prepare the paperwork for the children to be adopted. The children were required to undergo special medical exams and a significant number of legal documents had to be completed. I had expected that this would have been included in their job description, but Slava just scoffed at me whenever I said anything like that. Each time I discovered something like this, Slava again reminded be about Russia and his Wild West philosophy, claiming life was often each man for himself. Slava also alluded to fees being paid to governmental officials in the cities where the adoptions were arranged.

After that initial visit, I fully understood that from a cultural perspective, business was conducted extremely differently in Russia than in the US. People in Russia expected to be paid for every single thing they did. I witnessed that no one seemed to do anything without getting something in return. I learned that when traveling to always have small bills to give to whoever helped to do anything. In America, if you offered an official twenty-five dollars to sign a document for you, you would likely be arrested. In Russia, if you didn't offer that official the twenty-five dollars, your document would likely sit on the bottom of a pile forever.

The cultural differences were vast in number, from the business practices, to social norms, to manners, to the way people dressed, and yes, even morality. I recall one-time Slava told me that nearly everyone had a "lover" outside of their marriage. He said it was just accepted in society. It was difficult to believe that this was true, but it seemed that frequently I would encounter situations in which this statement was supported. For instance, in later years a governor from one of the areas where we worked in Russia came to visit the US at our invitation and with him was his mistress. His wife had remained in Russia with the children. No one thought this out of the ordinary.

Something that was out of the ordinary was the unavailability of blue jeans, another post-communism effect. I was surprised to see lines of people four or five blocks long, hoping to purchase a single pair of blue jeans. I promised to send blue jeans to several of the people I met and after returning to the US, sent them with the next couple that traveled to Russia. I continued sending blue jeans for three or four years, after which time their availability had improved so much that people no longer requested them.

I returned with Slava and Svetlana to the US with a much better understanding of what lay ahead for adopting parents. I realized I would need to do a much better job of preparing them for their trips.

After I got back to the office, I created a travel packet of information that over the years would grow to be many, many pages long. I tried to offer a comprehensive picture of Russia. Each time I traveled to a foreign country and learned something new, I would add it to the "Travel Packet." One of the more humorous suggestions I gave clients was that they *could* leave home without their American Express card because it was not widely accepted in Eastern Europe.

Many of our families had never traveled outside of the US, and the uniqueness of their travel added to the stress and fear they already had about the adoption. I tried to prepare them as thoroughly as possible, but regardless of how much detailed information the packets contained, there were always new scenarios presenting themselves to the parents in the foreign countries for which I could not have prepared them.

Slava and Svetlana continued to regularly travel to Eastern Europe to videotape available orphans, with me traveling with them at least one time per year. On each trip, I seemed to identify more issues which needed to be covered for clients in the "Travel Packets."

CHAPTER 34

FIRST TRIP TO BELARUS

NOT LONG AFTER THAT FIRST trip to Russia, Slava, Svetlana, and I flew to Belarus in the spring of 1996. We were going to videotape children available for adoption, and I would also learn how the adoption process operated in this country, which would enable me to better prepare clients for travel. What an experience this trip was! Although similar to Russia, Belarus was a different kind of place. The people seemed friendlier, even though it seemed perhaps to be an even more impoverished country.

That trip was so much fun for us. We laughed a lot, had some good meals, I met amazing people who all seemed committed to saving orphans, and the bond between the three of us deepened. We were traveling from Minsk to Gomel and were driving through mile after mile of farm land. There were no buildings, no gas stations, and no place to stop. I stated that I had to use the restroom but had noticed we hadn't passed a single one! Slava laughed and said we would pee the Russian way, out in a field. He asked the driver to pull over next to a cornfield, which was about four feet tall. I was leery of whatever animals may be out in the field, primarily snakes, of which I am deathly afraid. Laughing at me, Slava said Belarus did not have any snakes. Of course, I knew that was impossible.

All of us got out of the car and each of us went in a different direction in the corn field. I had learned my lessons well on my first trip to Russia and I *had* tissues with me. So, walking farther away from the group than anyone else, I took care of business. When I stood up, about fifteen feet away, Slava popped up and said, "Oooooooo, a snake," and began thrashing around in the corn stalks. Slava and Svetlana laughed heartily at the joke. I only fumed, not finding any humor in Slava's antics.

Also, during that trip, occasionally there were small roadside stands off to the side of the small two-lane highways. The little stands sold nasty, greasy dried fish! The fish still had their heads and they looked to have their scales, and I imagined they still had all their insides intact. I couldn't even watch as Slava and Svetlana excitedly partook of this delicacy from their past. I nearly retched. Again, they simply laughed at me. Despite our sad task of seeing orphaned children, Slava, Svetlana, and I always had a great time together on our trips. Slava's bursts of outrage at me were usually absent when we traveled.

It was also during this trip, while seeing more of the desolate playgrounds on which the children played, that the idea to build playgrounds for the orphans occurred. The external areas on which the children played consisted mostly of barren, treeless, grassless areas holding old wooden structures, having lost their paint years before, and amounting to little more than sheds to shelter the children from the sun. There were no swings, slides, or climbing structures. Once in a while, I would see a broken-down teeter-totter. Slava was not sold on the playground idea initially, but said he would speak with one of the orphanage directors about it. It would take a lot of coordination to pull off, but everyone seemed to buy in to the idea.

After returning to the US, I began to put together a team of people who wanted to assist with this new endeavor. I knew the first person I wanted to recruit for the project was Phil, a former client. He and his wife had adopted two children, were strong Small World supporters, and I knew that he had a lot of building and project management experience. I reached out to him; he was thrilled to be involved and was invaluable to each playground project. Small World paid the expenses for food and lodging once in the foreign country as well as the cost of the playground equipment, but the volunteers covered the costs for their airfare. Slava was not overly helpful with this project. I was frustrated by his lack of enthusiasm at this opportunity to improve the lives of the orphans. It took nearly two years of planning and coordination before the first humanitarian trip was made.

CHAPTER 35

A BOARD OF DIRECTORS

WITH THE HOLIDAYS OVER, IN early 1996, it was time to get back to the business of finalizing requirements for the State of Missouri licensure for a Child Placing Agency. According to the licensing regulations, Small World was mandated to have a functioning, managing board of directors which held regular meetings. When I explained to Slava that we needed to form a board of directors for the agency, he said he wanted to select the members. Slava created a board which consisted of his ex-wife, her husband, and a physician/friend, all of whom resided in New York City. After I adjusted to the fact that his ex-wife and her husband were on the agency's board, I had to battle the hurdle that none of the board members lived in St. Louis and they never had a meeting. At least none of which I was aware.

That first year in our new office, after I would argue with Slava about this, he would scribble some notes and tell me they had a telephone conference and I should create minutes from those notes. I took this to mean we were making progress; at least he wasn't totally ignoring me. Then one day, out of the blue, he started yelling at me that we didn't have a "real" board like the board a friend of his had (at another adoption agency also working in Russia), and that agency was raising thousands of dollars at dinner auctions. So, first he fought me about having a legitimate board and then it was my fault the board wasn't helping to do fundraising. Slava could be exasperating!

So, I took steps to create a legitimate Small World board of directors. I considered the current and previous adoptive families and put together a short list of those I thought could bring value to the board of directors; business people, lawyers, doctors, mothers, and I put together our first real board of directors. I invited a group of five to join the board. Our wonderful board of directors turned out to be one of the most valuable assets of the agency, and over the years it continued to have an incredibly positive impact on the work being done.

We were also blessed by the generosity of many of our Small World families. A former client ran the printing department for a local high school, and after my first feeble attempt at a newsletter, he offered to design and publish our newsletter for us. Of course, we paid the printing cost, but the volunteer work Mike provided to us was invaluable. He created impressive and beautiful newsletters for Small World. Another former client, Andy, had a website design company, and his company designed, built, and hosted our website. We were extremely fortunate to have our families share their many gifts so generously with us.

CHAPTER 36

BREAKING "SLAVA" POLICY

As WINTER TURNED TO SPRING, Slava and Svetlana prepared for another trip to Russia to videotape children for our waiting families. On this particular trip to St. Petersburg, I was extremely grateful I was not with them. However, Slava's mother happened to be traveling with them and after this trip, upon their return to the US, Slava shared the following story with me.

Usually, when traveling to Russia, the arrival time was sometime in the morning. I don't recall why their arriving flight was in the evening, after dark, but imagine that they had overnighted in Paris, which was something they often did. When Slava and Svetlana had landed in St. Petersburg, Russia, Slava made the supreme mistake of claiming all the cash he had with him, $70,000, when going through customs. He had been insistent that we, as well as our clients, never claim more than $5,000 when entering Russia. He always said this kind of minimal disclosure of funds being brought into the country was a safety precaution. Slava regularly carried huge sums of money which he used to purchase things for the orphanages, to pay staff, and to pay his expenses. I never understood why he completed the customs form as he did because he had schooled me explicitly on the need to refrain from doing this (I called these kinds of lessons "Slava Policy"). In retrospect, thinking about what could have made him breach his own "Slava Policy," I speculated that perhaps he had just had too much vodka to drink on the flight.

Upon exiting the airport, Slava's driver and car were waiting at the curb, as was the normal practice each time they traveled. They got into the car and went directly to the Small World apartment on Nevsky Prospekt, one of the more famous streets in St. Petersburg, Russia.

As they exited the car, gun shots rang out all around them. Slava yelled for his mother and Svetlana to "get down" and they, along with their driver, threw themselves to the ground between parked cars. As they lay in the street, armed men approached Slava and told him they wanted his $70,000. He opened his camera bag and gave them the money. They fled with all of Slava's cash.

It was dark and Slava could not see any of his fellow travelers and only called out, "'Momitchka' (mom), are you okay?" I smile as I recall how angry Svetlana was every time she talked about how Slava only called out to see if his mom was okay, but not her.

After returning to St. Louis, Slava told me he believed that the customs officer made a phone call to some friends. He deduced that the tip-off must have come from the customs agent because the thief had specifically asked for his $70,000. Both he and Svetlana talked about how terrifying the experience had been. Having stood in front of a rock wall at the end of a police officer's Uzi, I could only imagine the terror of being shot at! Slava's experience drove home to me the need to refrain from declaring any cash above $5,000 that I might be carrying, which was always the case when I traveled, frequently carrying more than $50,000 on each trip I made.

I remember the first time Slava wanted me to carry that much cash and how terrified I had been. We were all traveling together on that first trip to St. Petersburg and I had refused to do it, thinking it was illegal. He pressured and coerced me, calling me a stupid American until I acquiesced. Slava was very good at controlling others through degradation; unfortunately, it worked well on me.

Before leaving for the airport, he told me not to put all the cash in one place, so I split it up between my purse, my computer bag, and even put a wad in my bra! I was SO unnerved that first time. Eventually, distributing money around my body became so unbelievably routine that I ceased giving it a second thought. Slava had convinced me that carrying the extra cash, not fully declaring it, wouldn't be a problem for me and that even if my extra cash were discovered, I would only be required to pay a small fine. After the incident with the hold up on the street in Russia, I was convinced of the danger of declaring more than a few thousand dollars and felt the legal risk was far less scary than the mortal one.

CHAPTER 37

THE HUNGARIAN PROGRAM

After I had returned to the US with my little Alex, I had maintained contact with a few of the orphanage personnel in Hungary, with the doctor who had provided such good care to Alex, with Alex's foster parents, who had relocated to NYC, and with our translator, Abby. Our family had even traveled to New York City to spend a few hours with Alex's foster parents, Martha and Charles, after they immigrated to the US.

From that first moment when I committed to Slava to run Small World for him, I had a dream to replicate the Russian adoption program in Hungary. With Slava's blessing, in 1996, I began the research for opening a similar program in Hungary, enlisting the help of my former Hungarian translator, Abby. Abby and I first traveled to Hungary to do the preliminary work and then a few months later Slava, Svetlana, and I returned to Hungary so that he could see the country and get a feel for the program. I loved having the opportunity to share "my" Hungary with Slava and Svetlana.

During my initial trip, Abby and I had visited orphanages and had videotaped a few children who were available for adoption. We had returned to Szeged, which was special for both Abby and me. One of the children, Gabor, really touched our hearts. After returning to the US, I contacted the families from our original Hungarian adoptive group to see if anyone would be interested in adopting Gabor. A wonderful family from our *Szeged 28* group stepped forward to adopt him. The adoption was super difficult, lengthy, and ended up costing us more than we could charge the family. Thus, it became obvious that we were not going to be able to sustain a program in Hungary. I considered that my biggest failure during my tenure at Small World. More than anything, I had wanted to find families for the Roma children of Hungary. The treatment they received at the hands of non-Roma citizens of Eastern Europe broke my heart. The Roma were given so few opportunities to lead successful lives. But, in the end, I was only able to save one more Hungarian, Roma child. I had to be content with the saying, "Save one child, save the world." There would be no more children coming out of Hungary on my watch.

CHAPTER 38

VISA INVITATIONS GALORE

WITH HUNGARY IN THE REAR-VIEW mirror, it was time to look forward to our next summer picnic. For the annual summer picnics, Small World paid for various members of its foreign country staff to visit the US, like Maria, the main foreign country coordinator. Different foreign country staff was invited each year. They seemed to welcome the opportunity to visit the US. In order for staff to enter the US, they had to obtain visas from the American Embassy in their home country. To issue a visa to foreigners, the US government required that the visiting foreigner be officially invited by an American company or family member. The invitation had to cite the purpose of the trip and the sponsoring entity had to agree to be responsible for the expenses of the foreigner while in the United States.

One of my many duties was the authorship of the official visa invitations. Slava always told me his English skills were insufficient for creation of these documents. He regularly had me author documents for him for his other businesses as well. Through my tenure at Small World, I literally created hundreds of invitations. I created them for our foreign staff, but many more were for people with whom I was unfamiliar. As was the normal course of action, Slava would call, fax, or e-mail me a name and request a visa invitation for the person. In the beginning, I would inquire who the person was if it were someone with whom I wasn't familiar. Frequently, Slava told me that the people for whom I created invitations were the children of foreign country officials, such as governors, ministry officials, etc. Slava said that providing the invitations to the children of officials for an American vacation was one of the things that made our program so strong. To me, it seemed a bit like an American version of bribery, and I made the mistake of sharing my viewpoint with Slava. My comment made Slava furious, and after he declared how amazingly stupid and naïve I was, I didn't challenge him on their purpose ever again.

I did notice that we were primarily inviting the daughters of foreign officials and rarely any sons. When I mustered the bravery to question this, Slava stated according to Russian custom, boys had to get jobs at much younger ages and were therefore not available for foreign country trips. I didn't think too much about it but it struck me as sexist and unfair.

Eventually, I was preparing so many invitations that I stopped even asking who the invitees were or the purpose of their visit. Although I couldn't share my thoughts about this, I still had them. *Imagine if a company in the US provided vacations to the children of US Congressmen/women. I am positive it wouldn't go over very well and would most likely create a significant scandal in our country!* But according to Slava, it was an expectation that we provide this for the family members of the foreign officials. I grew to believe he was correct about this because I witnessed that he frequently solved problems in the foreign countries, issues I considered insurmountable, with the help of these officials.

CHAPTER 39

DEATH OF A HANDYMAN

SLAVA HAD A FULL CADRE of people helping us in Russia, but he also had a full cadre of people at his disposal in the US. During the first few years of working with Slava and Svetlana, I had more meetings at their home than in later years. In later years, Slava tended to come to our office late in the day, after finishing work at his surgery center. When I went to his home to work, there would always be a house full of Russian people visiting them. Two of whom I came to know that first year were a team of handymen who worked for Slava. One of them was married.

I recall feeling sad the day Slava called, in the spring of 1996, to tell me one of his handy-men had been found hanging from a tree outside his apartment in downtown St. Louis. Slava said he had no understanding of why the handyman had committed suicide, and I felt so sorry for his wife. Slava never wanted to talk about it and never really shared any details.

I had been told that both Slava's father and his brother had committed suicide and I questioned what kind of trauma this reignited for him. I understood his desire to avoid discussion about it. I never thought much about the death of the handyman until many years later, when I was questioned about it.

About a year after the death of the handyman, I needed a new nanny for Alex. Slava's daughter-in-law, our previous nanny, was getting a full-time job. Slava suggested that the handyman's wife could be our live-in nanny. He said she was struggling a little financially since the death of her husband. So, she moved into our home to care for Alex during the day and to do a little bit of light housekeeping.

However, one balmy summer afternoon, I stopped in at our home to find my fifteen-year-old son, Ryan, hanging out the window, watching the new nanny on our back deck. It seemed she had taken to sun bathing on our deck when Alex napped each afternoon, and the swim suit she wore barely covered her. She was not at all happy at my insistence that she stop doing this. Sunbathing in the nude or in barely-there bikinis was commonplace in Russia, and I think she thought of me as rather prudish. Perhaps so, but I just didn't want my teenager falling out of a second-floor window! After that, she only stayed a couple of more weeks. Conversation had become rather uncomfortable at the dinner table.

CHAPTER 40

IGOR

Shortly after one of their trips to Russia, sometime in the fall of 1996, Slava called me one afternoon and told me a man named Igor was coming by the office to leave some documents for him. Slava informed me he would try to stop by the office before the end of the day, after concluding his surgery schedule, to get them. He shared that the visitor, who was currently driving a cab in St. Louis, was going to organize an adoption program in Ukraine and he was going to be our new Ukraine coordinator. We were now expanding to a third country, with a taxi driver?

When Igor arrived, he was indeed driving a taxi cab and his English was so poor we were barely able to communicate. He was a tall and muscularly built man with an even larger personality who, over time, we would learn was both humorous and entertaining. Tanya, Maureen, and I just did not know what to think about him. He was interesting for sure, but he barely spoke any English and was driving a taxi - and this was our new Ukraine coordinator?

I was surprised to learn of this new program, about which I previously knew nothing. I wished Slava had let me be part of the planning process for new programs. But, Slava was a fly by-the-seat-of-his-pants kind of guy, and when an opportunity presented itself, he jumped in with both feet, usually pulling me in after. I later asked Slava what the back story was with the taxi-cab-driving, Ukrainian-speaking coordinator. Slava said Igor, purely by coincidence, had picked him up at the St. Louis airport in his taxi and had taken him and Svetlana home after their last trip to Russia. Igor, who also spoke Russian, got into a conversation with Slava, and I guess the result was that Igor claimed he had connections in Ukraine and was now going to help Small World facilitate adoptions from his homeland.

I believed that Slava, having driven a taxi in New York City upon arriving in the US while pursuing his American medical credentials, felt some kind of bond with this man. Igor turned out to be quite a character. He always had a great story to tell, frequently acting out the story as he moved through it. To manage the program, he frequently traveled back and forth between Kiev, Ukraine, and the US. His English improved quickly, and we were all better able to communicate with him. He frequently made us laugh when he came to our office. Igor grew to be just one more member of our ever-growing Small World family. Although she liked him, Marcia was, true to form, the most skeptical about him.

CHAPTER 41

EASTERN EUROPEAN ASSISTANCE GROUP

W ITH IGOR FIRMLY ENSCONCED INTO our process, Small World continued to thrive, meaning more funds to move overseas. After the robbery of Slava and Svetlana in St. Petersburg, Slava began wiring funds to the different cities in Eastern Europe to eliminate the need for him to carry such huge sums of cash each time he traveled. This was an expensive way to move funds overseas and our foreign country coordinators did not like the new responsibility of picking up large amounts of wired cash from banks. Slava had begun requiring traveling parents to carry and deliver several thousand dollars in cash to their foreign country coordinators. Tanya and Maureen were continually getting push back from clients who were not happy about carrying large amounts of cash overseas. We certainly understood. Since Small World was continuing to grow and thrive, more and more funds were necessary to make the foreign country process operate smoothly. Eventually, a year or so after the robbery, Slava and I met with a couple of board members and Slava made a proposal.

He explained that he had a friend with a company in Russia, Eastern European Assistance Group (EEAG), which for a small fee would allow us to make payments to their American subsidiary, which regularly transferred large sums of money between their offices in Russia and in the US. Slava would direct the Russian company to disperse the proper funds to Small World staff in the foreign country, and EEAG would in turn invoice Small World the amount distributed, plus a small fee for the service. EEAG would be responsible for payments to the drivers, translators, coordinators, orphanages, and officials as necessary.

The board had been concerned about the danger in which Slava and Svetlana found themselves that scary night in St. Petersburg. They were pleased that Slava had the connections to enable money to be moved overseas without placing anyone at risk. Additionally, the fee was less than the cost of wiring money on a regular basis. The board members were in complete support of this new way to process payments to overseas staff. In the early years, clients were paying fees in the range of $15,000 - $20,000. By the time I left the agency, some fifteen years later, Small World clients were paying upwards of $35,000 to $45,000. At least three-quarters of the fees paid by the clients were sent overseas. Slava continued to report regularly that the expenses in the foreign countries were sky rocketing and we had no choice but to increase our fees to meet the demands in the foreign countries.

The first full year Small World was in business, it completed around twenty-five adoptions, growing to a maximum of around 250 a year. In the last year I was with the agency, adoptions had dwindled to perhaps thirty adoptions.

And so, in 1997, the new process began. The foreign country staff, officials, orphanages, adoption and governmental fees, translation services, transportation expenses, Slava's, Svetlana's, and my travel expenses, etc., were paid by EEAG. EEAG would in turn invoice Small World. EEAG submitted the invoices directly to Slava's home fax machine and he would deliver the invoices to the bookkeeper, who then cut a check to EEAG. Slava picked up the payments to EEAG and submitted them to EEAG. Henceforth, all of the expenses in the foreign countries and many of them in the US were paid through invoices received by EEAG. Amazingly, I never had questions about this process, such as how did Slava transfer the payment to EEAG.

This new process seemed to be a far more efficient way of transferring funds overseas. Slava still required our adopting parents to "hand carry" a few thousand dollars in cash which they were to deliver to their foreign country coordinator upon landing in the foreign country. Generally, clients only hand carried around $4,000 or 5,000, but most were still uncomfortable, even with this reduced amount.

CHAPTER 42

SO MANY WAITING CLIENTS

Once again, Slava, Svetlana, and I traveled back to Russia to videotape more prospective children for our clients. We now had such a huge number of clients awaiting children, primarily the result of the attention from the Ann Landers article, it became critical for Slava and Svetlana to travel as frequently as possibly. Slava was opening programs in new cities as fast as he could.

On that trip, we traveled by a small, chartered airline to four small cities in Russia. As with every single trip I ever made, there were an abundance of adventures. At least on this expedition it didn't involve automatic weapons. It included the landing of our little plane in a field without a bona fide runway, giving me a true understanding of the term "airfield!" I was seated by the window and could tell our plane was descending. But, there was no airport in site. I questioned the missing concrete runway with which I was familiar and Slava explained that we were landing on a strip of land the charter company used. I looked out my window and could only see fields! As we got closer, I could see a flat patch of dirt that appeared to be where we were heading. As the plane set down, we bounced around like popcorn in a microwaveable popcorn bag. Slava and Svetlana were totally nonplused as my knees were knocking together. Invariably, on these trips with Slava and Svetlana I had flashes of never getting to see my family again.

During this trip, I had my first encounter with the pitiful orphans who were covered with mosquito bites. Not just a few, but bites so numerous their little faces looked like they had severe cases of chicken pox! To make matters worse, the caretakers had covered each little bite with a florescent blue medication. And EVERY child in the place had the bites; it didn't appear that a single child had escaped the ferocious attacks. I could see where some of the bites had been scratched to the point of being bloodied scabs and it was heartbreaking. As I looked around, it was evident that the mosquito invasion had occurred because there was not a single screen on any of the windows of the orphanage. I promised myself that as soon as we returned home, I would tackle the project of finding a way to get screens for every window of that orphanage. We were ultimately able to raise enough money through our fundraising efforts to enable us to install screens on the windows of that orphanage! These small successes gave me an immense feeling of satisfaction.

There were two other highlights from this trip. The first was our trip through the magnificent Caucus Mountains. I witnessed stunning splendor in this rather remote, idyllic area of the world. High up against the cloudless, azure sky were the dazzling snow-covered peaks of majestic mountains forming the background for the lush evergreens in every direction I looked. Down in a valley was a stream with water gently flowing over the coffee-colored stones. I spied a couple of wild goats traversing the cliffs opposite us, one with huge horns curling up over its back. The splendor seemed to be untouched by the harsh world on the other side of the mountains. It was truly spectacular, and I still enjoy pulling out the photographs from that trip and revisiting that piece of heaven on earth.

The second adventure during that trip was attending the Armenian wedding of one of Slava's friends. The wedding and reception were held in the courtyard of a very lavish home. Slava, of course, seemed to know many of the people there. The courtyard was decorated with brightly colored streamers and lanterns were hanging from the walls and from the lattice overhead. There was celebrating like I had never seen before, with nonstop dancing and singing and drinking. Some of the songs to which people danced were contemporary for the young people and others were traditional Russian folk songs. From the young to the elderly, they all knew the movements and routines for their time-honored, traditional Russian dances. I had never seen a group of people consume so much alcohol and still be able to stand. The evening had been delightful, exciting, wild, and full of drama.

CHAPTER 43

SVETLANA

Back at home, I sometimes found myself in damage control mode. Svetlana, although as pretty as could be, was not the best communicator and sometimes had a poor verbal filter. I believe her behavior was more in keeping with the forthright way Russians communicate and at times I felt the need to shield both staff and clients from her, as they were unaccustomed to the Russian way of communicating.

On one of our flights to Russia, I was sitting across the aisle from Svetlana, working on my laptop, when she made a peculiar comment completely out of the blue. Looking across the aisle toward me she said, "Brenditchka, you need to dye your hair blond. You would be much better looking." I thought, *How on earth am I supposed to respond to that?* I shook my head and laughed out loud, returning to my computer. Svetlana certainly liked to be honest when sharing her feelings about things. I learned to be careful and not take her too seriously. She did tend to be blunt and sometimes lacked tact.

She readily told staff when she thought they should lose weight or their shirt was unattractive. She was not at all involved in the US processes necessary for the adoptions and I was filled with angst when she spoke with clients about operational issues. She could as easily as not promise something which there was absolutely no way we could make happen. Never because she meant any harm, she was always trying to be helpful, she just didn't understand the process.

Because of her propensity toward unfiltered speech, I was always on edge when she was meeting with clients who had questions about a child or to review a specific piece of video tape. If at all possible, I worked my schedule so that I could be present for every meeting she had with our clients. But inevitably, clients ended up frustrated, even with me present to smooth things over. Part of the problem was that her English, at least in the early years, was still unsophisticated and she struggled with meanings of English words and clients struggled to understand her thick accent. To avoid these uncomfortable situations, I usually tried to handle things myself or I encouraged Slava to speak with clients when possible. His English skills were significantly stronger than Svetlana's.

It was necessary that Svetlana visit our office after their child identification trips so that we could review the videotapes together and she could provide me with the information which I would share with the clients.

Her visits to the office were always interesting. It was not an infrequent occurrence that clients would send "Thank You" gift baskets of candy, cookies, or fruit to our office after they returned to the US with their child. Svetlana had a habit of taking a bite from a cookie or piece of candy and then putting the remainder of the treat either back on the cookie plate or back in the candy box. Although, sometimes with boxes of candy, she would sample several different pieces and we would inevitably just throw the remaining box away after she left the office. Someone thoroughly examined the box or basket every time she had been near it to discard whatever leftover bites remained. Of course, I would never, ever have said anything to her because I wouldn't have wanted to hurt her feelings.

Svetlana had an interesting philosophy about child rearing. We were working hard to help loving families find children, yet Svetlana bragged about paying someone else to go to her daughter's school events. I had trouble understanding that. Svetlana told Maureen and me that she paid the nanny and handyman to watch her daughter's tennis matches so she didn't have to go. On a couple of occasions, she mocked Maureen or me for taking time off from work to go to watch our own children participate in sporting events. Those times were precious for us and we could never understand her inability to see what a gift they were. One time, she even bragged to us that she had never attended a single parent-teacher conference. I know she loved her children, and I believed her philosophy was another cultural difference between our two nations.

One time, Svetlana told me, "Brenditchka, you are the only woman I trust to be alone with Slava." This was a precursor to her request that I monitor Slava's activities while she was planning to be out of town for a few days. First, my challenge was deciding whether this was a compliment or an insult. Was it that I was an honorable woman who she respected or was it that she thought I was so unattractive that she felt assured Slava would not be interested? In the end, I told Svetlana, "Sure, I will keep track of him while you are gone." However, I knew that there was no way that was feasible. Not only would it have been impossible to do, it was simply not my place to be the watchdog.

One spring afternoon, Svetlana arrived at our little office to show us her new, red Mercedes convertible. She wanted all of us to come outside and look at her in her new car to see if she looked good in the car, and if the new sunglasses she just purchased matched it. She was very excited about her new car, so we all trooped outside and assured Svetlana that she looked fabulous in her new car and the sunglasses were perfect. She was always entertaining us in these ways.

Despite her eccentricities, I enjoyed and grew to deeply care about Svetlana as much as I did Slava. She seldom lost her temper and she was predictable, making her safe in my book. The rest of the employees had a more challenging time relating to her. Her lack of tact and her occasional inadequate filter sometimes caused people to be uncomfortable. She just had a very forthright way of communicating. Unfortunately, they did not have the opportunity to get to know her as well as I did.

CHAPTER 44

SLAVA AND LAURA

IT WAS EASY FOR US to see what kind of father Slava was. He was a devoted dad and he frequently spoke lovingly about his daughter and he sincerely wanted the best for her. He seemed to be truly proud of her. He told me he had never missed a parent-teacher conference and he tried to attend her events. I guessed that his philosophy about children was a bit more Americanized than his wife's.

Unless someone happened to encounter him on one of his "bad mood days," most everyone loved Slava. One time in the office he admitted to us that he went to "sad, chick-flick movies" by himself so no one would know he cried. In the springtime, when he passed a fruit stand on his way to our office he would often bring us a basket of fresh fruit. In those early years, he would frequently bring us cake from the Russian bakery that was near our office. Although he could be very challenging and we sometimes argued like cats and dogs, we sincerely appreciated one another. Slava knew he could always count on me to clean up messes and smooth over injured feelings, and I had the patience to listen to angry clients. I knew I could almost always count on him to fix crises happening overseas. We were an excellent team. I was generally able to take his ranting or raging in stride and usually I didn't let it bother me too much.

I had, early in our relationship, picked up on the fact that Slava was a bit of a womanizer. He quite frankly loved women. He always had an opinion about the women with whom he came into contact. Occasionally he would come into the office for a meeting with me and the meeting couldn't begin until he shared his latest venture to a strip club. He made inappropriate comments to all of us in the office about various women so frequently that eventually I didn't even hear them. He also made inappropriate comments to staff about their bodies or husbands or partners. I don't think he meant to hurt anyone's feelings and most likely thought himself funny, and I believe he just didn't know that some of the things he said came off in an unkind way.

Slava's most tender side especially came out when my daughter, Laura, got sick. She developed an autoimmune disease causing her body to kill its own platelets when she was thirteen years old. Laura spent a substantial amount of time, nearly two years, in and out of St. Louis Children's Hospital. She had multiple surgeries, her spleen was removed, and it regenerated, twice! On several occasions we were afraid we might lose her. The average person normally maintains between 250,000 and 400,000 healthy platelets in their body at any given time. At one point, Laura's platelet count was just over one thousand! That day she was in intensive care and a simple touch left an ugly bruise.

Slava frequently came to the hospital to see her and he would reprimand the nurses if he felt they weren't on the ball. He once got very angry when he saw the terrible bruising on Laura's arm, which was the result of a nurse's inability to insert an IV line. He told me that going forward I was to demand an anesthesiologist be summoned to insert Laura's IVs if the first attempt by the nurse was unsuccessful. It wasn't unusual for him to address with a nurse an action that he didn't deem appropriate or good enough for Laura.

I needed to be absent from work a great deal during much of that time. I tried to manage my time between the hospital and Small World. I always felt badly that the rest of our family got so little of my attention during those two years. But, Slava tried to help make life easier for me. He got me a new, faster laptop computer so I would be able to work more efficiently from the hospital. Even though I was gone from the office a great deal, he never once complained about it. He also was kind to me about all the time Laura had to spend in the office when she was too ill to go to school, as her doctors had instructed me that she could not be left alone. Because her platelet counts fluctuated so much, it was very risky for her to be alone in case she fell or even bumped into something. We set up a little area in the office where Laura could be comfortable. Laura grew very close to Tanya, Maureen, and Marcia, who became her de facto aunties, and they continue to play this very important role in the lives of all three of my children to this day. Through the years, other staff came and went, but these three, original employees/friends played special roles in my life.

During the time Laura was so sick, we were all working hard with Alex to encourage him to write his name. He was in kindergarten and simply refused to put a pencil to paper. Until the day he changed his mind and decided he would write his name.

Since Laura and I were frequent visitors to the hospital we nearly always utilized valet parking. For one of our hospital visits my car was being serviced, so we took Ryan's little, black Toyota Corolla, of which he was very proud.

As Laura and I exited the hospital that day to retrieve Ryan's car from the valet service, the passenger's side of the car was facing us. There, running down the side of Ryan's car, was Alex's name etched into the paint! Laura and I simultaneously said, "Alex wrote his name!!" The valet looked at us as if we were insane. Suddenly, it sunk in that his achievement was down the side of his brother's car. My exuberance about his accomplishment was somewhat dampened by his choice of medium. But, I decided I would take what I could get. When you are spending much of every day fearing for the life of your daughter, what are a few scratches in the side of a car? We had Ryan's car repainted and all was well; Alex had begun to write his name! A few months later, I discovered that he had taken a crayon and written his name all over the inside of his closet as well. That was our Alex, doing things his own way on his own timeline.

Laura's life-threatening illness had given me a new perspective on life and on what was truly important. It was incredibly hard to face each day fearing for Laura's life. Slava was tender and kind and tried hard to be reassuring to both Laura and me. Although we had excellent hematologists/oncologists at Children's Hospital, it was comforting to me that I could always turn to Slava for explanations or clarifications. Slava was supportive of our whole family during this truly difficult time. Laura was especially touched by how special he made her feel on his visits to us at the hospital. He often brought her flowers.

Our family was equally touched by the support and love we got from many of the clients. Those who knew about Laura never hesitated to ask about her each time they came to the office or spoke with a staff member on the phone. Many of our Small World clients became extended family members to not only me and my family, but also other staff members. I remain forever grateful to Slava, our clients, and our dear aunties, who gave us so much love during this terrible period of our lives.

Slava's and my relationship remained through the years very much one of brother and sister and it was frequently a love-hate relationship! We were both strong willed people. But I felt that we truly loved each other.

CHAPTER 45

MOSCOW!

T HAT SAME YEAR, I WAS fortunate enough to travel to Moscow with Slava and Svetlana. That was one of the most memorable experiences of my life. We were to be in Moscow for business meetings before going on to the smaller cities in Southern Russia where we would videotape available orphans. Slava arranged for a translator to give me a personal tour of Moscow while he and Svetlana attended to business. This was such an incredible gift. I had an experience of which I believe very few Americans have had the privilege.

Our first stop on the crisp autumn day was to the iconic Kremlin and its adjacent Red Square. It was an unbelievable fortress with the magnificent, breathtaking St. Basil's Cathedral looking as if it was standing guard. My translator told me that, although there were many, many beautiful buildings with brightly painted onion domes in blues and reds and golds, there was no equal in all of Russia to St. Basil's Cathedral. He said the cathedral was originally built in the 1500s and sat over the final resting place of the famous saint, Vasily. The cathedral had many domes and spires of varying heights, sizes, and many bright and beautiful colors. The sheer magnitude of the building was overwhelming, and standing next to it made me realize that the famous pictures of this structure in no way did justice to this incredible building. The cathedral had become more of a museum than a church, with church services held only occasionally.

I couldn't believe I was standing in Red Square in Moscow! The Kremlin itself was an imposing sight, surrounded by tall stone walls. It held a massive open concrete area surrounded by an array of buildings within those walls. There were soldiers everywhere you looked and they all appeared to be well armed. We walked across Red Square to the entrance of the building housing Lenin's Tomb. We entered a darkened chamber after standing in line well over an hour. There inside stood a clear, glass box that held the body of Vladimir Lenin. The case stood on a stone pedestal and was covered by a stone canopy. It was simply amazing that this man's body had been preserved to such a degree that it had been on display since the 1920s! My translator told me that the body had gone through many processes and even vodka has been used at some point in the preservation of his body. That fact was not at all surprising. The entire experience was surreal and morbid, but truly fascinating. The feeling was similar to wanting to look at the car accident next to the road, but then feeling badly after you did.

The next day, I had the pleasure of a tour of the city. The city was crowded, and the traffic crawled along many avenues. The statues in and around Moscow were ornate and striking, and I was enormously impressed that my translator knew the history behind all of them. He could describe which battle was represented or exactly what the hero being depicted had done. It was most impressive and clear that he was very, very proud of his Russian heritage. That same day, I had the rare opportunity to visit the Russian Diamond Fund, where the famous jewels, crowns, rings, and necklaces of the Russian monarchs from the past three hundred years are displayed. Peter the Great had decreed that valuable items such as artwork or large gem stones belonged to the

Russian government. Therefore, he had the items collected or confiscated and stored in St. Petersburg, where they remained until the outbreak of WWII.

The collection was subsequently moved to the basement armory at the Kremlin and the gems were eventually placed on display in 1967. The display, still below ground, consisted of two rooms, and the carpets were red velvet. It was as silent as a funeral home; the rooms were very dimly lit with gems on display behind thick glass walls, and each display had minimal lighting. It was an impressive collection of unique and large gems. The most impressive of the collection was the Great Imperial Crown worn by Catherine the Great. It was crafted for her in the 18th century and had a collection of over 5000 diamonds adorning it. Another impressive gem was the Orlov diamond. It is a nearly 200-carat diamond affixed to the middle of a gold scepter. It was such a privilege to get a glimpse of Russian heritage in this form. As would be expected, there were soldiers everywhere toting the familiar Uzis.

I am forever grateful to Slava for the opportunity I was given to visit the strange, beautiful, and forbidding city of Moscow.

CHAPTER 46

THE GRANDMA WHACKER AND OTHER STORIES

THERE WERE AS MANY STORIES about events at home as there were about our travels. I could fill another whole book about our experiences with our clients, but here are a few of the more memorable stories.

When people made inquiries, we sent out a detailed packet of information. The packet contained vitally important material necessary for making such a huge decision, traveling to a foreign country to adopt a child. Some of the many warnings given to parents regarded the laws governing foreign country adoption. In all the countries in which we worked, children were only available for adoption after the period of abandonment (different in each county) in which no family member visited a child, or if the birth mother signed legal relinquishment papers. However, the law also stated that even after a child had been offered for foreign adoption and the adoption was pending in the court, if a birth family member went to the orphanage and petitioned to have the child placed in their custody, the petition for international adoption would be withdrawn. Birth relatives were always given precedence over international adoption. We gave this warning because Slava cautioned me this was always a possibility. However, after several hundred adoptions, we fortunately had never encountered this.

Until the Grandma Whacker. A sweet, young couple had viewed a baby on videotape and had selected that baby for adoption. Their paperwork had been completed and sent to Russia. The family was simply awaiting permission from the adoption center, in St. Petersburg, to travel to finalize their adoption. I don't recall exactly, but it seems that it was only a few weeks before this young couple was supposed to travel when I received word from Slava that the Russian grandmother of the baby had recently learned about the baby's existence and had already rescued the baby from the orphanage. I didn't relish the task of informing the family of this news.

This was one of the worst kinds of phone calls I had to make. I called the young prospective mother and explained what had happened. I told her I was sorry and that as soon as she was ready, she and her husband could select another child. Having walked the adoption path, I truly understood the concept of bonding with a video image. The young woman sobbed and although I tried my best to console her, there just weren't sufficient words to ease her pain. We ended our phone conversation and I sat at my desk feeling as if I could weep for this woman. However, I recognized that if a child had the possibility to be raised in their birth family, it was the better option for the child. Although heartbreaking for the family, I viewed this as an opportunity to save one more child!

It wasn't long before Karena came to my office and said that the very angry mother of the young client with whom I had just spoken was on the phone demanding to speak with me. I picked up the phone and was given a monumental tongue lashing. The woman told me that I had better do whatever was necessary to fix her daughter's situation. I assured her that we had no legal recourse. She began screaming at me with such ferocity that I simply couldn't insert a word into the conversation. She finally told me, "Well, I know you people know how to make people disappear and you better do whatever is necessary to get my grandchild returned to that orphanage!" I believed she was asking me to have the grandmother in Russia, as the mob would say, taken out. I sternly told her that we were not in the business of making people disappear and that I felt it would be better is she didn't call my office again.

I got off the phone with the irate woman and sat in stunned silence for a moment. Eventually I walked out of my office to tell staff about my phone call, telling them that I believed I had just been asked to whack a Russian grandma! It eventually became something about which we could laugh. The young couple, by the way, did end up adopting a beautiful baby within the year.

During our first year in business, I had had a bad experience when I allowed a woman who became pregnant during the adoption process to remain in the program. I had been begged by the family to hold the child they had already selected until after their biological baby was born, not allowing another family to adopt him. They said they loved him and they truly wanted to go get their son awaiting them in Russia. I couldn't stand for a child to spend even one extra day in an orphanage, but I reluctantly agreed. I had to convince Slava who in turn had to convince the orphanage. As soon as their baby was born the family called and said they were not going to adopt the child awaiting them in Russia. Needless to say, there were a lot of people who were pretty angry with me, most of all Slava. But way worse than Slava's yelling at me was the guilt I felt for my poor decision which caused a baby to spend an additional five months of his life in an orphanage.

The result of this experience was introduction of a policy change, which made Marcia very happy. She had advocated for this policy from the beginning. This was in fact how many of our policies were created or changed - in response to events. Since a template didn't exist for operating an international adoption agency specializing in Eastern Europe, we just learned as we went along. The new stated policy advised parents that if they became pregnant at any time during the process, their adoption would be stopped until after the birth of their baby. This included pregnancies that may occur after the family had selected a child for adoption, in which case the already selected child would be released for adoption by another family that could travel sooner.

It wasn't long before a young couple who had selected a baby boy called me and asked to take me to lunch. They shared with me that they had recently discovered they were expecting a baby. Their faith in God was important to them and they disclosed their belief that God was placing both children in their lives, the birth child and the adopted child. I thought back to the influence I believed God had in my adoption experience. They were such kind and good people, I truly believed they would never leave their selected child behind. I allowed them to continue in the process. Fortunately, they had been able to travel to get their little boy before their baby was born.

Unfortunately, when a young mother has a newly adopted child and an infant deposited into her lap within a few months of each other, a large amount of stress is incurred by the family. Marcia, during the home study process, tried to prepare the adoptive parents that orphaned children would need time to adjust and to bond. The children could exhibit behavior issues resulting from the trauma of being removed from everything that was normal for them; their caretakers, their beds, even the foods were different after they were adopted. The parents were also warned of the potential, eventual risks such as learning disabilities or developmental delay. The little boy did in fact have some issues, as many of the children did in the beginning of their new lives. I remember quite well the day the adoptive mom called screaming at me that her adopted child was "not normal" and that we had given her a defective child. Her words during that conversation were unkind toward her son and my heart hurt for the little boy. I felt sure she was going to ask us to take the little boy back. However, they did not do that, and I believe that ultimately their world calmed down.

Slava was continuing to pressure me to try harder to find parents for a greater number of special needs and older children than we had been able to thus far. He berated me about this as if I could control the choices of other people. I suggested to him that it was likely more people would consider this if there was an even deeper fee reduction. So, he agreed to further reduce fees for people who were adopting "older children," which at the time was five years of age and older or special needs children, such as the boy found in the forest with severe rickets or a girl with a congenital amputation of her forearm. As a result of the fee reduction we were able to place a higher number of older children than we had before. However, I was always concerned about the long-term adjustment for these children.

During those early years, I also had my first encounter with an adoptive couple who traveled to Russia, came back to the United States, and relinquished their child to another family. The incident was heartbreaking. The couple had adopted two unrelated little three-year-old girls. The little girls were from the same group in an orphanage and were good friends. One of the little girls was being placed as a special needs child because her legs and forearms had "amniotic bands" around them. This was caused from the umbilical cord squeezing the arms and legs into deformity in utero, making deep grooves around sections of her arms or legs.

About a year or so after the children were adopted, we learned from another client that the couple had relinquished custody of the little girl with the bands on her arms and legs. We were told that the family stated they couldn't handle two three-year-old children at the same time. My heart ached for this little girl who had been placed for adoption in Russia, adopted by an American family, only to lose that family as well. Added to that was the fact that the little girl lost the friend with whom she had displayed such a close bond. In her short life she suffered way too much trauma and far too many losses. I had wondered how much loss that little girl could take and was despondent for days about the situation.

We also had prospective adoptive families who had suffered supreme losses. I recall one family who had a biological child, a handsome teenaged son. He was a star at his high school and was the apple of his parent's eyes. A couple of years before I met them, their son became ill and the parents took him to the hospital with what was believed to be a severe case of the flu. He was treated and sent home, where his fever continued to soar and the next day he passed away from an undiagnosed illness. As one would expect, the parents were totally devastated. I don't recall how they learned about us, whether it had been the Ann Landers article or not, but they were led to our door.

Marcia had been concerned because they had never deconstructed their son's bedroom and she worried about the family's ability to follow through with an adoption. But, I recall being told by the adoptive mother that their son would have wanted them to give an orphaned child a home. This couple completed the adoption process, and in the end, they adopted both a little boy and a little girl from Russia. The last time I saw the mother, she said the new little ones knew all about their brother who had passed away and sharing stories about him gave the parents great joy. She shared her happiness that both of her children knew their brother was watching over them.

We worked with another young couple who were reportedly infertile and thus came to us to build their family through adoption. After their first successful adoption of two children, the mother learned she was pregnant. However, during the pregnancy, the doctors discovered the baby had a severe chromosomal disorder and the baby was not expected to live long after birth. The baby girl lived for nearly eighteen months before passing away and I learned a lot about totally selfless love from that tremendously brave family during that time. Although the baby was severely developmentally delayed and blind, they loved her and gave her a peaceful and loving life knowing that they would have her only a short time. The grace and dignity that they displayed was awe inspiring. The couple eventually adopted two more children after the loss of their precious baby girl.

Another truly heart-breaking story centered upon a couple who were in the adoption process. During their process, they became pregnant and I placed them on "hold." I remember the day the prospective mother came to our office to tell us that something had happened to the baby in utero. The baby was essentially brain dead and there was no possibility the baby would survive outside of the womb, once the umbilical cord was severed. Our courageous client was told that she had to carry the baby to term, which was approximately another three months. My heart ached for this lovely woman as I considered the pain she must experience every time a person unknowingly referenced her pregnancy and the impending arrival of her baby. Months later, I was ever so happy when we welcomed this family home to St. Louis with their newly adopted child.

Many of our clients became friends, sent Christmas cards, volunteered for events, and continually offered their thanks for our assistance in helping them to build their families. Our clients came to us for a variety of reasons. During the home study process, clients are asked to disclose their motivation to adopt. We had many families who, for instance, had either two or three sons and wanted a daughter, or who only had biological daughters and wanted a son. One of these family's stories haunts me to this day.

The family had five sons, they really wanted a daughter and adopted a little girl from Russia. The little girl was around four when she was adopted and arrived with some challenging behavior issues. The parents were dealing with them, getting her therapy, and the family seemed to be moving forward. Not long after the adoption however, one of the sons got sick and he passed away. I went to the funeral and the mother angrily told me that her son was taken from her because I enabled her to bring this problematic girl into their home and disrupt the lives of the other children. To the best of my knowledge, the little girl's presence had no bearing on the illness which took her brother's life. The mother was terribly angry and let me know it in front of a group of mourners. I knew it was her grief speaking and she desperately needed to blame someone for the inexplicable and horrifying loss of her precious son. My heart broke for her and the rest of the family. I have always hoped the family found their way to heal and accept the young girl lovingly into their family.

These kinds of sad stories were more the exception than the rule and the positive stories brightened every day for us. The clients with whom we worked enriched our lives beyond measure. We were blessed by predominantly amazing clients and it was a fabulous time for our little company.

CHAPTER 47

A BIGGER OFFICE

EVERYONE IN OUR SMALL OFFICE loved the work we did. But with our growing client base and the need to hire additional people, we were outgrowing our current office. It was time to look for a larger one. I would just have to convince Slava.

Finally, in 1998, Slava agreed with me regarding the need for additional space and he announced that he had the perfect solution, as he frequently did. In one of the coincidences that seemed to so frequently occur, allowing Slava to work his magic, he announced that he was opening three new private businesses in part of an office building, and that Small World would be able to rent space there. The building was nearly vacant, with the top floor leased and a small office on the first floor occupied. He told me that since he was going to be utilizing much of the property for his businesses that he had gotten the building owner to give him a really "great deal" on office space for Small World.

Slava shared with me his plan to build a restaurant, which he would call "Zhivago's Russian Restaurant" on one-half of the second floor of the building. The other half of the second floor was to become a day spa, Spa of Eden, which would be run by Svetlana, explaining that she had grown weary of practicing pediatric medicine. One-half of the first floor of the building was to be a nightclub, Enigma Lounge, and Small World would share the remaining half with a small investment office.

We were quite fortunate that we had a former client who was in the construction business who agreed to do the buildout of the new space at a reduced rate. I set about designing the space in a way that would be workable for our needs, and we moved to our new office. Our little office had a reception area, my office, a conference room, an office for Marcia, an office for our revolving bookkeeper, a kitchen, a file and copy room, and an open area we called The Hub, where the case management staff all worked together. The office was small and poor Marcia had an office that was smaller than most first-floor powder rooms. But the contractor added a window that looked out to the hallway to make it seem bigger. I don't think it made the office seem any bigger, but everyone enjoyed passing her office window on the way to the restroom and making obnoxious faces at her! We also had a storage room for donations from which we regularly sent items to the orphanages with traveling parents. It was just perfect!

CHAPTER 48

THE FIRST FUNDRAISING EVENT – HEARTS OF HOPE

IT WAS A BIG YEAR for us! We moved into our new office and our dedicated board of directors led us through our first "Hearts of Hope" dinner, dance, and auction. The funds raised through the event were used to build the playgrounds, to buy gross motor equipment for the orphanages, to make facility improvements, etc.

Staff painstakingly hand-cut hundreds of red, cardboard hearts which were affixed to small wooden sticks to serve as the bid paddles for the event. Each paddle was numbered with one assigned to every attendee. Small World staff had enormous fun preparing for the events and we loved getting dressed up in formal wear for the black-tie functions. Laura had developed a love of photography, along with a little talent, and she carefully displayed and photographed items to be featured in the programs. The entire event was a true labor of love for each one of us. We adored those special opportunities to interact with our many clients who attended.

The first event was held at the country club of our board president. The generosity of those attending affirmed my belief in the kindness and generosity of mankind through their desire to make an orphan's life a little bit better.

During the planning stages of that first dinner auction, I accompanied Slava and Svetlana on another trip to St. Petersburg. During that trip, I purchased unique Russian objects, such as tea sets, beautiful china dolls, black lacquer boxes, and the famous Matryoshka (nesting) dolls to be auctioned off at the event.

One afternoon while in St. Petersburg, we stopped to get a late lunch at a pretty, street-side café at the edge of a park. Customers from a few tables away had gotten up and exited the area and their dishes had not yet been cleared away. I noticed a thin and frail looking child, no more than ten or eleven years of age, dart out from behind the nearby trees. He quickly began grabbing and shoving into his mouth, the food that had been abandoned by the previous diners. It was appalling to watch and even more shocking to see that no one cared, no one offered this child help, with most people refusing to even look at him. I insisted that Slava go to him to see if we could offer the child a meal, but while trying to convince Slava to do this, a waiter arrived to shoo the child away. My eyes welled with tears and I became more determined than ever to help the orphaned Russian children before they became children of the street. I took a photograph of the child so that I would never forget.

I wanted everyone to see that photo. So, at the dinner auction, we played a video. The video featured the voice of a local newscaster reading a poem I had recently come across. While the poem was read, the video showed pictures of sad and threadbare orphans alternating with happy children who had been adopted. One of the pictures featured in our video was of the child scrambling for a few morsels of food before being chased away at that sidewalk cafe in St. Petersburg. I had taken a variety of photos of orphans for this project over the previous couple of visits to Russia or Belarus. Each picture was more tragic than the last. Each one representing the reality of life for children in a place most people couldn't imagine, much less would ever see. I also used the picture of the clothes line on which hung row after row of gray and thin t-shirts and diapers. A picture I had taken of a group of orphans watching, from behind bars, out of a second story window was another one of the pictures included.

Watching the video and seeing the transformation of the children brought people to tears. I could only hope that their tears would translate to donations for the orphans. The attendees of the event were indeed quite generous and enabled us to build our first playgrounds the next spring! We were also able to use some of the funds raised to have those screens installed at the orphanage where I had seen the blue spotted children. I knew that both orphanage improvements would be immensely appreciated by both the children and the caregivers.

Through the years, we went on to have five more of these events, at one event raising as much as $400,000 for our projects. As part of our efforts to make orphanage improvements, near the end of one of our live auctions, we offered tokens of our thanks, little glass bricks with the words, "Hearts of Hope" engraved upon them, the bricks first offered for $10,000, then, $5,000, down to $100 each. Bidding paddles sprang up all around the room from patrons who wanted to help support our orphanage improvement efforts. I sat there silently, trying to keep a running total in my head as the auctioneer read off the paddle numbers, tears streaming down my face. Our office staff sat together and as I looked around the table, everyone had tears running down their faces. We squeezed one another's hands and watched in awe as those paddles continued to be raised toward the heavens.

We used the funds to improve the lives of the orphans for whom we would never be able to find homes by sending an oral surgeon to repair cleft palates in Belarus, building playgrounds, and purchasing rehab equipment for use at the orphanages. At one orphanage for disabled children, we installed a small swimming pool to help the children exercise and gain muscle strength. We were helping orphaned children to be united with their forever families, but we were also making life better for those children left behind.

Slava was never overly supportive of our efforts to make orphanage improvements. He seemed only to want to help those that could be adopted. I struggled internally with Slava's attitude about the humanitarian work. I always led the clients to believe that he was truly supportive of our efforts, it seemed important that they have this image of him. Although it felt disingenuous, I didn't think I really had a choice. When we first met, he had seemed committed to helping the Russian orphans, and his attitude about the playgrounds just hadn't jived with my initial impressions. I feared that he might suffer from the old Soviet mentality, that these children had no value so why waste time and money on them. However, my belief in our mission was so strong that I wasted little time trying to understand the discrepancy between what I had believed and what I sometimes witnessed.

I had encountered this attitude many times in Hungary, where I was questioned about why I would want to adopt an orphaned Roma child. I had been stunned and angry that someone would ask such a question; these were just children who had as much right to a loving home as anyone else. After the first time I heard these hurtful words, I crafted my pat response when asked that stupid question, "Because I was lucky enough to find him, isn't he beautiful?" That shut them up!

I refused to allow Slava to bully me out of our relief efforts that I believe made the difference for which I had hoped. I am optimistic that the play structures we built and other humanitarian projects we completed for the orphans continue to this day to bring joy and comfort to the children using them.

CHAPTER 49

"BRICKS OF HOPE"

Finally! In 1998, after nearly eighteen months of laying the ground work, we had concluded the plans to take a large contingency of people, around twenty-five, to Belarus for our first playground building experience. In preparation for the trip, I rented a satellite phone. At that time, the cost of using cellular phones internationally was prohibitive, even if there had been adequate cell service to facilitate any kind of connection. Slava insisted on my being accessible to him during this and all subsequent humanitarian aid trips. In later years, I was able to use my own cell phone and stopped renting the satellite phones.

Slava had begun programs in three different Belarusian cities and we had enough people going that we split into three groups and went to each location; Minsk, Gomel, and Borisov. Both my family and Maureen's family accompanied us on the trip. We felt it was important that our families experience the trip to understand the work we were doing and the life led by the orphans in Eastern Europe. We wanted them to truly understand the importance of our work. We wanted them to see how much difference they could also someday make in the world. Plus, they were all good recruits, except of course for our eight-year-old, Alex, and Maureen's nine-year-old son, Danny, both too young to be of much help.

When we went to collect our luggage after clearing customs, at the baggage claim area, one of my bags was missing. I was glad it was mine and not one belonging to one of the volunteers. So, after filling out the paperwork in the crowded lost luggage area, we headed to the hotel.

That night, I distributed cash to the other leaders of the groups who would be leading teams in different places. We had needed large amounts of cash because we had to pay the orphanage directors for the wood for the playgrounds in addition to our travel expenses. I gave each of the other two team leaders around $15,000 each. Fortunately, the other two leaders had traveled extensively internationally, and they had no reservations about carrying so much money with them.

Each group made their way to the different cities to prepare for work the next day. We had ordered wood to be delivered to the orphanages prior to our arrival and I had shipped the other pieces necessary to build the structures. We had plans to build a swing set and a climbing fort at each orphanage. We expected the projects to take about a week.

The team I led traveled to the city of Gomel and the hotel in which we stayed was without air conditioning; the nights stifling hot. All of us were on the same floor and fortunately we knew each other fairly well. We tried to keep our doors open that first night to let the air circulate. However, at the end of the hall on each floor of the hotel there was a little Belarusian lady, in a tiny office, who was essentially a hall monitor. She was like an RA in a college dorm. She would chastise us if we left our doors open, made too much noise, etc. So, the first night was utterly miserable. We went to the orphanage the next day to begin work with each of us suffering varying degrees of exhaustion and jet lag.

We were fortunate in that the temperature was somewhere in the low 80s, the sun shone brightly, and there was not a cloud in the pristinely blue sky. But this orphanage, like all the others I had visited, was in desperate need of paint and general maintenance. When I walked in to let them know we had arrived, it smelled as all the others had smelled. It was an odor I can't fully describe, but perhaps something along the lines of old boiled cabbage and hard-boiled eggs. The orphanage director explained where she wanted the structures placed and our group went to work.

I left the group working on the play structures to go into the orphanage to take care of business. I had paperwork to deliver to the orphanage director and Slava had asked me to take updated videotape of some of the children who had been selected and were awaiting their parents' arrivals. The parents in the US were awaiting permission from the Belarusian government to travel to finalize their adoptions. As was our process in Russia, whenever possible we obtained updated pictures or video for waiting families in the Belarus program. I was happy to be able to do this. Laura accompanied me, along with Maureen's daughter, Keri. It was such a sweet sight to see these two young, American women playing with the children in the orphanage. Today, both Keri and Laura have little girls of their own and they remain friends.

There was a designated restroom for guests at the orphanage. It was clean and functional, and it flushed! However, there was no seat, just a cold porcelain rim on which the ladies could sit. After my first trip to that restroom, I immediately went to the translator and asked to be taken to the local hardware store. He was curious about my request, thinking I needed something for the playground project. I explained that I wanted to purchase a toilet seat and he looked at me as if I had spoken an unintelligible language. I laughed and explained I wanted to purchase one for the guest restroom in the orphanage. He laughed at me, thinking I was as silly as could be. But I was determined to protect the derrieres of my fellow lady travelers. So, off to the hardware store I went with our translator, where I purchased a lovely white toilet seat, which one of the men affixed to the toilet for us! It made future experiences much more pleasant.

My next duty was to find lunch for our crew. But before I could figure out what to do about lunch, the orphanage director joined us on the playground to tell us they had prepared lunch for us! Our construction team traipsed into the building to a room that held a beautifully set table and surprisingly, pleasantly aromatic, authentic, Russian cuisine, which had been prepared by the caretakers. The caretakers were most gracious toward us, truly grateful for the work we were doing.

After lunch and after telling our translator how uncomfortably hot our evening had been, he said, "You go buy fans." He couldn't leave as he had to remain with the work crew, so he sent me off with our driver in a dilapidated minivan. The drive spoke perhaps five words of English, I spoke about that much Russian, and I had a bit of angst about wandering off with this Belarusian stranger.

But, I felt like our group was desperate for some sleep and I thought, *How much could fans cost and this guy doesn't look like an ax murderer?* I got into the van with the driver and he began driving across town.

He drove to what appeared to be the equivalent of a huge American flea market on an incredibly dusty field. It was a massive area with row after row of ramshackle tents and was packed with people. The driver did not park with the other vehicles but instead wove his way behind a series of tents to an area way at the back. He motioned for me to get out and he indicated that he wanted the, previously negotiated, $100 before we entered the back of a raggedy looking tent and into an even scarier looking part of this flea market.

The translator looked at me and said, "Nyet (no) speak," exactly as Slava had done to me in St. Petersburg! I was starting to sweat, the hair on my arms standing straight up. The driver made a motion to a man, wearing a stained, sleeveless white t-shirt, standing on the other side of this crowded and fairly large tent. We then backed out of the tent and the dirty-shirted man followed. My driver and the man had a brief, rapid conversation and the driver gave the man my money. The tent man disappeared, and the driver returned to the van and got in; I followed, not knowing what else to do. The place felt ominous to me because everything seemed quite secretive. The driver started the van and we wove our way out of the area and went to another section of this huge flea market. We parked behind another nasty looking tent and in a few minutes a couple of big men came around the corner carrying boxes of fans. The driver spoke briefly with them, they nodded to each other, and the fans were loaded into the van. It had all been quite mysterious and, in all honesty, rather exciting!

I later learned from our translator that I had just purchased floor fans on the Belarusian black market. For some inexplicable reason, we would not have been able to purchase so many in any other way. That night I distributed the fans to my team members, laughingly telling them I had risked my life buying them fans on the black market, which actually may have been close to the truth. After completion of our work, and before leaving town, we donated the fans to the orphanage.

One night during our trip, our group was invited to dinner by a local government official. It had been Maureen's birthday that day and I had told everyone to ignore it and not to wish her Happy Birthday. At the restaurant, everyone broke into song to surprise her. The restaurant had belly dancers as servers. It was fascinating to watch the dancers' actions. They kept shimmying up to the men in the group. It was particularly funny as they tried to shimmy up to one of our volunteers, Maureen's brother, John, a Catholic Priest! We were all laughing hard as we tried to explain to the ladies who he was. The youngest in our group, my little Alex, saw them coming and crawled under the table. Ryan was pulled up onto the stage to dance with the girls. They were terribly cute. It was a fun evening and one of my many fond memories of those wonderful years.

A few nights into our stay, I received a message that my bag had been found. I had to go to a central storage location in Minsk, where the entire cadre of lost luggage, during the past 100 years I am sure, was held, and not to a storage facility at the airport. We arrived at an enormous looking warehouse where I climbed an exterior, rickety metal staircase leading to a heavy, metal door. The door was locked, so I pounded on the huge door in hopes that someone would hear us. I was with one of the men in our group because I had been told that luggage may only be released to a "husband!" My husband had been too involved in the project to get away that afternoon. So, another team member and I pretended to be married. The door was opened by a soldier, with an Uzi of course, and we were ushered into an enormous, smelly, oppressively hot warehouse filled with thousands of suitcases and boxes.

I found myself standing on a metal catwalk about twelve feet above the floor of the warehouse that was larger than an airplane hangar. We were told to go ahead and look. I nearly burst out laughing, thinking there was no way we would find anything in this cavernous room. However, the presence of the Uzi assisted me with my self-control. The bag that had been lost was a huge, bright blue, duffel bag that had been filled with donations for the orphanage. Amazingly, I spotted it just a couple of feet from the bottom of the metal stair case. We retrieved the bag and then I was informed I needed to pay the fee for their storage of my bag. Was he kidding? They lost my bag, and I now had to pay to get it back? Silly me, I suddenly realized that these police were similar to those police who had held us at gunpoint until we paid a $50 fine for having too many people in a car!

Through our translator, I ever so sweetly, albeit rather smart alec-y, asked the officer how much the fee was to reclaim my bag, which they lost in the first place. I don't think the translator translated exactly what I said. The officer demanded, "$10." I handed him $10 and we headed back to the orphanage to deliver the donations to the children. Seeing the joy brought to their faces by the toys we had stuffed into that bag made it all worthwhile. I would have paid the guy $100 just to get to see the excitement of the children as they received their new toys. Watching the sweet way the children tentatively took the toys from our hands was enough to make us feel glad to be alive.

One afternoon, the Director of the local Adoption Center made arrangements for a Belarussian picnic in the birch forest. We all got onto a school bus and were driven about thirty minutes outside of the city to a picnic area. It was summer in Eastern Europe and it was quite warm. There was a lot of food, much of it was salami-like looking meats and other foods that were not recognizable. The flies clustered around the food made it wholly unappealing. There was no way I was able to eat anything. The only beverage available other than water, which was *not* bottled, so I had no idea from where it came, was vodka. So, on an incredibly hot and humid Belarussian afternoon, having had nothing to eat, we drank vodka. The bus ride back to the hotel was a wild time with everyone singing and my own personal repertoire of animal noises to entertain all, including my most famous rendition of the angry monkey.

On the last night of our trip, my fellow volunteers gave me a silly gag present of spiked high heeled shoes and a crazy outfit in honor of the wild time we had experienced. We had been blessed to share the joy of watching, for the first time, as the orphaned children ran to the play structures and began to play on them. It was a glorious site watching the awe on the faces of the small children as they swung on the swings and climbed onto the forts. We were snapping pictures like crazy, most of us with tears in our eyes. It was a very successful first humanitarian trip!

That evening, back in the hotel, as the construction team sat around the table at dinner, everyone agreed that more playgrounds needed to be built at every orphanage in every city from which we adopted children. Tom, one of the members of the team said, "We should name the playground projects 'Bricks of Hope.'" We had recently held our first "Hearts of Hope" dinner auction, and this seemed a perfect extension!

After the trip, one of our adoptive parents, our project manager, Phil, who would later become a board member, contacted me. He said that his company had a subsidiary that was willing to provide real playground equipment to us at their cost for our next humanitarian trip! The wood structures had been more challenging than we imagined, and Phil thought the plastic/metal structures would be better suited for the children and would last longer. What a generous gift! J. F. Ahern Company subsequently assisted us with building about fourteen more playgrounds for orphanages in Russia and Belarus over the next eight years, through the "Bricks of Hope" program. Except for one trip, Captain Phil spearheaded the building for all remaining playgrounds. I remain forever in the debt of both Phil and his amazingly generous company, J. F. Ahern, for their help in making the lives of many orphans a little brighter with their brightly colored red, blue, and yellow play structures.

We subsequently learned that some Belarus citizens had crept onto the orphanage grounds in the night and had sawed through the pipes supporting the swing sets, leaving their bases buried in the concrete, thus stealing the bones of the metal swing sets. They also sawed up the wooden forts for firewood. The caretakers had known to unhook the swings and take them into the orphanage at the end of every day, but no one had considered that the actual swing sets or forts would disappear. When I relayed this story to Slava, he shared that there were criminal elements in every town that would steal metals and sell them on the black market. Metals like steel, aluminum, and copper were hot commodities during this time in Russia. Thus, it was truly a Godsend that J.F. Ahern came to the rescue. The hard-plastic structures we built in succeeding years were rooted in concrete, and because of the material from which they were constructed they were thankfully left intact by the people in the communities.

CHAPTER 50

SLAVA'S EMPIRE

W<small>E RETURNED HOME TO FIND</small> Slava moving forward with his endeavors in the new office building. Previously, he had an import business which he had named after his daughter. For a short while, he imported things like shoes and marble. During the time I knew Slava, he was continually involved in developing new businesses.

But, those ventures had seemed to fall by the wayside. He had previously shared with me that he had a life-long-dream of owning a Russian restaurant. I knew he desperately missed the cuisine from his home land. When traveling with him in Russia, he seemed happiest when he was in a boisterous Russian restaurant at a table filled with Russian delicacies. I knew he had an entrepreneurial spirit and often seemed to be seeking novel endeavors. So, it was no surprise to me that he was preparing to embark on this new adventure in 1998, an authentic Russian restaurant.

Slava was proud of the Russian restaurant, Zhivago's, whose opening was soon followed by the lounge, Enigma. It was quite a popular night spot for a while. Svetlana's day spa was beautiful and it appeared that it would be very successful.

I usually had little knowledge of Slava's businesses outside of Small World, other than my assistance with the creation of or completion of some form. But, I ended up having an important role in his restaurant. Slava enlisted my help in the creation of the menu for his restaurant, needing my help to provide proper English descriptions of the Russian food to which Americans could relate. The best part was that I got to taste many of the dishes so that I would adequately describe them. I wanted the descriptions to match the beauty of the restaurant. Its interior was decorated in rich fabrics of blue and gold, with red velvet accents throughout. Tray ceilings and private booths for diners made the atmosphere warm and inviting. The table settings were exquisite with striking dishes and tableware. The menu holders were of embossed leather which Slava had commissioned to be hand-tooled in Belarus. The menu featured the tastiest of Russian cuisine, many of the recipes from Svetlana's own kitchen. Zhivago's was indeed a stunning, fine dining establishment.

The only thing that bothered me about the restaurant was Slava's request that our local adoptive parents deliver to him two-pound cans of Beluga Caviar, which he served in his restaurant. The Russian coordinators provided the caviar to our parents, who then transported it to St. Louis. I felt badly that our parents were charged with this responsibility, and he was usually insistent that they come to the office to deliver it the day after returning home. He became angry when the clients didn't comply and deliver the caviar as soon as he requested. I thought it was asking a lot of the parents to drive to our office the day after returning home with their new child. I, of course, knew how exhausting the trip was. But, as in most cases, what Slava wanted, Slava got. Much later, I wondered who paid for the caviar, Small World or Zhivago's. If Small World did indeed pay for all the caviar, it would have amounted to thousands and thousands of dollars, as a single ounce retailed for between $50 and $75, or approximately $2,000 per can. Eventually, I came to wonder who paid for the authentic Russian server's uniforms and the menu covers, both of which were transported by adopting families.

Slava's businesses, along with Small World, took up nearly two-thirds of the available space in the building. The new office building was only about a block from their new health club, which they had recently acquired. The health club was a nice facility and Slava gave me a membership. During my visits to the club, knowing that I worked with Slava and Svetlana, the staff was often eager to share stories about incidents they claimed to have witnessed. I would hear about public arguments Slava and Svetlana had had while they were at the club together and regularly I received stories about Slava blowing up about one thing or another at the club. There was always a lot of drama going on at the health club, and sometimes the stories made me uncomfortable. I eventually discontinued my membership, telling Slava I just didn't have enough time to work out.

The restaurant was truly beautiful, the spa for Svetlana was lovely, the nightclub became a hot spot on the weekends, and the health club parking lot was always packed. His businesses were indeed booming, and it seemed as if Slava was building an empire in this little corner of town.

Alex's Birth Home

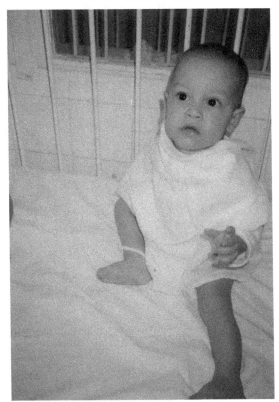

Alex tethered to crib

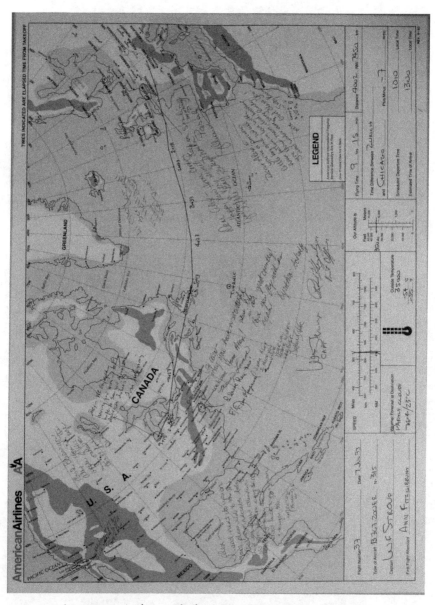

American Airlines Flight Map, Hungary to America

An Orphanage Kitchen

Baby Bottles in Russian Orphanage

Beds in Russian Orphanage

Bricks of Hope Playground in Russia

Orphans At Mandatory Potty Time

Orphans' Shoes Lined Up

Slava and Brenda in Hungary

CHAPTER 51

OFFICE ANTICS

Katy, our receptionist after Karena, left the agency to follow her dream of working with support animals. Katy had been wonderful, and we would miss her as we had missed Karena. I placed an ad in our paper and hired our next receptionist.

After interviewing several applicants, I hired Margo, who from day one day was an enormous asset to our office. She was bright, hardworking, and truly creative. Margo stayed with us many years and we were incredibly sad when she finally moved on.

Our office continued to grow and prosper, and we worked hard to always make the best of every situation, continuing to believe we were making a colossal difference in the world. Some days we laughed and some days we cried. We laughed the day Tanya was working at the copier and felt something cold fall into her hair. She reached up to feel the top of her head, which was a little wet. She looked up only to be struck on the cheek by a giant drop of brownish water. She smelled her fingers after wiping the water from her face and exclaimed, "Oh crap, something really nasty is falling from the ceiling." We all crowded around and quickly pushed the massive copy machine from underneath the drip. As we stood there contemplating the smell, someone decided it was fish!

Our office was underneath a portion of Zhivago's restaurant, and the drip had to be originating from there. I ran up to the restaurant and described to them the dripping water, and as we discussed the location the cook realized that the huge freezer just above our copier had stopped working. Fish within the freezer was thawing, and that was what was dripping through the floor and into our office. It was ever so nasty, but we got a lot of laughs, unfortunately at Tanya's expense. Within a month, Tanya lost a small patch of her hair that covered the spot where the fish water fell on her. Seriously! It did grow back, but it made that area of her head bald for a couple of months. Poor Tanya, we shared more laughter at her expense. But she was a good sport and laughed right along with us, so all was good.

Tanya, however, wasn't the only good sport! One afternoon, Slava called me to tell me that I had to send a copy of the "sex video" of Pamela Anderson and her husband, rock star Tommy Lee, to a judge who was hearing our cases in Russia! We continually had requests for gifts from the Russian officials, some super expensive, some ordinary. One of the officials in one of our Russian cities demanded the purchase of a diamond wedding ring! That was the most outlandish, but the sex tape was certainly a close runner up! This request occurred in the 1990s and although I was told pornography was available online and in specialty adult stores, I had no idea where or how to get a copy of this tape. On top of that, even if I knew where to get one, I could never walk into some place to make the purchase.

Our terrific, young, and creative Margo said she could find out where to get it and she would purchase it for us, and she was successful. The next hurdle would be getting it to Russia. There was no way I could ask an adopting family to carry this video, so we wrapped it up and buried it in a box of donations from local businesses that we sent with the next family that traveled to St. Petersburg. I warned our foreign country coordinator, Maria, to be sure to remove the videotape from the box before giving the box of donations to the orphanage!

Our Staff was a close-knit group, beginning with just me and growing eventually to a staff of ten, not counting Slava, Svetlana, or our foreign country coordinators. Laura continued to have her place in the office, moving from making informational packets to helping with more important clerical tasks in the office. Tanya had a summer cabin at a nearby lake. We would all go out to Tanya's cabin at least once each summer. We called ourselves the "Wooga Sisters." I don't really recall from where our little name originated, but we had many wonderful times together. During those weekends, we played games, usually brought by Marcia, who had the most amazing and fun, interactive group games. Everyone brought different dishes or was responsible for a specific meal. We drank wine, sang songs, told jokes, and swam in the lake.

Tanya's incredible husband was frequently there and made us drinks. We gave him the name Raul, the cabin boy. He was a fun-loving man who joined right in with our silly antics. My ever-present fear of snakes gave the group a lot of opportunities to tease me about seeing them, just as Slava had done. On a couple of occasions, we did see them, which would be a signal for me to drink a little, or a lot, more wine! At Tanya's cabin, we were just a group of really good girlfriends having a terrific time.

Every January, we drew names for "Secret Pals." Throughout the year, special little gifts would appear on desks from the employee's Secret Pal, and we would enjoy the big reveal at Christmas when we exchanged Christmas gifts. It was a big game for everyone to try to unveil the identity of their Secret Pal. It was a golden time for us.

One time, our super bright data specialist, Annie, made some comment about some ugly wallpaper in a magazine which she was looking at during lunch. I looked at the picture and said, "Wait a minute, that's the wallpaper in my hall powder room!" Everyone thought that very funny.

The next day, I arrived at work an hour before everyone else. I brought a left-over roll of wall paper from home and I took every item on Annie's desk and wrapped it up in my "ugly" wallpaper. I even covered the pictures on the wall by her desk as well as her chair. It was hysterical looking, and the staff got a huge kick out of my prank.

Another time, Marcia had made some comment about her office furniture; I don't even recall what it was. But, in response, Maureen and I came in early and we moved all her furniture out of her office and into the hall outside of our office space. Again, everyone thoroughly enjoyed the fun, especially Marcia! For one of my birthdays, I arrived at work to find nearly every inch of my office covered with toilet paper. It looked as if a literal blizzard had blown through my office. We had so much fun with one another.

Sometimes, when things were not crazy busy, we would have Spades Tournaments. We would play during lunch and then the next lunch, we would switch partners and a new group would play. We were close friends, working well together and even supporting each other through personal difficulties.

Staff came and went through the years, most leaving on good terms. But one thing was certain, I felt blessed to have the majority of them. When Laura was in high school, she became our youngest Wooga Sister.

Four times a year, Small World had a meeting of its board of directors. The board was comprised of adoptive parents who had a vested interest in its wellbeing. They were committed to its continued success, were critical to our successful fundraising events, and were often helpful with problem solving.

On one occasion, I was of questionable help to one of our board members. After a board meeting on a Saturday morning, I had been hurrying from the meeting to get to Alex's baseball game, which was nearby. We had placed Alex on a youth baseball team comprised primarily of his classmates. Although he struggled to follow directions, sit in the dugout, or to stop talking, he had a patient, kind coach, and overall the experience was very good for Alex. Because of his struggles, I was hurrying to get to his game as quickly as possible. Unfortunately, at the conclusion of the meeting and when leaving the office, I ended up following one of the board members down the street and we both turned the same corner, going in the same direction. When we changed directions, the sun suddenly blinded me, and as I reached for my sunglasses the board member put on his brakes! Yep, I ran right into the back of one of my bosses!

I was deeply upset. I nearly cried and kept apologizing and promised to pay for the damage to his car. It was a blessing no one was hurt. The insurance company eventually totaled the car, forcing the board member to get a new car. The funniest thing is that his wife called me and thanked me for running into his car! She had been begging her husband to get a new car and he kept refusing, claiming to be attached to the old one. So, all ended well, I got to keep my job and I made the day for my board member's wife!

CHAPTER 52

HE WAS LOVED...

THERE WERE MANY OTHER TIMES we all laughed together, but there were also many when we all cried together. A wonderful couple, Bob and Michelle, became clients and adopted two little boys, aged two and three, from Russia. They were a young, sweet couple and had recently begun the paperwork to return to Eastern Europe to adopt two little girls. One night, in the spring of 1999, after they had been home about a year and a half, my phone rang. I picked it up to the nearly hysterical voice of another one of our clients, Debbie, who was a friend of Michelle's. She said that Michelle and Bob's youngest little boy, Josh, had been rushed to the hospital, and the family was asking that I come join them there as soon as possible.

I rushed to Children's Hospital to find my two dear, sweet clients standing next to their precious little boy with tubes coming out from all over his body. The most shocking was the huge tube sticking out from the top of Josh's head. The tube was so large, it seemed to be half the size of Josh's head. Through hugs and tears, Michelle told me that Josh was already gone and was being kept alive by the ventilator. They explained to me that they did not want to let him go until I arrived to be with them. They feared what the Russian government would say about a child passing away at such a young age. They wanted me to be able to share their story if the adoption officials in Russia were concerned. Even in their pain, they didn't want their tragedy to hinder the adoption process for other waiting families. This was truly one of the most selfless families I have ever known.

As it turned out, Josh had suffered a massive stroke. He had complained of a terrible headache just minutes before collapsing on the bathroom floor that morning at home, never to regain consciousness. As the three of us stood there holding hands and sobbing, we watched as the ventilator was shut down, the bleeps on the monitor growing further and further apart as his little heart stopped beating and our precious angel was allowed to drift off to heaven. Josh was just barely four years old. The doctors had no explanation why blood vessels in the brain of a four-year-old child would rupture, saying this type of thing just happens, albeit extremely rarely.

A few days later, our entire staff attended his funeral. That young couple was amazingly strong, their faith in God helping sustain them. As I sat there with tears streaming down my face, Bob stood in front of the congregation and thanked me for bringing their son into their lives. He said that although they were only allowed to have Josh with them for a brief time, Josh would have suffered a stroke no matter where he was living, and they were exceedingly grateful that he did not have to die alone in an orphanage. This amazingly brave father was thankful that this little boy had been given approximately eighteen months of life with their family and Josh learned what it was like to be truly loved before leaving this earth. At the cemetery, everyone released white and blue balloons. For years after suffering this terrible tragedy, Michelle would describe her trips to the cemetery to tell Josh about things going on in their lives. She said she drew comfort from time spent by the graveside of their little angel. To this day the telling of this story brings tears to my eyes. This was twenty years ago, and I continue a close relationship with this family.

With events such as these happening in my life, how could this ever be "just a job"? How could it be anything less than a mission handed to me from God?

The flip side of this family were the families who only wanted perfect children, and we were occasionally under threat of being sued by a family who believed they had adopted a child they viewed as less than perfect. Over the years, a few of our clients actually tried to have their fees returned to them because their child had an undiagnosed health issue. I was continually revising our contracts to reduce the threat of a lawsuit. I was in constant risk assessment and management mode. This was one of the aspects of the job that was emotionally challenging for me; it made me sad that some people expected the same guarantees about their children as for their last new car.

CHAPTER 53

SLAVA THE SAVIOR

Shortly after we lost Josh, I underwent an extensive surgery on my knee. It was an invasive and painful surgery and the follow up procedure required that a home healthcare nurse visit me daily for the first two weeks. Screws had been placed directly into the bone and the chance of infection was great, so the visiting nurse came daily to clean the wound, change the dressing, and take my vital signs, etc. Laura and Alex were never far away during these visits as they found the whole disgusting thing to be fascinating!

From the moment I left the hospital after the surgery, I couldn't believe the excruciating pain I experienced. Every time I moved my leg, pain radiated through my body. I remained in this pain, lying on the couch at home for four days. I have an incredibly high pain threshold, but the pain was so intense I tried to remain medicated, thus sleeping continuously. I stopped eating and drinking, with the pain getting the better of me. On the fourth day, when the nurse visited me my blood pressure was dangerously low, and I was obviously very dehydrated. As my blessed good fortune would have it, right then Slava called and began asking medical questions which I was too drugged to answer. I handed the phone to the nurse. After a brief conversation between Slava and my nurse, he informed her that he was on his way to my house and he asked her to remain with me until he arrived. About 30 minutes later, he arrived with IV pain medications, bags of IV saline, and an IV pole from his medical clinic. He began an IV line, stabilized me, and said I needed to get back into the doctor immediately, something was very wrong. He called my doctor and demanded that they see me the next morning.

The next morning, I saw the doctor, where I learned that the "external fixator" (piece of metal screwed into my leg) had not been properly tightened before I left the hospital. This resulted in the unbelievable pain which shot through my body any time I moved my leg, as it caused the metal screws to wiggle or vibrate inside my bone. As soon as the doctor properly tightened the screws, I had immediate relief.

The home healthcare nurse had wanted to call an ambulance because my blood pressure had been so low. But I held Slava is such high regard as a medical professional, I wouldn't let her. I just wanted my Slava. My affection for him only grew as I saw Slava as my lifesaver. He had been so kind and gentle with me that day. I was incredibly moved by how much he seemed to care about me. His kindnesses made the occasions when he belittled me fade into the background.

CHAPTER 54

GROWING, GROWING, GROWING...

Our Ukraine coordinator, crazy, fun Igor, through some unknown means, found people in Guatemala who wanted to adopt through our program. By that time, we had those clients not only in Guatemala, but in France and New Zealand, and in more than twenty-five states. Sometimes I just sat back in wonder as I reflected on the lives we were touching all around the world. I had never envisioned such a far-reaching impact. Many of the clients outside of the US found us as a result of that famous Ann Landers article. Often the foreign families would tell us that an American relative had read the article and referred them to us.

As a child, Tanya's father had an international career, and she was raised in South America and was fluent in Spanish. Therefore, she easily took on working with our Spanish speaking clients from Guatemala. The two Guatemalan families even attended a few of our summer picnics. We were thrilled to have them come so far.

In anticipation of changes in international law, and necessary for our continued growth, I began the process to have our agency accredited by a national accrediting organization, Council on Accreditation. I attended training for the accreditation process and began the daunting task. It was one of the most stressful times for our staff. I am ashamed to say that I most likely increased the tension around this process because I was such a perfectionist. I probably still owe that amazing staff an apology.

The COA regulations had stringent guidelines, so new policies had to be written and manuals had to be created. I think we bought about one hundred different sized binders into which the documents were inserted. We worked late into the night and weekends for several months. Documentation of epic proportions had to be mailed to COA prior to two of its representatives visiting our office to do a "site visit." The day before we needed to mail the massive compilation of documentation, Ryan returned from England, having been in a Study Abroad program for the spring semester of his sophomore year in college. I couldn't even stop to pick him up from the airport. I don't recall who picked him up, but he arrived at the office without even going home, after being gone for nearly four months, to help us. Most of the staff stayed all night and we survived by eating chocolate throughout the paperwork amassing marathon. One of the case mangers went home and made breakfast for everyone, bringing it back to the office the next morning. Laura was recruited to help us, making hundreds of copies and collating the materials. We had stacks of documents stretching around the perimeter of the office. It seemed to be a truly formidable task.

The procedure to complete the accreditation process took about nine months and, in the end, we shipped five large boxes of documents to New York City. (We never told the COA officials about sending the X-rated video to Russia!)

The scoring for the process consisted of passing standards with scores of one or two or failing standards with scores of three or four. The perfectionist in me really wanted to get all ones and I posted signs all over the office – "Embrace the 1," encouraging staff to help us to be the best we could be.

I am proud to say that we received almost all ones with only a couple of twos out of approximately 300 standards and in 1999, we received COA accreditation. We had the option of arguing the scores, but the board president lectured me on the importance of learning to let some things go. My staff teased me about this for years. But each of us was extremely proud of what we had accomplished as a team. I was even more honored to lead such a group of outstanding people.

One of the best and truly special things about our growing family of clients and their children continued to be the fabulous picnics we held each summer. We tried to host the picnic during the same weekend each July, working around the beginnings and endings of the school year's calendar. As our numbers of attendees grew, we added bounce houses, games, clowns, and balloons. We hired a photographer who took pictures of the hundreds of people attending. During what I refer to as "the golden years," we lived for those summer picnics.

During one of our summer picnics, before we moved into an indoor venue, the temperature reached about 101 degrees by 2:00 PM. A couple of our family members had already been taken to the hospital from heat exhaustion. We had enormous cooling fans, tents, and huge tubs of ice cold drinks, but people were still dropping like flies. As the hostess of the event, I was continually in motion trying to connect with each and every family that was present. At some point in the midafternoon, I was walking toward one of the tents and I got so lightheaded I wasn't sure I was going to make it to a chair. I was focused on my destination, paying little attention to anyone around me. I was feeling as nauseous as could be and staff later reported that my face was bright red. I sat in the chair and placed my head between my knees. Marcia had been watching and rushed to my side with a small bucket of ice water, which she proceeded to dump over my head. I don't recall anything after that until I was in the ambulance. The paramedic told me I had been going into shock because someone had tried to "kill me." He knew it had been Marcia trying to help and said this with a big smile. He said dumping ice water on someone suffering with heat exhaustion can send the person into shock. He explained that they were taking me to the hospital for evaluation and fluids. I never missed the opportunity to remind Marcia of the time she tried to kill me.

CHAPTER 55

MY FAMILY

EVEN THOUGH I WAS BLESSED to lead that terrific group of people by day, by night I was more blessed to parent my marvelous children. Ryan spent a semester of college in a study abroad program in Harlaxton, England in 2000. We were all missing each other terribly and decided to visit Ryan during Laura's and Alex's spring break from school. Harlaxton is the birth place of the former British Prime Minister, Margaret Thatcher. Ryan had the tremendous good fortune to live and attend school in an old castle, Harlaxton Manor. The castle in which the students lived had been the setting for the 1999 Liam Neeson movie *The Haunting*.

After arriving in England, it was fascinating to walk through the spooky old castle, having seen the movie before visiting Ryan. Exploring the town and learning about the local history was also a treat. One afternoon, after touring the castle we decided to get something to eat. The castle sat about a mile off of the main road, and at the entrance of the smaller road leading to the castle sat a traditional British Pub. We decided to eat at this pub since Ryan spoke about it several times during our long-distance conversations. As we all sat down to eat, I turned to Ryan, who had lived down the road from this pub for more than two months and asked what was good to eat. He looked at me and said, "Mom, I have no idea, I've never eaten here." Initially, the protective mom in me didn't want to envision my little boy enjoying a "pint" of beer with friends and being so grown up. But I quickly came to my senses, he *was* twenty and living in a foreign country, and 18 *was* the legal drinking age. So, I just laughed out loud and enjoyed the humor in the moment. By the way, if you ever get the opportunity to visit Harlaxton Castle, I recommend skipping lunch at that pub and opting for a beverage instead.

While on our trip to England, we also made plans for our family to travel on to Budapest and Szeged, Hungary. It was important for me to share that piece of my life, which had hugely altered the trajectory of all of our lives, with the rest of my family.

They were excited to take this side trip. We arrived in Budapest and took the train to Szeged, as I had done many times years before. We sat down on the train, and at the next stop a number of Roma people entered our rail car. With the exception of Alex who is one-half Roma, we were a light haired, fair skinned group of people. The troupe of Roma sat together, staring at our little eight-year-old Alex, and there was much rapid conversation taking place between the group of Roma. It didn't take a quantum physicist to surmise that Alex was of Roma ethnicity, and he had most likely been adopted by this Caucasian family. They kept looking at him, making us all a little nervous. I was concerned but not quite to the point of alarm or fear. Unfortunately, there was still a great deal of conflict between the Roma population and the rest of Eastern European society. From my time in Hungary and from the reading I had done, I was aware that the Roma people were generally against mingling with Caucasian people. I will never forget that day and the way Laura held her little brother in a death-grip on her lap as the leader of the group approached us with suitcases, out of which they tried selling us silverware. It felt like something out of a movie. Also, none of us will ever forget the pungent aroma of the group of Roma. As they stood right next to us, with Alex's nose at their armpit level, his little eyes began to water.

We finally exited the train in Szeged and got into a taxi and everyone immediately clamored to see Alex's orphanage. For the first time in six years, I uttered the words Pósz Jenö Utca to the taxi cab driver and feelings of nostalgia washed over me. Although those weeks in Hungary had been some of the hardest of my life, they had been the seeds out of which had grown Small World. I felt that I owed a lot to that old preschool turned orphanage.

The driver took us right to the building, which was in worse disrepair and even more paint had peeled away. Everyone wanted to walk down the walk I had used that last day I left the orphanage. I stopped and hugged Alex and was overcome with emotion and shed several tears. It was a terribly sweet experience.

About three years later, Alex had reached the "ripe" age of a deodorant wearing preteen. I kept trying to coax him into wearing deodorant but was continually met with great resistance. I finally told Alex I just didn't understand and he matter-of-factly looked at me and said, "Well, mom, I just want to smell like my people." I burst out in fits of laughter, knowing exactly to what Alex was referring. What could a mom to say to that?

Alex brought enormous joy to our family, but he stretched to the max our problem-solving skills. He experienced difficulties in school, with relationships, anger management, tantrums, and general compliance with family rules. We were continually searching for therapists who could reach him and help him come to terms with the trauma of his infancy, help him develop healthier interpersonal skills, and ways to help him manage his rage. We tried numerous private schools, eventually homeschooling him, but the demons, born of abandonment, loss, and fear in his first nineteen months, loose within his heart, remained difficult to tame.

Although it was hard on my family whenever I traveled to Russia or Belarus, it was particularly hard on Alex. His therapist told us he had abandonment issues, so when I traveled I always tried to call home every day.

Some years, on our humanitarian trips to build the playgrounds, Ryan or Laura would accompany us. Laura made most of the trips with me, so I was always glad when Ryan accompanied us. He was smart, strong, and had already developed some building skills. Sometimes, if time permitted, our humanitarian crew would do a little sightseeing. One time while waiting in line to tour the Summer Palace outside of St. Petersburg, Ryan pulled out his hacky sack and began juggling it between his feet. A couple of teenage Russians were watching him from a small distance away. Before long, Ryan had both of them engaged in the activity. I watched with pride as these young people, who could not speak each other's language, were able to communicate, laughing, and enjoying each other's company, with Ryan teaching them how to manipulate the little bag, filled with sand, between their feet. As we needed to move forward in line, Ryan reached into his pocket and withdrew a second hacky sack and gave one to each of the teens, who were as excited as could be and kept saying "spaseeba, spaseeba" (pronounced spuh-see-buh), which is thank you in Russian! It had been touching to watch. If only our governments could get along as well.

On another trip, in Belarus, I entered a hotel lobby in Minsk to rendezvous with the rest of our group for dinner. Ryan, who was around 20 at the time, wanted to take advantage of his opportunity to legally purchase a beer in the hotel lobby, so he made himself comfortable at the bar and ordered one. He had come down to the bar by himself while everyone else was still getting ready for dinner. Of course, Ryan is completely adorable. So, I was unsurprised that a couple of local girls had begun conversing with him at the bar. They seemed to be fully engaging with him, loudly laughing, and looking as if they were having a good time. They did look a little older than he and they had on pretty risqué outfits for so early in the day. But, it all seemed harmless. However, Phil happened upon the scene about that time and, taking in the sight, he said, "Oh man Brenda, I better go save Ryan."

I naively asked why he thought Ryan needed saving. As Phil rolled his eyes, he said, "Brenda, those are a couple of hookers trying to pick up your son!" A surprised me watched as Phil went over to the bar to extricate my son from the clutches of the ladies of the night! Ryan claimed he knew what they were and thought it was hysterical, knowing that I was observing. Phil and Ryan got a lot of mileage out of the incident at my expense!

We returned to the US to learn that our beloved Tanya was going to retire. Her husband had wanted her to for a while, but I kept convincing her to stay a little longer. I was deeply saddened by Tanya's departure, but we never truly let her go. She continued to join us for picnics and parties and she would fill in for vacationing staff. We reluctantly wished her farewell. Connie, a fun-loving woman, was hired to replace Tanya and she fit right in.

CHAPTER 56

EVAN

OUR TEAM CONTINUED THE WORK of bringing orphaned children to the United States as quickly as possible. There seemed to be an endless supply of families hoping to adopt a child from Eastern Europe. But, the adoptions weren't always what we hoped they would be. One time, a local couple traveled to Russia to adopt a precious little boy. After the adoption had been legally granted, and as the couple was preparing to leave Russia, the mother called me and advised me they had decided they could not bring their recently adopted child home with them. The mother said her husband believed he could never "love this child" as he did their biological child back in the US.

At the time, there was very little research on bonding with adopted children, but I had several years of experience in working with the families, and this was not a common stance among the adoptive families with whom I had worked. The adoptive mom also shared that her husband expressed concerns about the child's development. As with all of the adopting parents, these parents were warned before traveling to meet their son that he could be developmentally delayed, small by

American standards, and initially even difficult to handle as the result of living in an orphanage, but their child was a fairly young baby and normally those children had fewer issues.

The mother was sobbing on the phone and I had no idea what to do, as the couple had completed a legally binding adoption. I told the mother I would call her back and I immediately called Slava. Slava stated that they would likely need to bring the child to the US and they could relinquish him to the American system. If they left the country without the child, they could be charged by the Russian government with child abandonment, perhaps even stopped at the airport. If they stayed to reverse the adoption, they would likely be there for many weeks. Their options were to remain in Russia for an unknown, extended period of time while the adoption was legally reversed or bring the baby home. The couple chose to bring the baby to the US.

Marcia contacted a local domestic adoption agency and explained that one of our couples was going to relinquish custody of a child they had just adopted in Russia and we asked the agency for its help. The agency arranged for the baby boy to go into one of their licensed foster homes. Marcia and I went to the airport to meet the couple and to take custody of the baby. Marcia had the legal forms necessary for the parents to sign, allowing us to take custody of him.

It was one of the most heart wrenching things we ever witnessed or did. The mother was visibly shaken and crying as we walked away with the baby. Both Marcia and I were weeping. As we were driving in Marcia's car toward the home of the assigned foster parent, I begged Marcia not to take the baby there. We were both still crying, and I wanted to just take the baby home with me or to do anything other than put this tiny little boy back into the legal system. Marcia, who was very skilled at handling these types of events, was adept at calming me down and we did take the baby to the foster home. The foster mother was so loving and kind toward our little guy that I was able to leave him with her. We turned and left this little boy, who just a couple of days ago had been rescued from the Russian orphanage system, and was now being placed back into the system, this time in the United States.

The following day, I called the next person on our waiting list to see if she would want to adopt this little boy. The client was a single woman living in another city. When I told her the story of the baby and then told her his name, Evan, she burst into tears. She said that when she had decided to adopt a child she saw the name Evan in a magazine, cut the name out, and put it on her refrigerator, planning for that to be her child's name. She immediately confirmed her desire to adopt Evan. We were exceedingly fortunate that Marcia had been a director of a local domestic adoption agency before joining Small World and was able to navigate the legal system, facilitating the termination of parental rights, and subsequent placement of the baby with his new family.

It was truly amazing that this little boy's name was Evan! I believe that God's hand played a part in this. The last I heard from our client, she and her little boy were immensely happy, and the little boy was exceptionally bright and thriving in all areas.

CHAPTER 57

AN EXCEPTION

THROUGHOUT THE YEARS, DOING BUSINESS in Russia, Belarus, and Ukraine seemed to get more challenging. The rules were constantly changing, which created confusion and angst for all of us. Initially, the foreign laws allowed single women to adopt children from Russia, Belarus, and Ukraine. Then the rules changed and it was not allowed. For a brief time, single women were once more allowed to adopt in all three countries, but in short order that option disappeared forever. Adoption by single men was never permitted in any of the countries with which we worked.

However, we did assist the first single man, Carl, to adopt from Russia. Carl had participated in a program to sponsor older children from Russia and had hosted three little boys for a summer. He had also traveled to Russia to see them many times. The boys were desperate to be with their perceived "papa," and he was equally invested in them. Carl heard about us from a friend and contacted me to see if we could help him. After sharing the story with Slava, he agreed to try to help and was ultimately able to get Moscow to agree to the adoptions. It took more than a year of paperwork, pleading, and the usage of all the goodwill Slava could garner in Moscow to make it happen.

To my knowledge, this was the first single, American male allowed to adopt from the country of Russia. The only other single male allowed to adopt a Russian child would also be ours, in the not too distant future. I truly believed that there was no one else with Slava's Moscow and St. Petersburg connections who would have been able to do this. I was continually amazed at what Slava could make happen when he was committed to a plan.

CHAPTER 58

ENIGMA LOUNGE

DURING THE YEARS WE WERE working in Russia, it was no longer officially considered to be a Communist country. However, years and years of Communism had created an atmosphere of complete distrust. Scandals were around every corner and behind every door. The smallest hint of a scandal could cause the ruination of both people and businesses. Small World was on the receiving end of a scandalous rumor that nearly closed its doors.

One day, in 2000, not long after the opening of Slava's nightclub Enigma Lounge, which was next door to our office, I got a call from Slava in his normally "revved-up" condition. He had received a phone call from one of his contacts in Moscow who was reporting that the adoption authorities had received a complaint from another American adoption agency that he, Slava, was the owner of a strip club named Enigma. If the complaint had been validated, Small World would have lost its right to facilitate adoptions in Russia. Enigma was of course not a strip club. The restaurant and club were physically located in a prominent suburban area, not prone to providing business licenses for strip clubs.

Small World could have suffered irreparable damage from this allegation, and Slava placed the solving of the problem squarely in my lap. I was terrified that Small World was going to be forced to stop providing services to families. This was my mission – saving children – and I wouldn't allow a rumor to cast a dark cloud over our work.

Moscow, having no way to verify Slava's statement regarding the club, requested a letter from the State of Missouri verifying the type of business Enigma was along with a letter of "good standing." They gave us a tiny window of time in which to deliver the letter to the Ministry of Justice in Moscow, and it was essential that I use all resources at my disposal to solve this problem. Fortunately, during the time I was trying to free Alex, I had cultivated a few strong relationships within the State government and I immediately contacted my political acquaintances requesting an expedited letter of good standing for Enigma. The letter needed to be notarized and apostilled (a special seal from the Secretary of State of Missouri). It also had to be translated into Russian and all of these tasks took precious time! My anxiety level was going up every day I didn't have that letter in my hands.

I received the letter about four long days later, and we were quickly running out of time. The only option I had to get the letter to Moscow by their deadline was to personally fly, with the letter, and hand-deliver it myself. Sending the letter through a courier service at that time would have taken six or seven days. We did not have that many days left. Thus, I got a flight out the next day to Moscow, which was about a twenty-four-hour trip from my home to my destination. I landed in Moscow and a friend of Slava's picked me up and took me to the Ministry of Justice, where I delivered the letter to the proper Russian authorities, and one day before the deadline! I was actually in Moscow less than five hours before returning to the airport to catch my flight back to the US. I recall that the trip to Moscow and back took me about fifty-five hours, and I never slept except for a few hours on the plane. The Ministry accepted the documents from Missouri and the incident was closed. I was incredibly thankful that we had won the battle.

CHAPTER 59

ZHIVAGO'S

SITTING JUST ABOVE ENIGMA WAS Slava's Zhivago's, one of the best restaurants in which I have ever eaten. The sea bass and the mushroom soup were to die for! Small World employees loved that the wait staff wore traditional Russian costumes and enjoyed dining at the restaurant. It was Zhivago's that introduced me to the drink "White Russian." Nearly every Friday afternoon at the end of the day, we would call the restaurant and order White Russians. Sometimes we would alter our routine and order the most flavorful Georgian wine imaginable. Even the non-wine drinkers in the office loved it. This became our kick off for the weekends. We loved our jobs, we deeply cared about one another, and we were a family. Sometimes Slava would stop in and join us for our cocktail hour.

Our Small World staff had grown so that the company could afford to provide the benefit of health insurance to employees. Sometimes Slava could be his own worst enemy. I think it was a constant struggle for him to differentiate between what was standard operating procedure in Russia and what was legally permissible in the US. I frequently found myself in the role of explaining the US legal system to him. These conversations frequently ended in heated discussions, as Slava felt he should be able to do whatever he pleased.

Slava came to the office one day and told me he was adding two young Russian men to our payroll and instructed me to add them to our group insurance plan. Slava stated they would be doing translations for the company and assisting Slava with some of the coordination of business in Russia. Slava had given them relatively small salaries. We were extremely busy at the time. I was often working 60-hour weeks myself, and I knew that Slava was working more than that because he had so many jobs to do: anesthesiologist, restaurant, nightclub, and health club owner, and assisting Svetlana with her new beauty spa business. Thus, it made sense to me that Slava was seeking relief from some of his duties. I met with the two young Russian men to do insurance paperwork. It was challenging as they spoke very limited English. I should have immediately questioned their ability to translate anything into English but was so busy I just processed them and sent them on their way.

A few months later, I was dining in Zhivago's restaurant and happened to go back into the kitchen. I had become friendly with the Russian community and it would not have been uncommon for me to step into the kitchen to greet someone who I knew was working. When I entered the kitchen, I immediately saw the two young men who had been hired to do Small World work, receiving a salary from it, and for whom the company was paying health insurance, working in the food preparation area. I suspected something was not right, and I was angry.

After one of our many bookkeepers failed to return to work one day, we hired a new bookkeeper, Dave. Slava and Dave developed a relationship, and before I knew it Slava hired Dave as the bookkeeper for all personal businesses as well. I expressed mild concern to Slava about the potential conflict of interest by mixing of his personal businesses and our non-profit, but Slava paid me no heed. Slava had from the beginning excluded me from nearly everything to do with finances, other than the signing of the checks.

I sought out the bookkeeper the next day and questioned him about the workers in the kitchen being on the Small World payroll as well as receiving health insurance benefits. He admitted he knew the men were working in the restaurant, but that Slava had instructed him to pay them regardless. He said Slava didn't believe there was anything wrong with the arrangement because from his perspective, he owned both businesses, Small World and Zhivago's. I thought about how to handle this for perhaps a week. I knew addressing this with Slava would be like making my way through an active mine field. I knew how headstrong and even downright unreasonable Slava could be and I did not relish confronting him about this.

However, eventually I did confront Slava and he told me that all the businesses were his and he could structure them anyway he wanted, just as the bookkeeper had predicted. He very succinctly informed me that it was none of my business. I tried to remind him that Small World was a non-profit organization and that no one owned it, and his paying restaurant employees with Small World funds was an illegal use of funds, from my perspective. I told him both men needed to be removed from the payroll and I was discontinuing their insurance. He was furious, but so was I. This was one of the very rare occasions during which I totally stood up to him and held my ground, even though he blasted me with unkind and offensive names. The next day, I called the CPA with whom we worked, and with whom Slava was good friends, and asked for her help. She said Slava just didn't understand the differences between doing business in Russia and in the US. She said this type of behavior would be sanctioned in Russia. But, again, I maintained my position and she said she would talk with him. I discontinued their health insurance and they disappeared from the payroll. Slava and I never spoke about it again. I shared the incident with both Marcia and Maureen, with Marcia proclaiming she was totally unsurprised by Slava's activity. As always, she reminded me that she held her trust of him in reserve. She was so very smart!

CHAPTER 60

ANGELS IN ADOPTION

THAT SAME YEAR, SLAVA AND I were nominated for the Congressional Award, "Angels in Adoption 2000." The award, which still hangs in my current office, says the award is given "In recognition of your outstanding example and commitment to promoting adoption." The award was issued by the Congressional Coalition on Adoption.

A ceremony for awardees was held in Washington, DC and I attended. Slava was unable to attend the ceremony, and Maureen attended in his place to receive his award. The award was signed by Senators Kit Bond, of Missouri; Mary Landrieu, of Louisiana; and Larry Craig, of Idaho, and by Representatives Tom Bliley, of Virginia and Jeffrey Oberstar, of Minnesota.

Slava and I were proud of this award. Our work together had been noticed at a national level and it moved me to want to do an even better job. I knew the important work we were doing was guided by a higher power, and receipt of an award by this name just solidified my belief, we *were* angels doing work in adoption.

CHAPTER 61

CONFERENCE IN BELARUS

PART OF THE IMPORTANT WORK we were doing was to be good ambassadors for international adoption. So, during one of Laura's remissions in the spring of 2001, I took her to an adoption conference that was held in Belarus. A client, Marie, and her little girl, Beth, went with us. The mother was a doctor and she joined us to address a group of doctors, offering the American perspective regarding both adoption and orthopedics. She had adopted Beth from Belarus, and Beth was missing her forearm, called a congenital amputation. She wore a prosthetic arm.

I think Beth was meant to be raised in this family. A year or so prior, Slava and Svetlana had returned from a videotaping trip to Belarus and little Beth had been on the newest video tape. I was standing in the main section of our little office, telling the staff about this beautiful little girl who was missing her forearm. I had been sharing my apprehension about finding a home for this precious little girl. At precisely that moment, Marcia walked into the office, having just completed a home study visit, and she heard my concern. Marcia immediately began to grin broadly, stating that she had just come from a home visit with a couple who were doctors. During the home study, Marcia had asked them the routine question regarding their willingness to consider a child with a disability and their answer had been, "No, unless it is a missing limb. We wouldn't even consider that a disability." Marcia and I quickly called the family, and little Beth was in the arms of her loving parents in just a few short months.

During her speech in Belarus, Marie spoke about Americans' willingness to adopt orphaned children regardless of whatever perceived limitations people might see. She was an accomplished doctor, speaker, and mother. She was a huge success at the conference.

During that trip, one night in Belarus, after spending the evening in Laura's and my room, Marie and Beth left to return to their room. A couple of minutes later Marie called, and when I answered, she asked, "Did you guys find an arm in your room?"

I readily responded with, "I don't know, let me look around." Sure enough, I found the prosthetic arm on the floor and told the doctor I would bring it right up to their room. Laura and I laughed about this for a long time, how funny it had been to be asked if we found an arm in our room and how normal and natural the exchange regarding the arm had been! Beth, who was perhaps five or six at the time, was as likely as not to remove the prosthetic arm because she didn't like it.

The next morning, we were to meet at the elevator for breakfast. We had been in Belarus for several days and when traveling, I frequently lost track of the dates. That morning, Laura hardly spoke to me and I couldn't figure out what was wrong with her; she seemed to be in such a bad mood! As we approached our friends at the elevator, Beth ran up to Laura and threw her arms around her, yelling, "Happy Birthday, Laura!" I hadn't realized it was Laura's birthday; I hadn't wished her a Happy Birthday. I apologized to her, hugged her, and ran back to the room for her gifts. To this day, she likes to tell people about the time her mother forgot her birthday!

We went on to breakfast and sat down. The hotel restaurant was a peaceful, pretty, and old-fashioned place. There were lace table clothes on the table and little doilies everywhere. The dishes were fine, thin china with charming flowers painted on the plates. This was normal for independent restaurants in small hotels. They were usually just lovely. However, the meals themselves were sometimes a challenge for Laura and me, and this breakfast proved to be particularly so. Often breakfasts in smaller, Eastern European hotels are just "served" and there is no real "ordering" from a menu. So, when an unknown brownish-gray piece of meat was placed before us, Laura began to study it intently. None of us could tell exactly what it was when suddenly Laura moaned, "Oh Mom, it's hairy!" Marie said she was thinking that perhaps it was an organ of some kind and had just decided it might be some of sort tongue. Needless to say, Laura and I did not partake of the tongue that morning.

That trip to Belarus left some truly lasting impressions with me, pictures which couldn't be filed away easily. One afternoon following a conference session, our translator/driver, Victor, asked us if we would like to visit a special World War II memorial in the Belarusian countryside. We agreed that would be interesting and it was a splendid day to be outside. The day was sunny, and the temperature was around 80 degrees with everything in full bloom. Some distance away, perhaps nearly an hour outside of the city, we arrived at a clearing in the middle of a birch forest. The birch forests, which ran throughout Belarus, were enchanting; every single tree within sight had the thin, signature white trunks for which birch trees are famous. I had never seen birch trees like this before. The sea of white trunks was a stark contrast to the brown trunks of the trees in the Midwest.

We parked in a small parking area and got out to walk. Our translator led us down a narrow rock path that ran between large slabs of concrete on either side of us. I immediately identified the slabs of concrete as building foundations which were quite old and weathered.

Victor explained that this village was a memorial to the Belarus people who perished during World War II.

Victor stated it had been commonplace for the Nazis to storm small villages in Belarus. If the people had enough warning, they would run and hide deep in the forests. He shared that the Nazis would perhaps then spend a little time trying to hunt people down, but usually just burned each village to the ground. The Nazis preferred doing this during the harsh winter months knowing that many of the surviving people hiding out in the forests would die from exposure and starvation.

We came upon a large statue of a man holding a deceased child. Victor then told us the story of this village, Khatyn, and the ensuing massacre which occurred in 1943. A group of Nazi sympathizers, consisting mostly of Ukrainian criminals, entered the village one night, driving all the citizens to a large shed which they secured and lit on fire. Some of the people trapped inside were able to break through the rear of the shed but were killed by machine guns while trying to escape. The Nazis then looted the homes and burned the village to the ground. Only six people survived the attack, one adult and five children. The adult had been shot, burned, and left for dead. One child pretended to be dead; one was thrown on a horse by his mother to escape through the forest; one hid in a potato pit; one hid in a cellar; and one hid beneath the body of his deceased mother. Victor ended the story telling us that the statue commemorates the surviving adult, a fifty-six-year-old man who found his mortally wounded son in time for him to pass away in his arms. This village had been home to 156 people.

After Victor finished telling the story, there were really no words to say. What unimaginable horror these people had experienced. The final thought Victor left with us, as we were returning to the van, was that the population of the Belarusian people had not yet returned to pre-World War II days. The result of those types of murderous rampages by the Nazis was that nearly one-quarter of Belarusian citizens perished in the war. The main leader of this execution squad was eventually caught and executed in Belarus in 1975. Few words were spoken in the van on our return trip as each of us was lost in our own thoughts about this ghastly story.

The following day, we were scheduled to make a visit to an orphanage which cared for children aged six to eleven. It was a wretched place, worse than any of the baby orphanages I had seen. Here there were no smiling babies, only sullen and rail thin children. Their eyes were blank and there were none of the easy, endearing smiles I usually received at the baby homes. We did not remain long at this orphanage. As I began to get into the van when we were leaving, I had a feeling of being watched and I turned to look over to my left side. There, on the second floor of the building, were a row of thin, pale children, all in raggedy clothing, standing on the heat registers and holding on to the bars on the inside of the orphanage windows. They made me think of birds trapped in a cage, wanting nothing more than to escape their confinement. The tragedy of their lives was visible on each sad and empty looking face. That vision haunts me yet today.

The final event of our visit was a trip to the circus. I had purchased tickets for the children in the baby orphanage who were old enough to attend a circus, and we joined them. The children arrived in a big bus and we had waited to go in with them. Laura and the rest of our American group were leading the crowd of children into the building, with the caretakers interspersed throughout. I was bringing up the rear. As our group climbed the steep steps to the seats in an area that had been reserved for us, I waited below.

As I waited for the large, noisy group to find their seats, I studied this big, round building, which stood in the center of town and in which the circus ran year-round. The smell was horrific, and it was clear by the looks of the crowded cages and the filthy floors that the animals probably didn't receive very humane care. I was wishing I had passed on attending the event with the children.

Finally, all of the children, my daughter, and my traveling companions had seats and were ready for the circus to begin. I looked wide eyed at my group, lifting my hands out in front of me in a shrug. There was not an empty seat anywhere for me! They all smiled, thinking this a great joke. I turned to sit on the bottom step of our assigned section when a large Belarussian orphanage caretaker, already seated in the stands, grabbed me. She had witnessed my little show for my friends and had made two small children move to share a seat. She hauled me up from the steps into the seat next to her and grabbed me around my neck, pulling my head into her enormous bosom for a huge hug. My head was caught in a squishy cavern smelling of BO and cheap perfume. She kept hugging and hugging my head until I feared passing out from lack of oxygen. She finally released me and although we couldn't speak one another's language, her message was clear; she wanted to thank me for bringing them all to the circus.

CHAPTER 62

TRAVELS TO RUSSIA

NOT LONG AFTER RETURNING FROM my Belarus trip, Slava, Svetlana, and I took off for another trip to Russia, later in 2001. They told me they had to conduct business relating to their other companies and had arranged for Slava's mother, who was also visiting St. Petersburg at the same time, and a translator to give me a tour of the city. I never had an indication of what their other business involved. Their business ended up taking a couple of days, thus I had the unforgettable experience of a personal guided tour around St. Petersburg. I had the joy of going through the famous Hermitage Museum, the Winter Palace, and touring the Peter and Paul Fortress.

During that visit, it was White Nights in Russia. This is a period each year, when far up in the northern hemisphere, the sun doesn't completely set. At the height of "White Nights," it may only be dusk during the hours between 2:00 and 5:00 AM. Although exhausted each day, it was difficult to fall asleep because the sun was still shining through my window at midnight. Experiencing White Nights was a fascinating event for me and I was glad to be able to enjoy them on this trip, giving us longer days to enjoy the sights.

One of my favorite sights was the Hermitage, one of the largest and oldest museums in the world, dating back to 1764. Its construction had been the lifetime pursuit of Catherine the Great; it is unbelievably massive and is reported to display over three million items. The majesty and splendor cannot be shared in this limited number of words, unable to do it justice. The structure alone is impressive with its marble and granite columns and archways, intricate patterned Italian marble floors, and the exquisite doors and windows. I easily felt the presence of previous Russian czars who graced its halls. The paintings and historical Russian artifacts on display were breathtaking. Having the opportunity to spend a day at the Hermitage was a blessing. However, to do the whole museum justice would have taken several days, very similar to the time required to fully tour the Smithsonian Institution in Washington D.C.

The following day, I had the pleasure of spending a few hours at the Winter Palace, again not remotely adequate time to fully enjoy the structure. That afternoon, I visited the Peter and Paul Fortress. Though less impressive than the Hermitage or the Winter Palace, the rich history and stories associated with the Fortress were fascinating. The Fortress was the first structure built in St. Petersburg and had served in many capacities from military base, to burial ground for Russian czars, to a very sinister looking jail. The Russian structures were astoundingly massive, regal, exquisite, and completely unlike any structures in the US, primarily because America is such a young country compared to much of the rest of the world.

At lunch on our second day of sightseeing, we enjoyed lunch at the Waldorf Astoria Hotel. I had been enamored by the mushroom soup Slava served at his restaurant at home and was thus moved to try it at the Waldorf. It was mouth wateringly wonderful. But, toward the end of our tour at the Fortress I began to feel sick to my stomach. By the time we returned to the apartment, I was violently ill. I remained deathly ill for several days and Slava attributed it to bad mushrooms. I was not recovering and continually vomiting, keeping neither food nor fluid down. On the morning of the third day, Slava began making plans to have me airlifted to Sweden, the closest place Slava felt I could get good medical care. He said there was absolutely no way he would put me into a Russian hospital. Plans were made, but a few hours before we were to leave for the airport, I stopped being as sick and began to feel a little better. Slava decided that I wouldn't need to go to Sweden, but he arranged for me to fly home on the first flight which he could arrange. He called my internist back in the states to prepare him for my return and we agreed that I would go directly to my doctor's office immediately after landing.

I was so weak and ill that Slava obtained permission to assist me in getting to my seat on the plane. I immediately fell asleep and didn't awake until landing at JFK airport in New York. I had slept the entire 10 plus hours without moving.

I was very happy to return to St. Louis to see my own doctor. My internist had actually gone to medical school in Russia with Slava, and he was as gifted a doctor as Slava. During the first year of working with Slava, I got very sick with bronchitis and Slava insisted I go see Dr. G. I smile as I recall Slava calling me and saying to me in his great accent, "Don't die, we need you." Dr. G. was funny and charming and a fabulous diagnostician. He is still my doctor. Eventually, nearly all our staff began going to see him, as did our family members.

Years later, Dr. G. was behind my very early diagnosis of stage three lung cancer with a less-than twenty-percent chance of survival. I had never smoked, and it was Dr. G's thoroughness which saved my life. I lost a section of my lung and most of my hair, but I beat the odds. Had it not been for Slava's insistence that I see Dr. G. years earlier, perhaps I would have ended up with a less talented diagnostician and my outcome might have been less positive. That is just one more thing for which I am grateful to Slava.

On every trip to Russia with Slava and Svetlana, I could expect some sort of excitement. The experience of going to Russia was always thrilling and it never lost its wonder for me. I loved every trip I ever made. About six months after our fateful mushroom-soup-eating trip to St. Petersburg, the three of us needed to fly to visit some orphanages that were closer to Moscow than to St. Petersburg. We were also working to establish some new programs in some cities further to the East. We would be meeting with officials in Moscow to help move the new programs along.

Slava, as was his habit, wasn't one to make many plans for events. So, when we landed in Moscow and tried to get into a hotel, we learned that there was an international summit going on in Moscow and there was not a hotel room to be had anywhere in or near the city. Slava seemed totally unaffected by this news. He said, "No worry, I have a good friend here in Moscow and I know we can stay with him." So, Slava called him and he was eager to be of assistance. We arrived at a teeny, tiny apartment, after navigating through another filthy apartment building entrance. Slava's friend was probably ten years older than him, was paunchy, and smelled of vodka. The apartment had a queen-sized bed in a single small bedroom, a tiny living room with a pull-out sofa, and a miniature kitchen.

We arrived late at night, and as I was assessing the quarters, I realized that Slava and his friend were discussing sleeping arrangements. Slava announced that his friend had graciously offered to give Slava and Svetlana the bedroom and he would "let" me share the convertible sofa with him. I looked at Slava as if he were a madman, saying, "Ahhh, no, I don't think that will work for me." Slava chuckled, saying that was what he thought my reaction would be.

After further discourse with his friend, in Russian of course, Slava said to me, "Well, I guess you can sleep with Svetlana and me."

Svetlana piped in with, "Okay, but I get the middle." Thus, Slava, Svetlana, and I shared a queen-sized bed in Moscow, Russia, which gave us laughs for many years. It warms my heart still to recall the night we all shared that bed. We had so many wonderful times together, but as the years passed they sadly became fewer and fewer.

CHAPTER 63

MORE ABOUT SVETLANA

S VETLANA TRULY WAS A VERY interesting person, marching to her own drummer. Slava's 50th birthday was approaching, and she announced that for his birthday she was giving *him* a "boob job" for *her*! I thought that was hysterical. She began wearing trendier clothing, with larger portions of her bosom exposed. As her tops got lower, her skirts got higher and tighter. Her mode of dress was attention getting, but she could definitely pull it off.

Since she and Slava had purchased a health club near our office, Svetlana had become quite committed to being and looking physically fit. The staff tried to quickly engage in external phone conversations whenever she entered the office because her ongoing suggestions to them about their needs to improve their fitness made the atmosphere awkward.

During this time, she would still meet with clients occasionally at our office, to review videos of prospective children and answer questions the clients had. I continued working to minimize meetings between Svetlana and clients. Clients had begun making comments to employees about her and I worried that wouldn't be good for our reputation. But, there were other things going on about which I should have been more concerned.

A few months after the opening of Svetlana's spa, we received a disturbing report from one of our clients. The client was in the salon having her hair cut when she overheard Svetlana bragging about how she owned an adoption agency and she made $10,000 on every adoption. The client was upset. I believed what Svetlana was saying was untrue and told the client that Svetlana's English, which was poor, was the reason for her misunderstanding of the financials of Small World. I explained that Svetlana still did not understand that she and Slava did not own Small World, as it was a non-profit business. From discussions with her, I knew she had no understanding of the way the business operated, so I chalked her comment up to being misinformed. I later speculated as to which one of us was misinformed.

We had established adoption programs in several cities around Russia; St. Petersburg, Maykop, Saratov, Pyatigorsk, and Stavropol, just to name a few. There was a beautiful government official, Anna, assisting us in one of our cities. She had long, blond hair and was tall and thin. She was married and had a son. Her husband made a substantial living for the family, according to Slava. In the beginning, I think Slava and Svetlana were friendly with the couple. But then Slava told me this story. For some reason (the details were never shared with me) while Anna was visiting in the US, staying at Slava's and Svetlana's home, something occurred in the middle of the night and Svetlana kicked the woman out of their home. Slava shared with me that he and Svetlana had an argument about Anna, and Slava was in vile humor for weeks. I believe he moved out of their home for a brief period of time. It was not long after this event that our program in that city shut down and we were no longer allowed to facilitate adoptions from that city.

About a year after the incident, Slava shared with me that Anna's husband had been murdered in Russia. While returning from a business trip in Moscow, Slava said his car had been purposefully run off a cliff. I was shocked to hear this and asked Slava why Anna's husband had been the victim of such an act. Slava said that he believed Anna's husband had probably been involved in some type of organized crime. I never really thought much more about this until years later.

I was also bothered by Svetlana's belief that the children being adopted had no medical, emotional, or psychological issues. Her belief was that if problematic behaviors arose in the children, it was because of bad parenting. I knew from the adoption of my own son that adopted children can experience some pretty severe emotional and behavioral issues and I believed I was a good parent. New research was flooding academia on the effect institutionalization was having on children. We began focusing more on preparing the adopting families for the issues they might encounter. Svetlana never budged from her belief that all children's behavioral issues were the fault of the adoptive parent. Her belief became particularly challenging when parents, who were experiencing distressing behaviors with a child, wanted to speak with Svetlana, and I had to work hard to keep that from happening. Because of her belief, I knew there was always a possibility that she would accuse the parents of poor parenting and wouldn't provide the parents with the support they were desperately seeking from the doctor who had read their child's medical records in the foreign country.

Eventually, I came to understand Svetlana's lack of trust in Slava. I recall one time in the middle of the day I received a call from a local hotel that wanted to notify Slava that he left his credit card at the hotel. I guess he had used our office address and phone number when he registered. I just called him and gave him the message. I didn't ask for an explanation and one was never offered. I was just left to my own imagination about the event.

Maureen and I still laugh about the time in our office when she was conversing with Svetlana about one of the children. I could hear their exchange from my office. Svetlana was trying to explain something to Maureen, but her English was poor, and Maureen was just not able to understand what Svetlana was trying to say. Suddenly, Svetlana said in a frustrated voice, "What, you don't speak English?" Maureen is a gentle soul, but I knew this really rubbed her the wrong way, and I feared an explosion. They were both extremely frustrated. I hurried from my office to calm ruffled feathers and interpret Svetlana's meaning for Maureen. I can still hear Svetlana saying these words in her thick Russian accent, and both Maureen and I continue to be entertained by that memory.

CHAPTER 64

IGOR AND UKRAINE

S LAVA HANDLED THE RUSSIAN AND Belarus programs, and the
Ukraine program was predominantly managed by Igor. The Ukraine
program was a strong program and Slava relied upon Igor a great deal.
Slava and Svetlana developed a close friendship with Igor and his wife.
They began vacationing together and their holidays usually involved
a foreign dignitary joining them, everyone's vacation at the cost of the
agency. This expense annoyed me, but Slava continually explained that
unless he entertained the government officials from the cities in which
we worked, our programs could not be successful. I chalked up Slava's
potential misuse of Small World funds to his lack of understanding of
the differences between Russian and American ways of doing business.
He had even been able to convince the board of directors that these
trips were vital to the health and survival of Small World. I had seen
him accomplish things no other agency would have been able to do,
so I surmised that the hosting of officials was indeed beneficial to our
success. Whenever I would bring these concerns up to our accountant,
I was always told the same thing, Slava was doing nothing illegal. So,

I paid little attention to the wormy concerns wiggling around in my subconscious. I had a job I loved, and I remained true to my objective of saving children.

Igor could be amazingly funny, but also terrifically annoying with his loud voice and intimidating demeanor. One time, Igor, who spoke with broken English, came to our office and told us the story of his recent car repair debacle. He was describing how he just left the car repair shop and he had been frustrated because the shop would not put a new mouse in his car. The service technician told him the difficulty with the engine was that there was a dead mouse in the engine. Igor described how he kept trying to get the technician to just fix the dead mouse, so his car would run. The technician kept telling Igor the dead mouse didn't need to be fixed, and that the dead mouse had *been* the problem. At which point Igor got frustrated and said, "but you just said the CAR ISN'T RUNNING BECAUSE ITS MOUSE IS DEAD!" After that, the frustrated technician simply said that they weren't going to fix the dead mouse, so Igor began trying to get them to install a new mouse and not fix the dead one if it couldn't be fixed. As Igor described the back and forth exchange between himself and the technician, he was waving his arms all over the place. He had just wanted to negotiate a new mouse for his car and he hadn't understood that the technician meant the dead mouse was a dead animal. We were rolling on the floor with laughter at his story.

But as Igor's feeling of importance grew as the result of his deepening relationship with Slava, and the increased number of adoptions we were doing from Ukraine, he began getting more and more difficult with which to work. He began giving orders to me and to staff, developing a condescending attitude, and yelling at them, seemingly following Slava's example. I was the director and my job was to protect staff from bullies when I could. One day in our office, Igor was being particularly ugly, hurling obscenities, so I literally ordered him out of our office.

I told him he was no longer allowed to enter our office and all of his interactions needed to occur with Slava, not the office staff.

Slava was not happy with me, but I held my ground. I usually tried to insulate staff from Slava's tirades toward me and to keep him from delivering them to the employees. Sometimes, they simply had to take it from Slava, but I didn't feel they needed to also take abuse from Igor.

Eventually, about four months later, I relented and allowed Igor back into our office to work directly with staff. It really was a smart move for the smooth operation of the program and I think staff was happy that I relented on my edict. But, Igor had learned his lesson and he never again spoke in an aggressive fashion toward any of the employees.

Slava and Svetlana eventually had a falling out with Igor and his wife. I never knew any details and just knew that their personal friendship had ended and that Slava's and Igor's professional relationship was quite strained. Igor began coordinating Ukraine adoptions directly with me and Slava had little involvement in the Ukraine program. That was perfectly fine with us as we liked Igor very much.

CHAPTER 65

SALARIES AND LIFE INSURANCE

SOMETIME DURING THE FIRST COUPLE of years of Small World, Slava, who didn't take a salary for his efforts decided that Small World would purchase life insurance policies for him and Svetlana in lieu of a salary. Again, the accountant said this was legal and Slava ended up with two one-million-dollar policies for himself and one for Svetlana. Small World was the beneficiary for one of Slava's policies, which made total sense to me. Without him, our program would suffer dramatically, and finding someone with Slava's skills and connections to replace him could have taken months if anything were to happen to him. I wasn't convinced about the appropriateness of our paying for their personal life insurance policies, but they weren't drawing salaries and the CPA said it was legal.

However, after Slava opened the health club, the restaurant, the nightclub, and the spa, I believed from statements Slava made, and from his even shorter-tempered behavior, that money began to be tighter for him and Svetlana. He announced, around 2001, that they would each begin taking $90,000 annual salaries in addition to their fully-funded life insurance premiums. Slava was very generous toward me as well. He wanted to continually award me with higher and higher salaries. One year, when he told the bookkeeper what my salary was to be, I told the bookkeeper not to tell him, but to divide the raise he was allotting to me among the staff. Although the CPA continually, through the years, reassured me that my salary was in line with that of other non-profit agency directors, I was never comfortable and eventually refused some of Slava's grand offers. I think my problem was accepting that I had that kind of value to the company. I am sure those insecurities could be traced back to my childhood feelings of inadequacy. In retrospect, perhaps paying me so much had been a way to keep me blinded to the reality of his business decisions. I truly struggle with that possibility.

CHAPTER 66

TIME ROLLS ON – MORE TRIPS
TO EASTERN EUROPE

E VEN THOUGH THERE WERE MORE and more bumps along the way,
I loved my job and the opportunity to fulfill such a meaningful
mission. Sometimes the bumps I encountered were overseas.

In the spring of 2002, Slava, Svetlana, and I planned a trip to Russia
and Belarus to meet and video tape children. We had never gone to both
countries on the same trip.

Although those trips were always extremely exhausting and gut
wrenching, and I was consumed by the terrible smells, the deprived
conditions at the orphanages, and the threadbare clothing the children
wore, I looked forward to these trips that would assist us with finding
loving homes for the orphans.

On this trip, we first flew into Russia. As was our regular practice, we
had utilized a small charter plane to visit as many of the smaller Russian
cities as possible in the shortest amount of time. Were we to drive to
the different cities, with the vast expanse of distance to cover, we would

have needed to be in Russia for weeks. Additionally, frequently in the smaller cities there were only flights into and out of each city a couple of times a week. This made commercial air travel extremely untenable.

Since we had flown by the smaller charter plane, once we had concluded our business in Russia we flew directly on to Belarus, where we continued to visit the smaller cities. After having arrived in Belarus on our chartered flight, we traveled between cities by car because the distance there would allow it.

I had only planned to join them for the first ten days of the trip, as Slava and Svetlana had planned to remain in Minsk to do business and visit with friends. Thus, on day ten, I bid them farewell and our driver took me to the airport in Minsk. I still only understood about 50 words of Russian and there was no way I could communicate on my own. But, I had traveled enough internationally that I knew the routine, I was familiar with the airports, and I knew how to go through immigration and customs. I had never been afraid while traveling on my own but was totally unprepared for what happened that day.

When I stepped up to passport control and handed over my passport and my ticket to be cleared to leave Belarus, the official began questioning me. I didn't have a customs declaration form to submit and had been hoping this would not create an issue for me. I couldn't understand his questions and just kept responding with "Nyet Parouski," which means "No Russian." With each repetition of the questions, his voice got louder, as if were he to scream it loudly enough at me, I would magically begin to understand the Russian language. The people in the line behind me began to stir and people were whispering to one another. Oh man, was this a familiar feeling – similar to my plane experience in Zurich!

Suddenly, three guards, armed with those darn Uzis again, appeared at the side of the official. After conversing with the customs agent, one of the police officers began to yell at me as well. I had visions of disappearing into some horrific Belarusian jail and no one knowing what happened to me. They continued to get louder and I began to get frightened. Miraculously, the most beautiful, tall, South African man, with one of those lilting South African accents, appeared from the back of the line. He gently said to me, "I am fluent in Russian, please allow me to help." I thanked him, and he began conversing with the guards.

The conversation between the guard and my new friend was growing quite animated. After their lengthy discussion, he relayed to me the challenge I was facing. Apparently, I had cleared customs in Moscow, Russia, where my passport had been properly stamped, but I had no entry stamp in my passport for Belarus. They were not even questioning my lack of a customs declaration form, thank heavens. They wanted to know how I got into the country and why my passport was not legally stamped upon entry into Belarus. I explained my previous travel arrangements to my South African friend, and that I had flown on a chartered flight from Russia to Belarus. He relayed the explanation to the guards. They instructed me to move over to the side out of the line so that others behind me could continue their process.

The yelling guard, through my kind translator, told me that I had not entered the country legally and asked if I had any proof of my travel history. Fortunately, I had retained my boarding pass showing my flight from Frankfort, Germany to Moscow, Russia, and I also had the charter flight information. However, it was in my suitcase. They told me to open my suitcase. My suitcase had a combination lock and my hands were shaking so severely that it took me several tries to engage the release. I opened my suitcase and reached into a side pocket and retrieved the requested proof. I was kneeling on the floor next to my suitcase when suddenly, one of the guards shoved me aside, onto the floor, and with the end of his weapon, he began tossing my belongings out of my suitcase onto the filthy airport floor. As I was crouching on the floor next to my suitcase, with my belongings strewn around me, my entire body was shaking in total, abject terror. The three guards were standing over me, each with their weapon pointed directly at my chest. Once they had reviewed the boarding pass and charter flight documents, as well as the contents of my suitcase, to their satisfaction, they told my savior that I could leave but that I had better never enter Belarus again illegally. I quickly threw everything back into my suitcase, hugged my wonderful savior, and ran for my gate, nearly missing my flight. I couldn't remember ever having been so frightened and once in my seat and out of Belarussian airspace, at the first opportunity, I asked for a drink! I didn't even care if it had any ice!

On our next trip to Russia, we visited an orphanage in Maykop. It was a small town and, as was my experience on nearly all my travels to Eastern Europe, the people were kind and genuine. On this trip to Maykop, our facilitator wanted to show us their newly expanded market.

The market turned out to be an open-air market, in which were rows of colorful, wonderful looking, fresh vegetables, fruits, and flowers. But the smell which permeated the air was the stench of dead meat and fish. Hanging from hooks and dripping blood were rows of beef, chicken, and other meats unknown to me. Smelly fish lay on nasty looking wooden tables. I am a city girl and was thus totally repulsed by the sight and smell of the meat area of the market!

However, the worst sight, which I can still envision, was the enormous head of a steer with giant horns, sitting on blood-soaked newspaper. It was also for sale. I was so disturbed by this sight that I became a vegetarian for the next eighteen months or so. The thought of eating meat was simply too much to bear after my trip to that market.

Around this time, the three of us stopped traveling internationally together because Slava feared the agency had grown so large that it would no longer be prudent for us to travel on the same plane. Not a pleasant thought, but a wise decision nonetheless.

CHAPTER 67

INSIDE SMALL WORLD

SMALL WORLD HAD THE GOOD fortune of dedicated board members, but also had clients who were dedicated to our mission. Former clients tended to be very supportive and generous to Small World. However, we did not accept donations prior to clients completing their adoptions to avoid expectations of favoritism.

Clients professed gratitude for the services Small World provided to them and for Slava's seemingly strong connections in Russia. One time, clients who returned from a trip told me how certain processes were expedited for them. For instance, when the parents went to the Russian Immigration Office in St. Petersburg to obtain the paperwork allowing their child to exit Russia, our Small World clients were ushered past 40 or more adoptive parents, working with other agencies, who were standing in long lines awaiting their appointments. Our clients were told by our foreign country coordinator that, since Small World paperwork was always perfect, the coordinator had received permission to "step to the front of the line." Clients reported being questioned about their paperwork very rarely. At the time, I was proud that we were preparing our clients and the paperwork so effectively, and that Slava was so well connected that we could simplify the process for clients once they got to Russia. Years later, I came to question this "privilege" enjoyed by Small World clients and exactly what the origin of the special treatment was.

After I was no longer with Small World, another client shared a story that would have greatly disturbed me had I known about it at the time. My former client told me that prior to going to the court hearing in Russia, at which they were awarded custody of their little boy, he and his wife were given a list of questions, by our Small World foreign employee, which the judge was going to ask them, along with the expected answers and they were told to memorize them for court. The adoptive mother shared with me that she had been exceedingly nervous at being asked to do this. It hadn't felt honest to her and she was terrified she would give an incorrect answer. Remembering myself how disconcerting it was to be in a foreign county, totally dependent on the few people around that spoke English, I can only imagine how terrifying this kind of situation was for Small World clients.

After walking away from Small World, I was unsurprised to hear this, but at the time I was running Small World, this would have created enormous discord in Slava's and my relationship because I would have demanded to know what was going on. Such a thing is unheard of in the US. In retrospect, I believe someone at the court house, perhaps even the judge him or herself, was most likely being paid a fee for which Small World clients were furnished the answers the judge was seeking at the adoption hearing. I think it is quite possible that the adoption hearings for Small World clients were totally orchestrated in an effort to eliminate glitches for adopting parents and to speed up the process.

I hope I would have found the information very disturbing. But, I also know that sometimes confrontations with Slava were too psychologically difficult or damaging for me and I might have just shelved that uncomfortable information rather than confront it. I believe his charisma and his bullying may have blinded me to some of the warning signs that could have alerted me to unusual things going on.

CHAPTER 68

UNUSUAL DEATHS

I NEVER RECEIVED MANY DETAILS surrounding the death of the nanny, it was just one more unusual event in our lives. Slava called one morning, agitated. He explained that early that morning, his daughter had found her nanny floating face down in their swimming pool. I didn't remember her being ill and she certainly wasn't very old. Slava said the ambulance had already taken her away, but he was sure she had drunk too much and decided to go swimming after everyone was asleep. The explanation made sense to me. After all, I had witnessed amazing amounts of alcohol consumption by many Russians, both overseas and in the US.

However, I was concerned for Slava's daughter and the trauma she experienced by this gruesome discovery. As with the handyman who had committed suicide, Slava never elaborated on any details. Before this, I had gone swimming at Slava's pool with some regularity. After this, I never swam in his pool again.

Around this time, we learned that our coordinator in Maykop had lost her husband. I had met Marina and her husband many times and I thought both were wonderful. Our clients loved Marina and she worked diligently for us. Sometimes, her husband assisted her with work for our clients. When I pressed Slava for details of the death of Marina's husband, he told me her husband had been found floating in the river with a gunshot wound to his head. Slava then told me he thought that perhaps Marina's husband had been involved in "illegal activity" and this is "just what happens" in Russia. It was the first time I had ever personally known anyone who had been murdered, having never met Anna's husband, who had been forced over a cliff a few years prior.

Several years later, Slava called me up and shared that another person had drowned in his pool. I don't even think I ever met the person. I knew the first one had been the nanny and I had even met her several times, but I had no idea of this person's connection to Slava's family. The second person was reportedly a visitor from Russia. I couldn't imagine anyone ever getting in Slava's pool again after two people drowned in it! As normal, Slava was disinclined to have any conversation about the details of the tragedy, other than to say she had gone swimming alone in the middle of the night.

The similarity in the events was completely missed by me. When thinking about the two murders later, I thought, *what a coincidence that had been - that the husbands of two of our foreign coordinators had been murdered.* It wasn't until several years later, during questioning by an investigator, when I had to admit that I had given very little thought to any of the deaths of Small World affiliated people, especially because they were so tangentially associated with the organization.

Around the time of the second drowning in the pool, Slava came into the office one day and told me that Olga, his former daughter-in-law, and Alex's former nanny, had been found dead in a New York hotel. He said it was apparently the result of a drug overdose. I had not been aware that Slava's son and Olga had divorced and was shocked to learn that Olga had moved to NYC alone. She had seemed so sweet and innocent. My family was very saddened by the news, we had truly cared for Olga.

CHAPTER 69

OUR GENEROUS SLAVA

Miles

As we added staff and were acquiring an increasing number of files to maintain, it was time to move to yet another larger office. There was recently vacated space on the third floor of our office building, so we moved our office to that area of our building. Our wonderful clients who had built out our first office stepped in to complete the second one for us.

The same family, who assisted with the construction of our offices, was instrumental in beginning the "Links of Hope" golf tournaments. This became a cousin to our signature "Hearts of Hope" dinner auctions. The golf tournaments alternated years with our dinner auctions. Through these events, Small World raised funds for the many humanitarian projects it sponsored. The support and generosity from clients, as well as from strangers, was always impressive and heart-warming.

One golf tournament particularly stands out in my mind. The tournament planning committee, of which Laura was a part, decided that they would purchase a golden retriever puppy to auction off at the event. Laura, a college student, was still working part-time in the office. Usually there were about ten exceptional items in the live auction and, recently in the St. Louis area, auctioning off puppies had become quite a popular method for bringing in large returns on an investment.

The golf tournament was always held on a Monday. On the Saturday before the event, Laura and Alex drove a couple of hours away to a breeder of golden retrievers and purchased an 8-week-old beautiful white puppy. By the time they arrived home, they were both in love with him. From the minute they came in the door, I told them, "We are not keeping that dog, we already have one full grown golden retriever!" They kept saying, "We know, but isn't he so cute!" Alex told me he decided the puppy should be called "Miles" because they had gone so many miles to get him. I maintained my position, we were not keeping him!

On the day of the event, it was Laura's job to walk around with the puppy and get people to fall in love with and bid on him. She carried that puppy around and cuddled him all afternoon. After dinner, the live auction began. When we got to the puppy and people began bidding on the dog, Laura, who was standing by Slava, got teary. Slava suddenly began bidding on the dog. That seemed to make Laura happy because Slava and Svetlana already had a couple of dogs and Laura knew the puppy would be well loved. Finally, after an exciting bidding war, Slava won with a bid of $5,000! Laura went to hand him the dog and Slava took the microphone and said that he actually bought the puppy for Laura, handing the puppy right back!

I had been sitting down and jumped out of my chair, yelling across the room, "Slava, did you forget she lives at college?" Everyone in the room burst into laughter, realizing what had just happened to me. So, that night I took home an eight-week-old golden retriever named Miles, that I hadn't wanted, but turned out to be the most fabulous and loving dog of which anyone could have dreamed. Laura, who already adored Slava because he had been such a support to us when she was sick, was now totally and forever more committed to him. Alex was actually thrilled that Laura lived at school and considered Miles his personal puppy.

Miles grew to be a 112-pound, beautiful, white haired, golden retriever, who never actually learned to retrieve. He was as timid as a mouse and only wanted to be a lap dog, making him even more endearing. Up until the day I left Small World, I often took Miles to the office. He was the official Small World dog and the staff, clients, and especially the children loved to see him and cuddle with him.

Cabo San Lucas

Slava and Laura continued to enjoy a very special relationship, seemingly to equally adore one another. They teased each other, and he was as much like an uncle to her, as he was like a brother to me. At a "Hearts of Hope" dinner auction the year before, Slava had purchased a week at a beautiful home in a gated community in Cabo San Lucas, Mexico. He won the home with a bid of $10,000 for the week, but never used it. Laura kept giving him grief about not using it and one day he said, "Laura, Svetlana and I are never going to use it, you take your family and you go." We didn't have to be asked twice.

My son, Ryan, and his girlfriend, Rachel, Alex, Laura, my best friend, Cathy, her daughter, Natasha, and I had the most fabulous week imaginable. When we arrived, the courtyard had a tremendous stone fountain right in the center of an amazing blue and green tiled courtyard, and was bordered by impressive, brightly colored plants and flowers. We had arrived at a mansion worthy of the queen.

The house had not had the hurricane shutters removed and Ryan had to figure out how to "break in" before we could begin our vacation. The house itself was a massive two-story villa with five bedrooms and at least as many bathrooms. The enormous spiral staircase had no fewer than twenty steps as it wound its way from the lower level to the upstairs. As soon as we walked in, everyone clamored to select a bedroom, with each one being more spectacular that the last. The furnishings and Persian rugs were exquisite. The mansion sat high on a hill, in a gated community, with a stunning view of the Pacific Ocean on one side and the Sea of Cortez on the other. It was spectacular.

From the lower level, we walked out to a gorgeous deck with a hot tub and a pool, from which the water ran over the edge and into another pool below. The rock work and plants throughout the pool area were beautiful. There was an explosion of huge tropical flowers of red and pink everywhere I looked. None of us could believe our good fortune.

Rachel made us fabulous authentic Mexican meals, we went snorkeling in the ocean and swimming in the pool, visited the local street vendors, and had the time of our lives.

Unfortunately, I learned several years later that Slava had never paid Small World for the vacation week. That knowledge tarnished my memory of that magical week.

Slava really could be generous and kind-hearted. We had built an incredible relationship. We would find ourselves discussing the economy, politics, or the latest movies. There wasn't a topic that he and I couldn't discuss and more often than not our points of view were in agreement. But I was always intimidated by him, leery of his quick temper, and never fully relaxed around him. My childhood experiences had prepared me to be proficient at handling volatile personalities like his. In many ways, he reminded me of my father.

CHAPTER 70

THE PLAYGROUND THAT
TOUCHED MY HEART

The "Bricks of Hope" projects were a welcome break from the intensity of the office world. In 2003, on one of the trips, our group of volunteers was able to participate in the most moving and memorable project of all. Over the years, we constructed many playgrounds at many orphanage sites in many towns. But none impacted us as much as our poignant project in a small village somewhere in the southwestern area of Russia.

The trip to the small hamlet took us over bumpy and unpaved roads. We felt as if we were driving to the end of civilization. It was a depressing and desolate feeling area, no beautiful Russian forests, mostly flat terrain with large patches of brown earth, consisting of either dirt or dying grass. As the village came into view, we spied a melancholy looking place. Many of the cottages had thatched roofs and seemed only to be still standing by the sheer will of the crooked walls. There were no brightly painted buildings; everything was either gray or bleached-out brown in color. No structure was more than one story high. The village had no paved roads and initially appeared to be deserted. I didn't believe any Americans had ever been to this place before.

I was puzzled as to why the Russian government had requested that we build a playground here, surprised that the community was large enough to support an orphanage. To our amazement, almost in the center of the town was the decrepit, diminutive orphanage building. Housing only about forty young orphans, it was run by the most sanguine group of loving caretakers. Their positive spirit moved me nearly to tears, exuding an air of energy and excitement that didn't totally make sense to me.

As was our practice, we immediately went to work, knowing we were on a tight time frame.

Throughout the day, villagers would saunter by, some stopping to lean against the orphanage walls and watch us work. Small children would peak at us from behind the legs of their parents. Some of the older children brought balls to kick around in the street next to the orphanage. It was clear to me that we were making quite a spectacle and our visit was a highlight in the lives of these townspeople. We had power tools unlike any they had likely seen before and groups of men would watch and excitedly talk among themselves. The orphans and the caretakers would observe us from behind thinly veiled windows. What had originally looked like a deserted town was bustling with townsfolk by mid-afternoon.

Earlier in the day, I heard a tinkling sound coming from up the road. I watched and listened and an enormous brown cow with a rusty, old cow bell came ambling around the corner as if she owned the road. No one was tending to her, and after passing by she turned the next corner, seeming to know exactly where she was going. It was a most charming place.

Near lunch time, we were invited into the orphanage. This impoverished town had laid out the most beautiful table; delicate china, cloth napkins, and mounds of inviting looking and smelling food they had lovingly prepared for our team. The orphanage director and the caretakers sincerely wanted us to enjoy our lunch, and we did. After profusely thanking them, we returned to our duties and continued to work into the evening.

The next day, we arrived in the morning to find even more observers around the perimeter of our work area. Near noon, we had tightened the last bolt and tested all of the equipment. Our brightly colored, red, blue, and yellow play structures were complete and were truly a beacon of dazzling color in their otherwise drab world. A few of the orphans came out of the building, and as I looked up a side street I saw a dozen children running toward us, laughing and yelling to one another. From another direction, another group of children were running as if to catch the last bus. The children of the town joined the children of the orphanage and stared wondrously at the playground. I motioned for the children to try out the structure, helping a small child up onto a slide.

Tears began to leak from my eyes as I finally understood. This playground was for the whole village, not just the orphanage, and I realized what a tremendous gift we had given to this kind and generous group of people. But an even greater gift had been given to us. We had been able to truly change the life for this small town, and I felt such gratitude for getting to play even a small part in this wondrous adventure. With the help of our translator, the orphanage director explained in halting English that the town had been anticipating our arrival for months. She shared that there were no other play structures in the town, no place for the children to gather and have fun. In fact, most of the people had never seen anything like the colorful playground we had constructed. The mothers and fathers began to shake our hands and shyly whisper "spaseeba," the Russian word for thank you. I whispered back, "pashalsta" (pronounced pa-zhal-sta), the Russian word for you're welcome.

I looked around, working hard not to weep, and for the first time noticed that this orphanage, unlike many of the others to which we had been, was not surrounded by a fence. This building was not isolated but had been included in the community. These orphans were not outcasts but played side by side with the children of the town, something I had never witnessed before. In some cities in which we had worked, the orphans had not even been allowed to attend the local schools. The acceptance and love I witnessed in this small community made me hopeful for the future of these people. The name "Bricks of Hope" was such an appropriate name, especially for this project, as I believed it brought hope and happiness to a very depressed area of the world.

CHAPTER 71

SHAKEDOWN #3

MANY TIMES, THE "BRICKS OF HOPE" trips were something to "write home about." I had led these trips before with board member, Phil, and we had done it so many times that we had become master playground builders. Phil, our Captain, had the plans, would organize the group, and assign tasks. I usually had many thousands of dollars in cash with me, hidden in different places, enabling me to pay the in-country expenses.

On one of the trips to Russia, one of our volunteers became ill on the flight. I can't recall what his ailment was, but think it was dehydration or something along those lines. It was not a life-threatening illness. Upon landing, he was helped off the plane by St. Petersburg medical personnel and taken to an infirmary on the grounds of the airport. He was given vodka as the remedy for his illness!

In the spring of 2004, on our final trip to Belarus, we had about fifteen volunteers with us, including Laura. When we arrived in Belarus, the first thing we did upon landing was to go through customs. On this trip, our group was asked, at gunpoint, to step over to the side. One of four guards asked us in broken English, "Who is your leader?"

I immediately knew something was terribly wrong and was alarmed. I had only had trouble leaving foreign countries before, never entering them! I looked over at Laura, who tried to grab my arm as I stepped forward and said, "I am." They walked over, surrounded me, and told me to come with them. I was taken down a dingy corridor to an empty, small, gray room, with the plaster crumbling off the walls, somewhere in the bowels of the airport and told to sit down on an old, cold, rickety, metal folding chair. As I sat in that tiny cell-like room, I concentrated on holding my rising panic at bay and trying to figure out what these guards could possibly want from me, I kept my hands clasped together to keep them from shaking.

I sat alone in the room for several minutes before an obviously higher-ranking guard came into the room. He sat across from me and said, "Why are you here?" His English was surprisingly understandable. I explained why our group was in Belarus and showed him some pictures of a completed playground we had previously constructed, which I carried with me to show the orphanage directors upon our arrival.

He did not seem particularly interested in our endeavor. He was intensely interested in how I was going to pay for everything for this many people while in Belarus. He demanded to see my money. I was frantically trying to remember where each stash was hidden and the amounts of each. I did not want to show him all of my money. I showed him our agency credit card and about $10,000 in cash. He then left the room. I sat for a while longer by myself as my panic continued to rise. I had traveled so many times to Eastern Europe and had guns waved in my face several times, I had been followed, and I had even been to the black market. But by far, this was the most frightened I ever was during my tenure as the Director of Small World, more frightened than I had been on that floor in the Belarusan airport. I was terrified thinking about Laura and the group and what was possibly being done to them. I knew I was totally at the mercy of these soldiers, trying hard to figure out what they wanted from us. If they demanded all our money, I knew that would be okay. I would call Slava and he would arrange to have more wired to us from a bank or EEAG, or someplace else in Belarus. I just didn't want anyone to get hurt.

After several minutes, another guard in a full-dress military uniform returned. He told me to get up and follow him, which I quickly did. He led me down a different, dimly lit corridor to another small, dreary office in which sat a stern-looking lady behind a small, metal desk. She ordered me to sit down. She told me that none of my group would be allowed into Belarus without my purchasing health insurance for everyone. I was overwhelmed by a myriad of emotions. I wanted to argue and refuse, and I wanted to laugh all at the same time. I wanted to cry with relief that this was a problem I could easily fix. I said to the lady behind the desk, "We all have health insurance in the United States and we will be reimbursed for medical expenses we might incur in Belarus, so this isn't really necessary."

She just stared coldly me at and told me rather emphatically, "That doesn't matter! You are required to have insurance issued by our government." All the while, the military guard was standing by her side, staring at me. Suddenly, I really needed to laugh, silly woman that I was. Hadn't I been coming to this part of the world long enough to know a shakedown when I saw it? Hadn't we been forced at gun point to give the police in Russia money for having too many people in a car? Hadn't I had to pay a "storage fee" to the Belarus government to obtain my luggage which had been lost by their luggage handlers? When would I learn?

I sweetly said, "I understand, and what will the cost be per person?" She barked, "$25 – per person!" I retrieved my previously revealed stash of cash and withdrew the exact amount she requested and handed it over to her.

Knowing that no such thing existed, I just couldn't help myself, and asked if we would be issued documentation to give to a medical provider should one of us be in need of medical care? She looked at me in a sideways kind of manner and said it wasn't necessary because all of the medical providers in Belarus would know that we, as foreigners, had purchased insurance when we entered the country. In that moment as we looked at one another, she knew that I knew exactly what had just happened. She flashed an extremely fake smile, waved me away, and told me to have a nice time in Belarus. I had just gone through yet another "shakedown!"

My team had been moved through customs and they were waiting on the other side of the gate. I came through the gate and everyone rushed up and hugged me, Laura telling me how scared she had been for me. I felt badly, and a little angry, that everyone had been forced to be so frightened for such a stupid thing. Laura later told me that the group became even more frightened after our translator, Victor, met them after they had cleared customs. When they described how I had been taken away, Victor's statement to the group was, "Oh, this is not good." But despite our initial shakedown, we enjoyed another very successful "Bricks of Hope" building experience.

CHAPTER 72

THE END OF THE
BELARUS PROGRAM

Sadly, and tragically for the thousands of orphans who would never have loving homes, Belarus closed its doors to adoptions by foreigners. President Lukashenko initially only placed a limit on the number of orphans being allowed to visit other countries during the summer months, somewhat like exchange students. Many of the former communist countries had programs whereby orphans were allowed to spend summers with families who promised to get medical and dental care for the children during the visits. The visits were called "recuperation holidays." However, in 2004, the president announced that the children would no longer be allowed to visit other countries because of the "consumerist" values they were bringing back to Belarus. The President had taken on a very anti-west stance and in short order he also placed a "hold" on international adoption, claiming that Belarus could take care of its own children. However, we had heard this kind of messaging from President Lukashenko in the past, and eventually

289

international adoption had resumed.

In all our countries there had been closures, usually for short times, with the programs always reopening within a few months. As with other closures, we were told Belarus would allow adoptions to resume. We had a dozen or so families who had selected children and were expecting to travel to adopt their children. But Slava told me he had a different feeling about it that time. He was not nearly as hopeful as I had seen him in the past.

I tried to be as honest as I could with our clients about the situation. I told the waiting families that I wasn't sure how long the country would be closed. Belarusian law had changed a year or so before and had begun requiring adopting families to make two trips to Belarus. During the first trip, the prospective parents met their prospective child and submitted paperwork. Then, approximately four to eight weeks later, the families were invited to return for a finalization hearing. At the time the closure was announced, a few of the families had already made that first trip to Belarus and had already met their intended child.

Waiting families would call our office and they would alternate between sobbing and screaming at us. I understood. I had seen Alex on video, during the time we were waiting to adopt him, and I understood "video bonding." I couldn't imagine being forced to give up on Alex, especially after holding him in my arms. Slava and I worked hard, wrote letters, paid lawyers, and Slava even went to Belarus. But in the end, there was nothing that could be done to hold the adoption doors open in that country. President Lukashenko had made his final decision. I believe he felt that it made his country look weak by allowing its orphans to be placed with families in other countries.

I had loved the Belarusian people, the culture, and the country. I was sad beyond measure. But my heart was truly broken for the orphans who would most likely live out their childhood years in a desolate orphanage, only to be turned out to the streets as teens. I had tremendous pity for our families who had to accept that they would never bring home the children they believed would be theirs. Many of the families were able to make the transition and were able to select children in either Russia or Ukraine. However, there was a handful who wanted to wait longer. I believe that group of families waited nearly another year before giving up and moving on. I spoke with one of the families several years later who said they kept the picture of their "lost Belarus child" because for a time he had been a member of their family. What an enormous heartache for the families.

CHAPTER 73

LAURA – A NEW BOOKKEEPER

IN EARLY 2005, OUR BOARD president had a lot of questions about the financials, the way they were presented, and some inconsistencies in them. Over a period of several months, the board president tried to work with Dave, the bookkeeper, but was consistently disappointed with the quality of work and the number of errors in the reporting.

By then, Laura was a second-semester junior in college, seeking a degree in accounting, and she had volunteered to serve on the finance committee, setting up the accounting processes and procedures for the upcoming Small World dinner auction. The board president served as the chairperson for the third or fourth time for our "Hearts of Hope" Dinner auction. Laura had worked with him on the previous one but was substantially more involved in the current one. The board president was impressed with Laura and would frequently tell me how bright and capable she was. Therefore, it came as no surprise when the board decided that, when the current bookkeeper needed to be dismissed because of numerous reporting errors, he wanted Laura to fill in during the interim while they searched for a new accountant.

The accounting firm, which provided us with our audit and with whom Small World had been involved since its inception, stepped in to train Laura on the specifics of the agency. They were likewise amazed at how quickly she grasped the full scope of the accounting practices for Small World. Within a month, she had the financials cleaned up and provided accurate reports to the board. The accounting firm, who had been assisting in the search for a new bookkeeper, recommended to the board that they retain Laura.

Laura had literally grown up in the company and had an in-depth knowledge about the way the organization ran. She was excited for the opportunity to learn new aspects about Small World. The board discussed potential conflict of interest, since my daughter would now be the new accountant. However, the CPA firm worked with the board to put many checks and balances in place, and her work was monitored by the accounting firm on an ongoing basis. Plus, Laura reported to Slava rather than me, as had been the case with all previous bookkeepers.

So, Laura came to work for the agency in a bookkeeper capacity, and for the first time I was allowed a true view into the finances. I finally got a chance to understand how all the funds were routed, what the expenses were, and the exact level of income for Small World. Laura insisted I learn everything about the finances of the company. This was the start of my mild concern about some of the financial decisions Slava had been and was still making. Laura confirmed with me that Slava's expenses on his trips to Russia, and when he vacationed, were primarily being paid by Small World. I knew that frequently on their way to Russia, Slava and Svetlana would stop off in Paris or St. Marten for several days to vacation. The company should have been responsible for expenses to Russia, but not for their vacations. When I asked our CPA about this, she said that Slava had the authority to do this as it was part of his job. Invariably, Slava would tell us he was "hosting a foreign official" on these trips. I wanted to argue that, for instance, when Slava spent two days in Paris on his way to Russia that the trip to Paris was not part of his job.

But clearly our CPA was on Slava's side and I knew it was pointless. But seeds of concern were planted for both Laura and me.

Shortly after taking over the bookkeeping position, Laura graduated early from college and began graduate school seeking an MBA, and started her own accounting business. The position at Small World was a part-time commitment. Laura was determined to get her MBA and eventually have her own company.

CHAPTER 74

OUTBURSTS

Although Slava had always been volatile, I had been able to handle him. After all, I had grown up in a home never knowing what behavior my father or mother would exhibit from one minute to the next. I was a good compartmentalizer. I had a compartment in my head for good Slava and one for abusive Slava. Usually I was able to ignore the cruel Slava compartment unless it was necessary to access it for storage of information. That need to access this compartment became more frequent as time passed.

I recall one day when I heard the receptionist greet Slava, but I did not hear him respond. I was busily working while seated at my desk. As he entered my office and I looked up, the expression on his face informed me of his furor. He burst through the doorway, holding his motorcycle helmet in one hand, and took a few steps across my office. He suddenly stopped and hurled his helmet at me. He was at least a dozen feet away from me, so I had time to duck as the helmet slammed into the wall next to my desk. I was a mixture of emotions, embarrassment, anger, and fear. My staff was hearing the whole thing. I didn't say a word. The rest of the office staff was suddenly silent as Slava began to scream at me. I don't recall what it was that he was so angry about, but he introduced a new emotion (for me) into our relationship—fear of him.

He was becoming less reasonable regarding our clients. If a client changed his/her mind about adopting a specific child, he would scream at me and tell me they had to adopt that child and I needed to make them. He began to put crazy demands on our clients, again demanding that they hand carried large sums of cash to the foreign countries, which I refused to ask them to do. Unless absolutely necessary, the clients were never informed of his crazy demands.

His answer to any problem was to fire someone. If a document had gone to Russia with an error, he would demand to know who had done it and insist they be terminated. I often found myself defending myself or staff to him. The work we did was mentally and emotionally challenging and people are human, so occasionally mistakes were made. But anything less than perfection would send him into a tirade. I never followed through with his demands to fire people and he always forgot about the directive, usually never bringing the event up again. Life was often just about riding out the storm with Slava.

Slava had never been happy when I took vacation, and during the fifteen years we worked together, I only took four vacations. He would be so angry at me, making it miserable for me to be away. He refused to allow anyone else in the office to take on any of my tasks when I was gone, and it was always a nightmare to return to the mountain of work awaiting me. He would continuously call me while on vacation, as if I was sitting at my desk.

Our relationship was becoming more and more complicated. He seemed to be two different people and I had been forced to become even more adept at reading him.

Perhaps Slava's foul temper could have been chalked up to issues with his heart. One of our clients who was a heart surgeon had told Slava about a new test which was easy, although expensive, that could evaluate the condition of the arteries of the heart. Slava thought this was an amazing new test and he had to have it. It turned out that the test saved his life. He had the test and the next day entered the hospital to have by-pass surgery. I believe three of his arteries were 90% blocked. Slava had a penchant for Kentucky Fried Chicken, which was next door to the surgery center where he practiced. We knew that KFC had been his downfall. The doctor told him he had to stop eating lunch at KFC every day, but I don't think he ever really did.

As Small World had grown, Slava and Svetlana's interactions with clients became fewer and fewer. But, Svetlana did continue to interact with clients who had concerns about available children after viewing them on video tape. She occasionally came to meetings, after leaving the health club, in tight yoga pants and low-cut tank tops. I finally garnered the courage to ask Slava to speak with her and ask her to dress a little more conservatively when coming to the Small World office. From his description of the conversation, she became furious at him, after which time he became furious with me, and it was an unpleasant scene. But the end result was that she reduced her visits to our office, and when she did come she looked more professional. One of the brainstorms I had to alleviate our angst about Svetlana's choice of attire for Small World functions was to purchase matching, high quality, embroidered shirts for everyone to wear. She wasn't thrilled with the shirts, but at Slava's insistence, she did go along with the group. They looked very professional and she looked lovely in hers.

Slava's outbursts weren't the only taxing behaviors with which I was dealing. At home, Alex was stretching our emotional reserves to their max. It seemed like I would sometimes spend my days taming Slava and my evenings taming Alex. Alex developed a very adversarial relationship with both Allen and me. We were simply not equipped to handle Alex's raging outbursts, his aggression, uncontrollable behavior, and were frustrated by Alex's challenge with authority figures. Alex couldn't abide being told what to do; it was a recipe for disaster.

Both Ryan and Laura were no longer living at home by this time, so the three of us were left to be angry and frustrated with one another. Allen's consulting business continued to struggle, which had become a consistent point of conflict between us, and our marriage was under unbelievable strain. Unfortunately, instead of pulling together to fight the external battles, we began to withdraw from one another. Allen is a good and kind man, but we just couldn't find our way together. The chasm that had developed in our relationships was too broad. We separated, Alex staying with me. I had hoped that by removing the negative force field that had developed between Alex, Allen, and I, Alex would be better able to cope with life, having that stressor removed. Unfortunately, I still couldn't find the right supports for Alex and he continued to struggle at school, with friends, and with his own family.

It wasn't long after the motorcycle helmet hurling incident when I woke up one morning and discovered I had totally lost my sense of taste. I underwent every possible medical test to learn why this had happened to me. Ultimately, my doctor determined that it was simply the result of the intense stress under which I operated. Although my taste returned somewhat over the years, it never returned to normal, and many foods remain tasteless to me.

CHAPTER 75

PEOPLE DON'T COME ANY BETTER THAN THIS

In spite of issues with Slava, I was incredibly blessed to encounter, get to know, and become close friends with some of the most wonderful people in the world. People who were exceedingly generous with their time working on fundraisers, making huge donations at those fundraisers, paying their own ways to travel multiple times to build playgrounds, and those who agreed to guide our agency by serving on the board of directors.

Some of the stories about the clients are not only gut wrenching but awe inspiring as well. The wife of one young couple who had chosen to adopt with us had a medical condition of polyps that sporadically and uncontrollably grew near her vocal cords. Over the years, she had had many surgeries, which had caused a great deal of damage to her body. She had a feeding tube, a tracheotomy allowing her to breathe more freely, and could only speak by holding her finger over the small hole in her neck. Both she and her husband were amazing. They completed their first adoption of a baby boy without a hitch and returned about two years later to adopt a little girl.

At the time they completed their second adoption, Russia required adoptive parents to travel to meet their child, submit paperwork, and then return a few weeks later to complete the court process, as had been required in Belarus. This couple had made their first trip; they were preparing, within a few days, to take their second trip. The mom regularly had a surgical procedure to essentially "clean up" the area in her throat, thereby increasing her ability to breathe more easily and speak for a while, and she planned the procedure just prior to their second trip. She wanted to be able to speak as clearly as she could when she went to court. During the routine surgery, the doctor nicked an artery and her lungs filled with blood too quickly for her to be saved.

Her husband was devastated, as was everyone who knew her. She was such a kind and gentle soul and she loved her son more than life itself. I will never forget meeting with her husband, even before her funeral, and listening to him sob and beg us to help him return to Russia to adopt his daughter. However, this would be a tall order, because at that time single people were not allowed to adopt from Russia, and adoptions by single men had never been an option. He was now a single parent and he knew that he faced the potential of not being allowed to bring home the little girl he and his wife had already met, and with whom they had fallen in love. I can still hear him telling me how badly his wife would want him to move forward to adopt this little girl. I promised to do everything I could to help him and run interference for him in Russia. However, Marcia squarely objected to allowing this to happen. She felt the adoptive father was in too much pain to make rational decisions and she was concerned because this action was against basic social work ethics. That time, I just could not make myself listen to her.

I wrote a very heartfelt letter to the judge, I had our client write a similar letter, and Slava called many people in Russia who he thought might be able to help this young father. I remember breaking into tears on the day Slava called me to tell me that our young father would be able to travel back to Russia to get his little girl. He completed his adoption as a single father and I stayed in touch with him for a while, long enough to know that he was an excellent father and loved his children enough for both him and their mother. She would have been proud of him.

Another couple whose story is embedded in my memory involved a prospective mother who had cystic fibrosis. She was in her late thirties and had undergone a double lung transplant. Biological children were not in the cards for her. She and her husband adopted a little girl. It was not easy getting the foreign country to sanction an adoption for this couple. Her health issues would normally have been a disqualifier for the family. But again, after impassioned pleas in letters and Slava's utilization of his connections, we were able to help them. I remember her thanking me after their return from Russia with huge tears rolling down her cheeks, saying she was the happiest and most fulfilled person in the world. The adoptive mom described her daughter as a dream come true. Sadly, within a year or two, the mother passed away. But I remember feeling blessed to have gotten to play a role in her miracle adoption and to witness the love the family had for one another.

CHAPTER 76

A FEW BAD APPLES

OVER THE YEARS, I ALSO experienced a couple of people who were the exact opposite of the angels described above. Two families particularly stand out in my mind, though I am pleased to say there were few families like this. One family traveled to Belarus to adopt a little girl during the time only a single trip was required. They had selected a little four-year-old girl and traveled to finalize the adoption. They went to court, the adoption was finalized, and they returned to their apartment to await the issuance of the court decree allowing them to exit the country within a few days. Shortly after the court hearing and after taking their little girl out of the orphanage, the family contacted our foreign country coordinator and demanded that their child be returned to the orphanage.

The staff called Slava, who was furious with me. As was more frequently the case, everything was my fault. I immediately contacted the adoptive mother in Belarus. She said that ever since they picked up "the child" (her words) from the orphanage, she had been alternating between running around the apartment and then crying and she would not listen to them. As was our practice, before we sent Americans to any of our foreign countries, we tried to help them understand that the children, especially older children, could be difficult to manage. They are terrified, they have been removed from their home, the orphanage, where they knew the people, were familiar with the smell, and above all, they understood the language. I kept trying to explain to the adoptive mother that their little girl didn't respond because she didn't understand what they were saying, and I offered to have their translator remain with them through the night.

They were not interested in any assistance. The adoptive mother told me she was a "counselor" and she recognized "attention deficit disorder" when she saw it and that she and her husband were not prepared to parent a child with this type of disorder. However, the mother never allowed me to speak with the father and I felt that perhaps the issue was hers, not her husband's.

I called Slava back to report that I could not get the family to reconsider and they were not going to bring their daughter home with them. He explained to me that he had made some calls and was told that the laws in Belarus differed a bit from those in Russia and the family would be legally allowed to immediately sign abandonment papers and leave the country without their little girl. So, this poor little girl was returned to the orphanage. She was old enough to know what had happened to her – that she was being rejected by a family for the second time in her life. I couldn't imagine what that scene must have looked like. I had wondered if the adoptive parents had hugged her goodbye, what explanation had been given to her, and what her reaction had been. But Slava thought my questions were foolish and would not ask the coordinator for details. The family signed the legal relinquishment documents, but the little girl was not able to be adopted by anyone else for another eight months while the first adoption was legally reversed through the normal court process.

The family later filed a lawsuit against us and wanted their fees returned to them because they did not get a child. They did have a finalized adoption and the fees they paid were fully expended for that adoption. They just chose to leave their daughter in a foreign country. We provided the documentation of the adoption and the signed abandonment papers to the American courts and the incident went no further legally. But I was angered by what had been done to this innocent little girl.

Fortunately, we found another family for this little girl and she was ultimately adopted into a loving home eight months later. I kept in contact with the new family who at our request provided us with documentation from their pediatrician that this little girl was perfectly healthy and had no physical or psychological diagnoses. The family also wrote a letter saying that their daughter was frightened the first day they met her, and she did indeed "run around" that first couple of days. But, as they adjusted to one another, she learned to speak English, and the little girl felt secure, she never again exhibited similar behavior. I was grateful that the original family did not get a chance to parent that little girl.

Another story, which I believe to be a sad commentary on humanity, involves a single mother who traveled to Ukraine to adopt two children. She had selected two children from videotape, and during her trip across the ocean one of the children was removed from the orphanage by a family member. This was perfectly legal and prospective adoptive parents are warned that this could happen to them. When the client got to the foreign country and learned that one of the children she had selected was not available, she, unbeknownst to us, contacted her bank and stopped payment of her final check to the agency.

However, the first day she was in Ukraine, she was taken to the same orphanage and allowed to select a second infant and return to the US with two infant children within the expected, normal timeframe. A week after she finalized her adoption overseas, we learned she had stopped payment on her check. When I contacted her, she said she would not pay the remaining sum because she did not get the two children she had originally selected. Yet in accordance to her contract, she had adopted two children.

We were forced to hire an attorney, pointed out the sections of the contract that cover potential incidents such as what happened to her, and she eventually did end up paying the fees she owed to Small World.

It was depressing that a person could behave in such a dishonest and self-serving fashion. The adoptive mother had not been one of our clients who had to borrow money to facilitate the adoption. She had been a very successful business owner. We did everything we could to help her have the family of her dreams and yet that was the way she behaved. I hoped that she loved the children and gave them a good life.

Thankfully, most of our adopting parents were understanding, loving, and supportive people who only wanted to give their children fabulous lives.

CHAPTER 77

OUR LAST NEW OFFICE

I N LATE 2006, IT SEEMED as if everything in Slava's world began collapsing at the same time. Small World had been a strong fabric, painstakingly woven together over years, which began unraveling five or six stitches at a time. The crumbling seemed unstoppable. Enigma had been void of activity for months and the restaurant and spa were failing. Slava was not a good business manager. He was a brilliant doctor and he had enormous dreams, but he didn't have the temperament to personally manage a business. He didn't want the expense of hiring an experienced and qualified restaurant manager and relied either upon himself or other Russian acquaintances, who were likewise not experienced in managing a restaurant.

Slava not only made a series of poor business decisions, but he also earned a negative reputation in the community and people were making comments online about their experiences. If someone had a complaint about a meal, instead of trying to appease the customer, Slava would generally become defensive and invite the person to never return to his restaurant. Word was spreading. As business fell off, Slava began to cut corners and I witnessed a definite decline in not only the quality of food, but also in the quality of the service. In the end, Zhivago's quietly just went away.

The Spa of Eden, Svetlana's spa, was likewise failing. Svetlana was interested in it at first and paid close attention to the details that made it popular and successful. But she struggled to maintain consistent staff. Her tendency to be too blunt and abrupt with people, many of the same behaviors which caused me to protect our clients from her, also created issues for the spa. As Svetlana got bored with the spa, it began to decline, and as with Zhivago's, it too went quietly into the night.

I surmised that Slava and Svetlana took a huge financial loss on their three failed business endeavors. The failure of Slava's businesses forced him to break the leases for the space in the building. The next thing I knew, Slava announced to me that I needed to find a different space for our office. I am not sure what transpired between Slava and the landlord, but the result was that we were asked to relocate. I ultimately found a beautiful new office for us about two miles away.

During this time, the adoption process was becoming more challenging. The Hague Convention was in the process of being ratified, which made international adoptions more difficult, but also more secure. Political differences between Russia and the US were having an impact on adoption regulations. Tragically, a few Russian born children who had been adopted through other agencies were murdered by their adoptive parents, and that had created increased tension between the two countries. The children had died at the hands of their adoptive parents who were unprepared for parenting a child with psychological or emotional issues and had been unable to control themselves when upset with their child's behavior. Statistically, fewer adopted children were victims of filicide than biological children, but forces within Russia, already against international adoption, used the tragedies to benefit their agenda.

Some American agencies had become lax regarding the required progress reporting on children after they had come to America and submitted the reports to the Russian government either late or not at all. These issues had created a climate in Russia whereby officials were no longer as cooperative as they had once been. The adoption process was taking longer, and the regulations were continually changing, creating barriers for the smooth adoptions for which Small World had become so well known. Business was definitely slowing down. Slava and Svetlana were less and less involved and traveling much less frequently to identify children for adoption. It was becoming more difficult to get Svetlana to engage in the process of evaluating the health of the children. I was becoming increasingly more frustrated but vowed to persevere even though Slava had begun to be more and more demanding and intractable.

CHAPTER 78

ANOTHER PLAYGROUND
FOR RUSSIA

IN THE LATE SPRING OF 2007, grateful to be leaving Slava behind, Phil and I led our annual "Bricks of Hope" trip to build playgrounds in a couple of cities in Southern Russia. One of the cities was Solikamsk, a city in the region of Perm. The city is known for its salt mines, and we were told that Solikamsk means "Salt City." It was a harrowing trip in an old van, over bumpy roads, with a crazy-fast Russian driver.

Laura was with us on this trip, as was my best friend Cathy. Since I had no relationship with either of my sisters, Cathy had become the sister for whom I had yearned throughout my life. Cathy's son, Michael, was one of the Szeged *28* children, and a few years after adopting Michael she and her husband, Dave, adopted their daughter from Russia. Michael suffered institutionalized autism, most likely the result of his early, solitary, and prolonged time in a facility in either Romania or Hungary. During the first Szeged *28* reunions, my family and Michael's family formed a close bond. I never saw Michael as just a child with a disability, but a golden spirit who taught all of us about love, laughter, honesty, and he was a constant reminder to never take things too seriously. I became Auntie Brenda to Michael and his sister, Natasha. Cathy and her husband became Uncle Dave and Aunt Cathy to my children. We had bonded during the "war" to free our children from Hungary and during the process built an incredible friendship. Cathy's daughter was adopted from the Perm region, though not the area we were visiting, but making this trip was meaningful to Cathy. She welcomed the opportunity to give something back to the region that had given her the beautiful Natasha.

Upon arriving in Russia, I learned that my luggage had not arrived, and I was forced to share clothes with Cathy all week.

We arrived late in the day in the city of Solikamsk and went directly to the orphanage to scout out the premises and make our game plan for the next day. The orphanage was in what appeared to be a very economically depressed area of town. The orphanage building had an empty lot next to it where we would be building the new playground. There were many apparent vagrants milling around outside the building and each of them appeared to be drunk or well on their way to getting there. It was a little disconcerting for us. We had made many trips and I had never feared for my safety while working on a playground. But this town felt foreboding, as if danger were lurking just around the corner.

Phil explained to the orphanage director that our work would be easier if she were able to arrange for us to have an auger to assist with digging the holes into which we set the playground posts. On our original trip we had dug the holes with shovels, so we had learned from experience to begin each project with a request for an auger. (An auger is a machine that looks a little like a small tractor with a big drill on the front for digging holes in the ground. They come in a variety of sizes for digging different sized holes.) Most of the time, the orphanage directors successfully had one brought to the orphanage along with someone to operate it.

Plans were made, and we went to dinner and then we went on to what we were told was the only hotel in town. We arrived at what I can only describe as an amazingly decrepit hotel. The woman who appeared to be managing the hotel had on just enough clothing to keep her most impressive private parts covered. There was a bevy of rather scruffy men milling around the area and I had a slight feeling of fear. The sort-of-lobby area was in extreme disrepair with peeling paint and dirty floors. In my experience, this was uncommon for a Russian hotel. Every other Eastern European hotel in which I had been was super clean. They may not have been luxurious, and may have been plain and simple places, but they were always clean, and I always felt safe.

We requested that all of us be placed on the same floor and were assigned rooms. There was not a working elevator, so up the stairs we went. We entered a hallway unlike anything I had seen before. The bare light bulbs were hanging by wires from the ceilings and there were bundles of exposed wires tacked all along the sides of the walls, which were losing their paint. The plaster was hanging in large chunks from both the walls and the ceiling. Cathy and I were sharing a room, identified which was ours, and bravely entered. The bare room had a single chair and a very low double bed with what looked like an old-fashioned doily on top. The bathroom was interesting in that a shower head came out of the middle of the wall in the small room, with no shower base or curtain.

Cathy and I chuckled at the environment, knowing a person can sleep anywhere for a few nights. Cathy sat down on the bed and said, "Bren, this bed is like a board, feel it."

I sat down next to her and ran my hand over the bed and burst out laughing. "Cathy, this is just a box-spring! There isn't even a mattress on the bed!" Our bed for the next two nights was a box-spring with a doily for a cover.

We looked out the window to see a large group of men milling around the corner outside the hotel, the majority of them appearing quite intoxicated. We eventually fell asleep on our box-spring, sleeping in our clothes.

The next morning, we all met for a peculiar breakfast of some unknown meat and made our way to the orphanage. When we arrived about 9:00 AM, we were shocked to see a group of young teens from the nearby neighborhood leaning against the orphanage. With them were a few little boys, who looked no older than eight or nine years old. They were holding huge bottles of beer. These children were obviously drunk, and my heart ached at what I imagined their lives must be like.

The orphanage director came out and shooed the children away and we began to assemble the pieces of the playground which would soon become an awesome play structure for the children of the orphanage.

Around lunch time, the orphanage director kindly summoned us inside to serve us lunch. She explained that to save time the man with the auger would dig the holes while we were eating. We had carefully marked where the holes were to be dug. After lunch, we walked back out to the assigned playground area to find that the man with the auger had a machine commonly used for telephone pole holes and instead of one-foot holes, we were faced with holes that were about three feet wide and about that deep. There had been a huge misunderstanding in the translation of the size of the holes we needed. I couldn't wait to hear how Phil was going to handle this!

He said nothing to the hole-digger or the orphanage director and after they had gone, we ended up shoveling most of the dirt back into the giant holes that the kind, Russian man had dug for us. We mixed and poured our concrete, set the poles for the structure, and, as dusk was settling upon us, we busily worked on the rest of the structure. It had been common practice for us to work into the dark on these trips. We had limited time and usually were building two or three play structures in differing cities in about six or seven days. We were always racing to beat the clock and took advantage of every bit of light we could.

A group of scruffy looking men appeared again that evening and were just hanging around the area watching us. The orphanage director came out and said, "The women *must* leave immediately and return to the hotel." She was extremely adamant and practically stomped her foot, saying that the women would not be safe. Phil and I talked and decided that a couple of the men would walk the four women back to the hotel and the remaining four men would put everything away securely in the locked shed belonging to the orphanage. We returned to the hotel and waited for the rest of our group. We were a little nervous about their safety.

They returned within the hour and we ate a quick dinner together as everyone wanted to shower and go to bed. As on all our trips, we were exhausted by the end of the day, having done a full day's worth of physical labor. When we went to take showers, we discovered that only a few of our rooms had hot water. We all met in the hall and set up a schedule so that everyone could take a shower in one of the rooms with hot water. Were we not exhausted, it might have been comical.

The next morning at breakfast, Phil had quite a story to tell. Phil's fifteen-year-old nephew had joined us for the trip. He was a sweet, hardworking young man. Phil and his nephew were sharing a room. The night before, while getting ready for bed, his nephew had switched on the television and immediately up popped a pornographic scene. Embarrassed, Phil's nephew quickly switched channels, to yet another pornographic scene. Again, he quickly switched channels and sure enough, another pornographic movie appeared. At that point, he switched the TV off and they agreed there wasn't really anything good to watch on TV!

We returned to the orphanage to finish the play structure and I began conversing with our translator as we were wrapping up our work. I learned two interesting things. First, I learned that the hotel in town, where we were staying, was actually the town brothel. There wasn't an actual hotel in this town, just a brothel that would also occasionally rent rooms to non-brothel customers. Second, I learned that the city was located right next door to a major Russian prison for men, one for "high crimes." When the prisoners were released after serving their sentence, she said many of them ended up in their city, living on the street. This information explained the unusual hotel, the choice of movies on the TV, and the large number of disorderly, drunken men in the vicinity.

It was an interesting trip to say the least, and we were all relieved to be getting back into the old van with the crazy-fast driver. This time, we didn't mind his speed so much as we traveled on to our next city.

CHAPTER 79

VIETNAM

W ITH THE DIFFICULTIES DEVELOPING FOR Eastern European adoptions, Slava began to pressure me to identify adoption programs in different countries. I researched India, South America, and Vietnam. It seemed like developing a program in Vietnam could be the most promising, and it was where Slava wanted to go. I developed some relationships with individuals with connections in Vietnam and I began working to learn about Vietnamese adoption processes and the required paperwork.

Ultimately, Slava and Svetlana ended up traveling to Vietnam to personally work on building relationships and establishing a framework for Small World to facilitate Vietnamese adoptions. The process took many months, but eventually Slava felt that he had developed enough connections that we could begin working in Vietnam. In 2007, I had begun to publicize our new program in newsletters and on our website.

It took a few months before one of our waiting families signed up for the Vietnam program. Sadly, at the time I left Small World, the single mom who was adopting in the Vietnam program was in Vietnam and had been there for several months. The country suddenly ceased allowing children to exit due to concerns of corruption among agencies that had been working in Vietnam for a long time. There were reports that agencies were paying governmental officials for preferential treatment, as well as concern over the legal status of some of the children being adopted. Our adoptive mother was already in the country with her son when the closure was announced.

I had worked for weeks to assist our adopting mom to find a way to bring her child to the US. Vietnam basically told the adoptive mom, she was welcome to immigrate to Vietnam and raise this child, but she was not taking him out of the country. She had vowed to stay in Vietnam with her son, who had already been placed in her custody, until she could legally take him out of the country. I got the board of directors to agree to help with her expenses for a few months because she had lost her income. Her employer promised to hold her job for her and the people in her community held fundraisers to help support her while she was trapped in Vietnam. At the time I left, mom and son were still living in an apartment in Vietnam together. I never learned if she was able to bring her son home. I hope and pray that Vietnam recognized the love she had for her son and allowed the family to return to the US.

CHAPTER 80

THE FINAL
"BRICKS OF HOPE" TRIP

WHAT TURNED OUT TO BE the final humanitarian trip to be made by Small World staff in the spring of 2008 was a dark omen of things to come. One of the men on the trip got desperately ill and was unable to assist during the entire trip. He was so ill, we were fearful for his life. He had a fever and chills and seemed to have a bronchial illness. His father was a physician back in the U.S., and after speaking with his son, was able to explain to our translator the medication he believed his son needed.

In all the years we had been building playgrounds, it had never rained. On that trip, it rained most of every day. It was cold and miserable. It wasn't a joyous experience as the previous trips had been.

A few hours before leaving Russia, Laura began to feel ill. She was terribly ill the entire way home with some kind of intestinal issue. Upon arriving in the US, I took her directly to the hospital. She was hospitalized for four days and diagnosed with an intestinal parasite that hadn't been seen in the US before. The parasite remains in her body, causing life-long symptoms.

It was hard to ignore that so many bad things occurred on one trip after never experiencing a single issue or bad day on any other trip. It was stressful and unsettling for me. Slava was completely disinterested in what had happened. It was as if a gray cloud was settling over all of us.

CHAPTER 81

MARK

AS UNPROMISING AS EVENTS AND relationships seemed to be at Small World, at least my personal life was on an upward trajectory. A few years earlier, one of my best friends from college wandered back into my life. For three years in college, there was a group of friends who had been inseparable. One member of our group was Mark, who was from the same town as Jeffrey. We had gotten close in college when I had tutored him in the fundamentals of studying. I introduced him to the ever-important college tool, the highlighter, when he complained that he had attended a high school that had provided no preparation for the rigors of college life. When my son, Ryan, was born, Mark was named godfather. When Jeffrey and I left Springfield for Kansas City, we completely lost touch. He had gotten married and had two children.

Ryan and Laura kept in touch with Mark a little, and occasionally saw or spoke with him. He did not live in St. Louis but regularly traveled through the area on business. They told him about Small World and where I worked and that he should stop by to see me. So, in 2006, he came walking into my office and I was thrilled to see him.

I was divorced, and he was separated. Over the next couple of years, we began spending more and more time together. Our already deep friendship blossomed into a loving relationship and he provided stability in my tumultuous life. Since Ryan and Laura had known Mark all their lives, he fit naturally into our family circle. I was worn down and weary from the stress between Alex and me. Mark seemed to hit it off with Alex and he felt like he could be a good influence on him. He certainly provided some much-needed emotional support where Alex was concerned. He was kind and he made me laugh all the time.

In 2007, I had introduced Mark to Slava and Svetlana, and he thought Slava gregarious and a likable guy. Svetlana said little to Mark, but his impression was that she was a quiet and pleasant person. But, he agreed there was an undercurrent of something going on between the three of us.

In May of 2008, Mark and I got married and he and his two children moved into my house. It was the bright spot in my troubled world of the disagreements with Slava and my concern over the future of Small World.

CHAPTER 82

THEY WERE SUPPOSED TO CARE – THINGS HEAT UP

SVETLANA, WHO HAD ALREADY DISENGAGED herself from much of the business, was becoming even less involved. If clients had questions about the health of their waiting children, she appeared highly annoyed when I requested that she check on the children or ask questions of our foreign contacts. Her responses had become curt and she expressed impatience at being asked to assist with information. Adoptive parents had begun to have the video tapes of prospective adoptive children evaluated by American physicians specializing in the care of internationally adopted children. This always annoyed Svetlana, as she was of the belief that the opinions of the other doctors didn't matter, they hadn't viewed the children and she had. But, the reality was that this was not always the case any longer.

One of our clients had a close friend who was a doctor, who had agreed to travel with the client to evaluate the prospective child. Both Slava and Svetlana became furious and would not allow it. Slava tore me apart verbally when I gave the client's request to him. I had just been the messenger, but he raged at me for even giving the idea enough importance to bring it to him. We were supposed to be partners and I hadn't deserved his wrath. I understood how insulting that action would have been to the pediatricians in the orphanage. But, it was an indication to me that the clients no longer trusted our opinion. It was evident that the clients who had returned from recent adoption journeys had adopted children who were less healthy than ever before and were sharing this with prospective clients.

Slava and Svetlana seemed to be constantly fighting and they were refusing to travel to Russia to identify children. Tapes of waiting children were being prepared by foreign country staff and brought back by adoptive families. I was furious about this development, as this wasn't the process I had promised to the waiting families. Slava and Svetlana were supposed to personally see the children. They were supposed to care! I didn't understand what was happening.

During 2007 and 2008, things were changing, seeming to fall apart. We began to have financial difficulties for the first time ever. Slava was becoming more and more unpredictable and mean.

There were a lot of rumors floating around about Slava during that last year we were all together. He himself told me that he had been gambling at the riverboats most nights, and had begun seeking private, high stakes games because of gambling limits imposed on the boats. I was shocked by this because I had never heard him talk about gambling before. He was still practicing anesthesia every morning, and I hoped he wasn't staying out all night. Sometimes people would tell me they had seen him on the boats.

Slava told me one day that he and Svetlana were no longer living together. He didn't elaborate on any of the details, but I witnessed the deterioration of their relationship, so I was unsurprised by this. I eventually heard he lost his house and had moved into an apartment, Svetlana moving to her own. I didn't know the reason for the loss of their house but wondered if it could be related to his high stakes gambling. Slava never discussed the details of this with me. That last year we had no conversations that weren't business related.

About twelve months before I left the agency, as the finances were getting tighter and tighter, I would occasionally look at our bills with Laura to decide what we needed to pay that week and what could wait. Funds were growing tighter by the month. Slava continued to be less and less engaged in the operations of Small World and his focus was clearly mentally and emotionally elsewhere.

But apparently, he was paying attention to what bills I was choosing to pay. At a board meeting, Slava addressed the board and asked that they order me to pay the invoices for the Russian company, Eastern European Adoption Group (EEAG), before paying salaries or rent. The prior month, I had elected to pay the staff salaries, all of them having been frozen and mine dramatically reduced, and had put off some payments to EEAG for about six days. Slava shared with the board that a couple of EEAG invoices had been a few days late because I had chosen to pay the salaries of our domestic employees. He explained to the board that failure to pay EEAG on time could result in closure of the program. He gave an impassioned speech to the board about how critical it was that EEAG be paid immediately, the day invoices were received.

The board voted that EEAG invoices would be paid ahead of any other financial obligations. I simply did not understand Slava's insistence to the board that EEAG be paid above all else. I felt that Slava had wanted to put me in my place and he was successful. I could not get him to understand that our employees made the agency function and without them, we wouldn't be able to operate. I believed that our employees should come first; they were our most important asset. For the first time, I began considering if Small World was still where I was supposed to be. Slava's and my views had become dramatically different. I was becoming less sure by the day that our partnership would survive.

As our relationship was deteriorating, my mistrust of him was increasing. He would become angry over ordinary procedural questions and he was furious if a client made a complaint or had a concern. Although he had always been prone to calling me names, he became relentless with the habit and was becoming crueler with his choice of adjectives for me.

Over the past two years, Slava had continually increased the prices for our clients, saying that the prices were going up in Russia and Ukraine. Fewer people were applying because our prices were now considerably higher than other agencies. Plus, Russia had begun creating numerous roadblocks to slow the entire adoption process. The country had begun requiring families to remain in Russia longer when completing the adoptions, they were rejecting documents which had previously been easily accepted, and were increasing the entire time line for the adopting parents.

During that time I came to realize that some of the things I had believed about Slava and Svetlana may not have been true. I came to believe that Svetlana was not actually checking up on prospective adoptive children when the prospective adoptive parents requested it. She had once upon a time been so efficient with this task, now I believed she was not doing it. More children were coming home with significant health issues. I was also learning from our clients that some of the children, who Svetlana had "personally selected" and assured clients the children were healthy, in some cases had devastating health issues.

One day, Slava came into the office quite angry about something over which I had no control and he slammed his hands down on my desk, startling everyone in the office. Although Slava had been verbally abusive almost from the beginning, I had never been physically afraid of him. I always made excuses for his behavior, making myself believe this was just another cultural difference and was how Russian businessmen behaved.

Slava seemed to be building an alliance with some of the staff in the office. They were frequently on the phone with one another, and I could feel something was not right. Most of the staff generally avoided Slava because of his outbursts. But a couple employees became distant not only to me but to the rest of the staff as well. They would often whisper to one another and would follow Slava out of the office when he was leaving after meetings with me.

The split in our office was becoming cavernous. The days of loving to come to work were over. The stress in the office was so thick I could have choked on it. I had been an employer who always considered the employee's family to be a priority. I always encouraged staff to attend their children's room parties, doctor appointments, or whatever family event was occurring in their lives. I wanted everyone to be happy while insisting they do their jobs. If staff worked hard, did a good job, and took care of our clients, I was never a clock watcher. I even provided paid vacation to part-time staff. I wanted everyone's job to be fun and had been able to develop a warm comradery among staff. Employees always seemed grateful for the way I treated them and in return stood ready to work overtime or on a Saturday if it was necessary. We had been a group of women who were loyal and supportive of one another. Now, I could do nothing as I watched with horror the happiness that had been a constant in our office for nearly fifteen years melt away.

The obvious change in the behavior of some of the staff was not only baffling but hurtful. I began to see a connection between their behaviors and Slava's behavior. But it was still a mystery to me. I just couldn't put all the pieces together. If I hadn't known myself so well, I may have believed I was becoming paranoid. I continued to be convinced there were negative forces at work in our office.

During that stressful last year, Laura avoided being in the office if Slava was going to be there. She did much of her work remotely and if coming into the office, she would call first to see if he was expected. She had begun this plan of action because, as abusive as Slava was becoming toward me, he was much worse toward her. He cursed at her and accused her of not doing her job correctly. He was angry at her all the time for no reason. He continuously stated that it was her mismanagement of funding which created Small World shortfalls. For about a year, she had been vigorously pressuring Slava to submit receipts for his expenses because he had ceased being cooperative regarding documentation of expenses. She had been trying to encourage him to pay for items and make good on donations to which he had publicly committed at our last dinner auction. Ultimately, he told her he was not going to f-ing pay what he owed for the auction and told her she had better not ask again.

Sometimes he would submit receipts, but more often than not, he didn't. Laura had been told by the accounting firm that she had to do a better job of collecting receipts from Slava. But, he refused to cooperate, failing to submit them when asked. She shared this with the auditors, who had become concerned. She wanted to leave the agency desperately, but remained not only because she was my daughter, but because she also truly believed in our mission. We both hoped the accounting firm would be able to talk some sense into Slava. But it was not successful either.

Laura expressed fear of the damage that could be done to her reputation due to the financial issues of the agency, which seemed to be growing worse by the day. She had developed a thriving accounting and business development company and couldn't afford any scandal.

At the last board meeting which I attended, in April of 2008, the previous year's audit was distributed. The accounting firm pointed out that it was a substantial problem that there was a lack of receipts for Slava's expenses. Slava told the board it was Laura's fault because she failed to request them. I almost laughed out loud. After the meeting, I told the board president that he needed to speak with the accounting firm, which was aware of Slava's refusal to submit receipts and had also been working to convince him to cooperate. In fact, following this audit, the accounting firm discontinued its relationship with the agency because of Slava's refusal to cooperate. They too were concerned about damage to their reputation by continuing to maintain a relationship with Small World.

Laura and I often talked about what could be going on with Slava. He had had that open heart surgery a few years earlier and we had been told this could bring about depression in some people. I tried to chalk up some of his behavior those last few years to that.

Slava had begun writing checks and not telling Laura he had written them, so it was always disconcerting to never have a handle on how much money we had in the bank. He was always wiring money somewhere and giving Laura no supporting documentation.

In January of that last year, Slava told me he wanted me to lay off more staff. I had already, through attrition, been minimizing the staff over the last year. I wanted to lay off one of the case managers, who was assigned to helping clients prepare their adoption paperwork. We had so few clients that Maureen could easily handle all of them. But, Slava told me I had to lay off the office manager, who was at the time more valuable to the organization than a second case manager. I didn't understand, as this move was not the best business decision to make. But, I let the office manager go and I could almost feel the tension in the office increasing by the minute. I had no clue what was going on, but Slava and I were in increasingly greater adversarial positions.

He would scream at me because a client refused to accept the referral of a child when they believed the child to be unhealthy. Most of the time, I agreed with the client. The healthier children we had been placing were being replaced with sicker children. We fought about this. We fought about his incessant raising of prices to the point that it seemed like he was almost blackmailing prospective adoptive parents. Slava would wait until someone had selected a child and then determine that there was some special fee the family had to pay. He would offer weak reasons why additional fees needed to be paid. He was nearly manic about fees and he got into arguments with our clients. I got into verbal showdowns with him in my efforts to protect our clients. Life was increasingly more difficult every day.

In late April of 2008, Laura and I began seriously talking about leaving. My heart was breaking. I had spent nearly fifteen years believing that I was in the place God wanted me to be. I was doing God's work, saving children. But now everything was very unstable, and I felt this huge wall of secrecy surrounding us. Everything seemed to be developing an almost sinister feel.

I felt intense anguish about the loss of clients, the deterioration of my beloved office, the increased expenses in Russia, the changing Russian processes, Slava's worsening spinning out of control, and I wasn't sure how much more of it I could emotionally handle.

CHAPTER 83

THE WORLD FALLS APART

AND THEN ON THE LAST Friday of May 2008, just a few weeks after our final "Bricks of Hope" trip, my world changed forever. It happened in a split second, when what I thought I knew for so many years turned out to have no actual relationship to the reality of the world in which I worked.

At about 3:30 in the afternoon, on a beautiful, bright and sparkly day, everything came crashing down around me. Spring was in full bloom with summer just around the corner. I was sitting at my desk, in my sun-drenched office, when Laura walked into my office, her face unusually pale, and her eyes wide with alarm. She sat down next to my desk and said eleven words that changed our lives forever. "Mom, EEAG is not a company. It is Slava's bank account." I simply stared at her.

Eventually, I said, "What do you mean?" She repeated those same eleven words. The significance and meaning of the words were slowly sinking in. I asked her to please explain what she was saying. It almost felt to me as if she were speaking a different language. I was hoping she would tell me some piece of information about Slava which I could explain away and would set my world back on its axis.

But that was not to be the case. Slava usually made the bank deposits and did both his personal as well as Small World banking at the same institution. Laura explained that when she went to the bank to make a deposit, there was a new teller who Laura had never met before. She was obviously not as familiar with Small World as the other tellers. When Laura presented the checks for deposit, the teller glanced at them and asked Laura if she wanted them deposited into the Small World or the EEAG account. The teller was obviously not aware that she was disclosing to Laura that there was a bank account named EEAG which was not related to the bank account of Small World. Laura had not had any legal right to that information.

As she finished speaking, I felt as if the oxygen was being let out of the room like air out of a balloon, with the walls closing in on me. In those few seconds, my mind played back to the hundreds and hundreds of checks I had signed which were made out to EEAG. That had been the extent of my involvement with the finances for years, simply signing the checks. Slava had presented us with the invoices which were always faxed to his house, previous bookkeepers, and then Laura wrote the checks and I signed them in his absence. We were talking about millions of dollars in checks over the fifteen years we had been in business! The information was slowly sinking in; all that money had gone into a checking account belonging to Slava! There was no company named Eastern European Assistance Group. The thought that came barreling into my brain was, "How much trouble am I in?" That thought was followed by the realization that Slava may truly be a dishonest person who may have at the worst embezzled funds, and at the best, misappropriated them. The board had believed him. I had believed him. Nearly 1500 clients had believed *in* him.

My next heart-crushing thoughts were for the hundreds of Small World clients who might well have been victims of whatever nefarious actions Slava may have been taking.

I told Laura we needed to leave the office immediately and go somewhere to talk. I did not want to take the chance that Slava might stop by the office. I simply could not face him.

After our initial conversation, which was mostly Laura explaining the legal implications as she understood them relating to financial mismanagement, we made the decision that I needed to meet immediately with the board of directors. I called the president of the board and told him I had a serious emergency and that I needed to speak with him over the weekend. We agreed to meet the next morning, at a coffee shop.

I did not sleep at all that night. I tossed and turned and tried to make sense of everything Laura had told me. I was anxious about how I would disclose all of this to the president of the board. I was fearful he would think I had known about Slava's bank account and I was terrified that people might assume I was complicit. My concern for my clients was adding to my inability to sleep. What would all this mean for them? I kept asking myself if there would be a way to explain all of this away and return to those "golden years."

The next morning, after telling the board president what I knew, I told him that I had no prior knowledge that EEAG was just a bank account belonging to Slava. I reminded him that we had believed EEAG was a company in Russia working with us to transfer funds for our Russian operations and that we were talking about the transfer of millions of dollars. We spoke for about thirty minutes before he left for his child's soccer game. He said he would need to think about this information and would get back to me as quickly as possible. He had adopted three children through our organization and I wondered if this information was as painful for him to hear as it had been for me. I told him I wanted to resign immediately, and he asked me to please wait until the board could meet. After only a few minutes, I had the feeling that he just wanted to escape from our conversation, and as I was driving away I was not at all sure he had believed anything I said.

Over the weekend, I called my attorney at home and told him the story. He said he wanted to refer me to the best employment attorney he knew, feeling I needed to be protected. He arranged for me to meet with the employment attorney early Monday morning. That weekend was a blur of sleeplessness and sitting in a chair staring out the window. I felt so terribly lost and afraid.

On Monday morning, I was in the employment attorney's office at 8:00 AM. After hearing the story, the employment attorney said I needed to personally contact the remaining board members and claim, "whistle blower status." He said making a documented record would give me as much protection as possible. One of his staff members came into the office to record my narrative of the situation and we both signed the document. He said it was imperative that I use the phrase, "claiming whistle blower status." He said people making this proclamation are supposed to have special legal protections. After the meeting, not for the first time, and certainly not the last, I sat in my car after the meeting, sobbing uncontrollably.

That week, I subsequently met with two more board members and spoke via the telephone with one who was not in town. I believe they were all as stunned as I was and that they completely understood the gravity of the situation. Many members of the board were prominent professionals and I could tell that after the initial shock, their concern was to protect their own reputations. But I believed they also felt that they owed it to the Small World clients to protect them as well. I did not meet with all ten of the board members; I simply could not force myself to keep retelling the story. The five with whom I spoke said they planned to get the board together as quickly as possible.

I just wanted the nightmare to be over and sadly for me, it was only just beginning.

CHAPTER 84

TRYING TO RESIGN

IN SPITE OF MY PROMISE to the board president that I wouldn't resign, I couldn't stand to go back to the office and faxed my resignation to Slava. He sent me a message and told me he would not accept my resignation. His text message said, "Things will be okay." At that time, Slava had no idea that I was aware of the truth about EEAG. I believe his impression was that I was resigning because of the deterioration of our relationship and that I no longer had faith that Small World would survive.

I called the board president and told him what had occurred, and that I really needed to resign. I asked him if he would accept my resignation and he again asked me to please remain with the agency for the time being. He said the board needed me to be in the office as they were working out the details regarding Small World's future. Those words struck a chord with me – Small World's future. I began thinking about our many clients who would be caught up in this terrible event. I decided I owed it to them to try and see the crisis through. If Small World was going to close, I wanted to be there for my clients. I had been there for the beginning and felt I should be there for the end. I reluctantly agreed to stay.

That same day, I told Marcia and Maureen that EEAG was not a company, but a bank account belonging to Slava. I shared the exchanges between Slava and me and the board president and me, and I learned from Marcia about something Slava had done. During the month of May, Slava's and my battles had been intensifying. Marcia shared with me that a few days before we learned that EEAG was merely a bank account and not a company, Slava called her and asked her to meet him. She agreed to meet with him and during that meeting he offered my job to Marcia, telling her, "We both know she has to go." Marcia told me she had been stunned and stated that she didn't feel there was a future for Russian adoption. She declined his offer.

Both Maureen and Marcia were as devastated by these new revelations as Laura and I had been. We discussed our shared desire to resign, but I explained the board's request that we not resign. We collectively agreed to remain.

Marcia had spent a lot of time, as had Laura, avoiding Slava that last year. Marcia had the least tolerance for Slava's bad behavior, his bullying, his continuous racist and sexist remarks, and his meanness. I remembered Marcia telling me that Slava had invited her to strip clubs, telling her she might like the same kinds of girls as him. She had been disgusted by his behavior on so many occasions. There wouldn't have been enough money in the world to entice Marcia to take my job. She later shared with me that had she not been so intimidated by him, she would have told him there was no way Small World would survive without me. Marcia shared with me that many times doubt about Slava and Svetlana would creep into her consciousness, but then she would see the kids and it seemed to make the doubt fade, at least a bit. By this time, we were all intimidated by him.

The next weeks were a hazy existence for me. I went to the office and conducted business as normally as possible. The board president called me at home and said the board had retained legal counsel and that I should continue to run Small World as if nothing was wrong. He said it would take a few weeks to iron things out. There had been board members on vacation with whom they had not had the chance to meet and he wanted to get everyone to sign off on the plan which would allow the board of directors to take over the agency.

I was not only concerned, but consumed, with how long it would be before I could escape. I hated the charade I was living. But, I couldn't abandon the clients about whom I cared so much. It was hardest of all to speak with them by phone or see them in the office and behave as if the world was fine. Maureen, Marcia, and Laura also had to play the same game and they were equally distressed. We were four honest, hardworking women and felt like we had been reduced to playing the roles of bad actors in a B rated movie with a terrible plot.

I had begun to have a headache most of the time and sleeping through the night was a thing of the past. I was in almost daily communication with the board president, who was giving me support and guidance. In just a few weeks, the annual client picnic was being held. I could not imagine attending this function and pretending like Small World was a righteous organization and one deserving of people's affection. But, I had my marching orders, carry on as normal while the board created a plan through their attorneys. Business went on as normal with the bills being paid, including Slava's "fake invoices" still being paid to EEAG, which infuriated me! I never understood why there was such a delay in their taking action after learning about Slava's EEAG account. I was in a torturous situation, moving through my days like an anemic sloth, barely able to put one foot in front of another.

CHAPTER 85

THE LAST SMALL WORLD PICNIC

JULY 12, 2008, THE DAY of the picnic unfortunately arrived, and I still had no more resolution than the first day I spoke with the board president. I was very frustrated. Several hundred people attended the picnic. People about whom I cared deeply, some of whom had become dear friends through the years. I knew I couldn't say anything. Again, the lessons learned from my childhood enabled me to get through. As a child, I had become adept at putting the abuse of my home life on a shelf in my brain and going out into the world all smiles. It is an art form and one which I assume many abused children have perfected. I was nothing if not the consummate secret keeper and eternal smiler. No one would be able to see the blackness that was eating away at my soul.

And so, one of the most stressful days of my life began. I pretended my way through the day. I tried to focus on the good things we had done, watching with joy as the children we had rescued from Eastern European orphanages ran about happily enjoying the many activities we had for them. I tried to avoid Slava. Svetlana was not with him;

he had come alone. I had learned from another Russian person in the community that they had indeed separated and that their house had been repossessed. I now had heard this for the second time, not knowing really what was true. But the scenario made sense since Svetlana was noticeably absent when Slava arrived. They had always been together for every function held during the past fifteen years. She did arrive later by herself and stayed for about thirty minutes. She and Slava did not interact with one another.

True to form, as he had every year we had gathered together, Slava arrived late and he left early. I had always made excuses for both he and Svetlana, they were busy doctors, this was an extra activity they worked into their life because they wanted to save children, I should be grateful for the time they gave us, etc. Suddenly, I was replaying my childhood in my head, finally seeing the parallel. All the years of making excuses for Slava's behavior, justifying his treatment of me, his raging and meanness... making it okay in my head – I realized I had slipped back into the same survival mode during the past several years in which I had grown up. I angrily realized that I had been comfortable with his behavior; I was once again excusing the unforgivable behavior of another person. Internally, I became angrier and angrier, mostly at myself. I would no longer be his victim.

The pressure of whatever was happening in Slava's life was evident. He had gained weight, he looked tired, and his whole demeanor was one of anxiousness. He drank too much and acted erratic. During the picnic, he seemed to be out of control, dumping beer on one of the children, thinking it funny. Slava had always had some challenges with boundaries, but this was the most outrageous thing imaginable. Marcia, Maureen, Laura, and I watched his behavior in horrified, stunned silence. The parents were understandably furious. I backed out and didn't intervene this time. I would not make any excuses to the people looking on. I would not try to cover for him, I was finished with that. The parents scooped up their child and angrily fled the picnic.

He then poured beer on Maureen, soaking her shirt. He was quite literally someone who I did not recognize at all. As I watched in horror the screaming parents and the angry Maureen, calm descended upon me. I knew that whatever lay ahead in the coming weeks, I was finished forever with this man.

CHAPTER 86

THE UNIMAGINABLE

DURING THE NEXT COUPLE OF weeks, I was in daily communication with the president of the board of directors as I was given directives on moving forward. I was informed that the board's legal counsel believed the best course of action was to immediately close the agency and take control of the company. This included the bank account, and I was told that I should not sign any more checks. All the checks would be signed by the president of the board. Laura could continue preparing them and doing the accounting, but she would need to meet with him when she needed to have checks signed. The board had a brief discussion about potentially merging Small World with another agency facilitating Russian adoptions, but they discarded that possibility. I was told to make final arrangements to close the office within two weeks and to let the staff go once the office officially closed. I was told not to share the information with staff, or at least as little as possible. That was the only directive to which I didn't adhere. I asked my two longest term employees, now my support system and my friends, to meet with me privately in my office to tell them the board's plan. Marcia and

Maureen had been my first employees and had been with me fourteen years. I had, of course, already shared with them the truth about Slava.

There would have been no way I could have survived those final weeks without Maureen's calmness and Marcia's strength. Among many other things I had to do, I had to prepare letters to our clients, trying to find just the right wording. I was told that the attorneys would need to sanction any correspondence being sent to our clients. I shared with Marcia and Maureen that I would be finishing the letters to be mailed to all the clients with instructions as to what they should do if they were in the process of an adoption. The greatest challenge would be working out the financing for something as unprecedented as this. I felt sick knowing that Small World did not have the funds to return to clients the fees they had already paid to adopt, and I knew that the new agency would not complete the adoptions for free. I simply had to block this out of my mind. It was inevitable that my clients would lose money.

I found myself busy with the unbelievable, and never imagined, business of finding a way to close a business which I had begun with a partner I had loved, doing work I thought incredibly noble. Saying I was heartbroken doesn't come close to describing the overwhelming pain in my heart and soul. I was just trying to make it through each day, praying for the grace to survive.

I also needed to arrange to have all closed files sent to another agency in accordance with the legal requirements for the closing of an adoption agency. This would be a monumental task as we had more than eighteen file cabinets filled with closed adoption files. I would need Marcia's and Maureen's help to forward the current clients' documentation to another international adoption agency which had agreed to take the cases and finish their adoptions. Missouri law required that adoption documents be kept for a hundred years, therefore we had been unable to shred or discard any of the official documents in the files.

The board president called to let me know that the board's attorney was meeting with Slava that evening to advise him that the board was taking over the agency and he was being relieved of his duty as Executive Director. I would temporarily continue in my position of Director of Operations. Slava would also be told that all the Small World assets had been frozen. I shared this information with Marcia and Maureen.

I can clearly picture the three of us sitting around my desk and simply staring at the floor. We were finally accepting that we really would have to say goodbye to this company which we had all loved and the many clients who had become friends. I think we sat there several minutes digesting the uncertainty which lay ahead for each of us. We were broken-hearted for our clients and the orphaned children who would be the biggest losers.

I had this conversation with them late in the day on a Tuesday, during the last week of July of 2008. By this time, there were only the two employees who appeared to be in the Slava camp, Marcia, Maureen, Laura, and I working for the company. Everyone else had been let go. I couldn't help wondering how the other two employees were going to be affected when they learned the truth about Slava. I was genuinely concerned for them. I had begun to tell one of them, but she had rebuffed my efforts to speak with her, so I gave up. I wanted them to know the truth, but it was obvious to me that Slava had already spun a different story for them, and I was clearly the evil doer in their world.

I was dreading the next day and the sadness I knew awaited us. But, I was thankful that the board would be speaking to Slava and taking control of the company. I was hopeful that I would never have to see him again. I told Marcia and Maureen that we needed to get busy with the work of closing our beloved agency in the morning.

That Wednesday morning, July 30, 2008, I was finalizing the letter that would be sent to clients, incorporating a phrase the board had requested. Suddenly, about 10:00 AM, Slava burst into the office, stormed directly into my office, and told me he had decided to accept my resignation. He threw a letter from him on my desk stating that he accepted my resignation. He instructed me to vacate the office immediately. He then walked out into the main office area and said he would accept the resignation of any other staff members who wanted to go with me.

I followed Slava and told him, no, I didn't think that was going to happen. I told him I had been advised that the board had taken control of the company, knowing that he was already aware of this. He told me that was no longer the case as he had hired an attorney. He had his personal handyman with him who he had instructed to change the locks on the doors, and who was already dismantling the locking mechanisms on the door. I told him he could not legally change the locks in leased space and that only the building management company could do that. He told me he could do what he wanted. He was pacing around the office like a panther in search of its prey and fury was radiating from him.

Marcia immediately typed out letters of resignation for both herself and for Maureen. Laura was not there, but I am sure Slava knew she was walking out with us.

I walked back into my office as I told Slava I was calling the board president, who immediately answered the phone. My voice and my hands were shaking uncontrollably in response to Slava's rage, which by then was palatable. The board president had not been aware that Slava was coming to the office. I told him how agitated Slava was behaving and that I was uncomfortable being in this situation with him. The board president said he thought it might be best if we just left the office, taking our belongings, and "let things go." He said he didn't want to place us in an uncomfortable or dangerous situation. He said they would work with the attorneys and he would call me that night.

I was utterly stunned but shared my conversation with Marcia and Maureen. In a fog, I began to gather my possessions. I had a lot of personal belongings in the office after fifteen years, so I had a great deal of items to gather up. Likewise, Marcia and Maureen had a substantial number of personal items in the office. I called Mark and asked him to come to the office to help us load our things. I was also a little frightened by Slava's behavior and I knew Maureen and I would feel better if Mark were there. Marcia felt it was important for him to be there to support me. He immediately came to the office.

When Mark arrived, Slava told him to get out, but Mark refused, saying he was present to assist us with loading our cars. Slava called the police, who arrived shortly. I explained the situation to the police and they did not make Mark leave. Slava was even more furious. His pacing became frenetic, like a caged animal. I probably should have been more frightened but was in too much shock. I was grateful that Mark was able to be there and had not been out of town as he so frequently was.

We cleaned out our offices and Laura's as well. We finally got our cars loaded and the three of us went to my house, not knowing what else to do. We sat around my living room with glasses of wine, completely at a loss for words. Laura arrived soon after and we all sat together for a long time, speculating on what could have happened, what would happen going forward, and what it all meant. Our greatest concern that afternoon was not about us. We were all extremely upset about our clients. Some clients were preparing to travel to finalize their adoptions and others were in varying stages of adoption readiness, all of them with a financial and emotional investment in the organization. The board had asked us not to contact the clients for the time being.

That night, the president of the board called me at home and said that I should go back to the office in the morning, that the board had filed an injunction to stop Slava, and they had secured the funds at the bank. The board president made it clear to me that Maureen, Marcia, Laura, and I still worked for the board of directors for Small World Adoption Foundation. They wanted us to close the agency as quickly as possible. I told the board president that Slava had changed the locks on the doors and that my keys would not work. I told him that the other two remaining staff members most likely had keys. He told me to call one of them and tell them the board was requiring that they come to the office to let me in and that they were no longer employed. I had such a cascade of changing, uncontrollable emotions running through me: fear, anger, and sadness heading the list. In twenty-four hours, I had been employed, unemployed, and then employed again. I seemed to be caught in a downward spiral, like water going down the drain, with no chance of stopping it.

The next morning, instead of calling one of the remaining employees, I just went in a little late to the office as I was sure that Slava's two employees would be there. I simply did not have the courage to call either of them on the phone. Marcia and Maureen met me at the door. Sure enough, they were both there. I explained to them that the board had filed an injunction with the court to remove Slava from his position and to take control of Small World. I told them what Slava had done, I told them about EEAG and that millions of dollars had gone into a bank account owned by Slava. I calmly advised them that the board of directors was letting them go and that I was closing the agency. They immediately left, making sure to let me hear them calling Slava on one of their cell phones. They did not take any of their belongings with them. It was clear that they felt confident that they had chosen the right side and that they would be back.

Before finalizing the letters that would go to the clients, I did something that I feared might have been risky. But, I understood from the employment attorney that what had happened with Slava and EEAG was extremely serious. I wanted to do what I could to protect myself. Using a CD, I downloaded everything on our server, including the financials. I realized that I was perhaps doing something illegal, but I could not chance the proof of Slava's actions disappearing. That day, I didn't care what happened to me. Since learning about what Slava had potentially done, I had become resolute about making sure he couldn't hurt anyone else.

I finished copying the information from the server and slipped the CD into my purse and was preparing to start making personal phone calls to the current clients preparing to travel. My private line rang and it was the board president. He said that Slava had filed personal lawsuits against all of the board members to stop them from taking over the agency. I was stunned that Slava had been able to make this happen in less than two hours. I was asked to leave the office immediately. The board was going to continue to work through the attorneys, but they didn't want me caught in the middle any longer. They wanted me to know that the board was going to retain control of the agency funds. He, once again, promised to call me at home that night. Marcia, Maureen, and I gathered our purses and exited the office.

For the final time, on July 31, 2008, I walked out of the office that had been my "home" for fifteen years. I had started this agency in my basement with my partner, Slava. I was consumed by immeasurable sadness as I exited the building for the final time.

CHAPTER 87

FALLOUT

SLAVA AND I HAD BEEN through and accomplished so much together. We had saved nearly 1800 children together, worked with more than 1500 families together. I vowed to never lose sight of the good we had done together. Wherever it was that Slava had gone wrong, I knew in my heart that once upon a time he had been a good man, and I believed that goodness still lay within him.

I returned home, quite unsure what to do with myself. For the first time in my adult life, I didn't have a job.

I was totally lost. I think I spent several days alternately crying and being semi-comatose. Then a few days later, I got a call from the local police that I was going to be arrested for having stolen a vehicle that belonged to Small World. I was asked to come to the police department to turn myself in! On my final day at Small World, I had asked the board president what to do with my company car. He said to keep it and get another as quickly as possible and to return the car to the leasing company. I agreed to do this.

I gave the police officer the name and phone number of the

president of the board and told them that the car was not stolen. I explained that the board had given me permission to use it for a few days until I could purchase one. I then called the president and told him what had happened. He said he would call the police department and he would take care of it. He then told me not to return it to the leasing company but to return it to the Small World parking lot. I never heard about the car again. I got a new one and left my company car in the parking lot. I sent an e-mail to one of the remaining staff members, telling her the car was in the parking lot and the keys were under the mat.

In the following weeks, I met with the licensing consultant for the State of Missouri with whom I had worked for several years and made him aware of what had happened, as per the licensing regulations. He said he would relay the information to his superiors. At that time, I understood that the agency was still open, and business was ongoing, in spite of the board having control of the funds. I was convinced that after getting the information about the bank account and EEAG, the State of Missouri would revoke the agency's license. For reasons unfathomable to me, that did not happen.

As per Council on Accreditation's regulations, I submitted the same information to them. They likewise took no action to close the agency. According to the one board member with whom I remained in touch, the board was never contacted by either the State of Missouri's Licensing Division or by any representative of COA. How could these two entities have failed to contact the president of the board of directors? It seemed that Slava was going to get away with it, although at the time I was not really sure what it actually was he was getting away with, but I knew it had been illegal. It seemed that for both the State of Missouri and for the Council on Accreditation, there was no concern about a child placing agency where the Director had been removed and the board had taken over management of the funds. It was incredibly disappointing.

I met again with the employment attorney to update him on what was happening. He was appalled that the agency was still in operation. He asked me if any of the board members had notified the authorities. I said I didn't know. He instructed me to immediately notify the federal prosecutor's office. He said to fail to do that could make me look guilty. But how could that be, I thought, I hadn't known that EEAG was not a real company. He said that could be a point of contention since I had signed many of the checks. He again counseled me on using the term "claiming whistle blower status." I was in a constant state of disbelief about what had just happened to my life, terrified of what lay ahead, and just floating through each day in a fuzzy state, where the edges were no longer sharp and crisp. I had trouble making decisions, even simple ones, like what I wanted for dinner.

I subsequently notified the federal prosecutor's office after speaking with my attorney and getting direction. The federal prosecutor for our region at the time, Catherine Hanaway, had been one of my clients, so I couldn't imagine how everything was going to work. After communicating with her, she informed me that, as a former client, the case would be assigned to the assistant federal prosecutor and that he would be contacting me. It was a surreal experience to have a conversation with one of the highest lawmakers in the country, who had been appointed by the President of the US. I was uncomfortable and intensely anxious. My communications led me to believe that one of the board members had already notified the authorities.

After I contacted the federal prosecutor's office, I tried to go on with my life. I began to look for another job. I needed something in my life. I had spent my entire adult life working to make the lives of children better and I needed to find a job that would allow me to do that.

About a month after everything had happened, I received a text message from Slava saying that he "never wanted things to happen this way" and asked if I would meet him. I never responded to the message, ultimately giving it to the federal prosecutors.

A few weeks after my final day at Small World, I received another call from the local police department advising me that I was going to be arrested, this time for theft of a company laptop and I needed to come to the police station to turn myself in. Again! The computer was four or five years old and I hadn't used it much since my last trip to Russia. I had even forgotten about it in a drawer in my home office. I called my attorney, David, and asked for his help. I removed my files from the computer, not wanting to take the time to sift through documents. He was well acquainted with our police department and he said he would call them. He called me back a few days later and told me that he had arranged to meet with the police at the Small World office and return the computer to the agency.

David knew that I could not emotionally return to the Small World office. I was grateful that he picked up the computer and took it to the office himself. Amazingly, I imagine because I had removed all the files from the device, and it did not look as they expected, they told the police and my attorney that it was not the correct computer and that they would not accept it. My attorney suggested that they pull the records for the computer and compare serial numbers. He assured them this was indeed their computer. They argued that it was not the correct computer but refused to take steps to verify serial numbers. The police officer told my attorney that the police would take no further action, recording that we attempted to return it and they declined to accept it. David returned the computer to me and it went back into the same desk drawer for a couple more years. I finally donated it.

At about the same time, Marcia received a call from the same police department advising her that she was also being charged with the theft of a company laptop. She was livid. She had purchased her own laptop and informed the officer of such. The police officer told Marcia to mail a copy of the receipt to Slava, which Marcia did. Marcia never heard from them again.

Subsequently, Maureen received a similar phone call and the funniest thing about her call was that she didn't even have a company laptop and never had. She told the police office she had never had a laptop and I couldn't imagine what the police must have thought about Slava and Small World after four attempts to prosecute three different people and all allegations had been unfounded.

CHAPTER 88

MEETING FEDERAL
INVESTIGATORS

IN SEPTEMBER, I RECEIVED A call from the Assistant United States
Attorney for the Eastern District, Jeff Jensen. He explained that he
understood I might have some information relating to Small World and
the possible misappropriation of funds. He again stated that the lead US
Prosecuting Attorney, his boss, Catherine Hanaway, had recused herself
from the case, which of course I already knew as I had been the one to
assist her with her adoption. He explained that his office housed the
US federal prosecutors for the Eastern District of Missouri, reporting
directly to the Attorney General of the United States.

I said I believed I could provide their office with information,
and that my daughter, Laura, could likely provide an abundance of
information as well. He asked if we would speak with two forensic
federal investigators who reported directly to the US Attorney's office
and who specialized in embezzlement cases. I agreed to meet with them
and a date and time was arranged. My hands were trembling as I hung

up the phone, after which time I sat down and wept again. My life had taken such a disturbing turn and the path forward seemed impossible to navigate.

A week or so later, two men arrived at my door, wearing suits, carrying badges and brief cases. They introduced themselves as Investigators for the Office of the Federal Prosecutor with the US Attorney's office and said they had come to discuss Small World with me. Their names were Paul and Greg. They were both tall, with close cropped brown hair and extremely serious expressions. I couldn't fathom that I was standing at my front door inviting investigators, from the Attorney General's office, into my home! That was not something that happened to normal people. I realized that my world had stopped being normal the day Laura discovered the truth about EEAG.

I introduced them to Laura. They handed us their business cards, which displayed the raised seal of the US government, over which I kept rubbing my fingers during that first meeting. The whole surreal experience was incredibly interesting. They asked us a lot of questions, many of which had complicated and expansive answers. It was clear from that first meeting that Slava was in serious trouble and that this would not be a simple process. It was at the first meeting that the investigators told me that they did not want Laura or me to speak with any of the Small World clients during the course of the investigation. They asked that we not even accept phone calls from them. They asked us to avoid any discussion of Small World with any external individuals.

That evening, I recall sitting on my deck with my golden retriever, Miles. I was looking out over the grassy field behind my house and once again spoke with God. I had known that in my life, I would someday face the inevitability of losing people close to me. I believed that my faith had helped to prepare me that someday I would lose my parents, older relatives, even a friend. But God had not prepared me to lose over a thousand people about whom I cared in a five-minute span of time. I could not even wrap my mind around the possibility of never getting to see some of the people who had been so special to me again. I considered the tragedy of never knowing about how "my kids" were doing. I might never know of their great successes, their graduations, their weddings. There would never be another picnic. I had lost too many people who I had considered family. As would be a repeating event in my life over the coming months, I sat and wept.

So began a twelve-month relationship with a variety of people: a US postal inspector, federal prosecutors, federal investigators, and the FBI. I found myself living in a world I had only seen on TV and never imagined would become my life. I simply became a robot operating my life on autopilot and just trying to survive each day.

In the end, I never got to hear about the families who were in the process of adopting when I left. I hoped they had been able to conclude their adoptions. I did learn from my contact at the MO State Children's Division that Small World finalized only a small number of adoptions after I left and before it closed for good.

CHAPTER 89

SHOULD WE BE AFRAID?

FOR MANY MONTHS, INTO THE fall and through the winter of 2008-09, Laura and I regularly met with the federal investigators, always bizarrely sitting at my dining room table. The situation in which we found ourselves did not feel real. It was always the same two investigators, Paul and Greg, Laura, and me. They wanted to hear the story of everything I could remember about Slava from the first time I met him. That story alone took several meetings. They asked Laura to recount the same thing. They also questioned us quite expansively about our own families, our finances, and our lives in general. I later learned from Paul that during those first few months, they were also fully investigating Laura and me, our finances, etc., vetting us to be sure that we had not played a participatory role which we were attempting to cover up.

As would become the rhythm of our meetings, nearly all the questions were asked by Paul, with Greg quietly observing the majority of the time, and both of them taking copious notes.

At some point during my explanation of the adoption process and the way it worked, I was asked how much information about Small

World was distributed utilizing the US mail system. I explained that everyone who completed an adoption had received a full information packet through the mail; we did fundraising through the mail, as well as distributed contracts that way. Next they asked me if we would meet with a US postal inspector because the postal service may have been used illegally.

Laura and I met with the postal inspector for a couple of hours a few days later. He asked a lot of questions about the dissemination of information as well as fundraising requests made via the US mail. Laura and I answered all of his questions, he left, and we never heard from him again, and Paul would not tell us anything about the Postal Service investigation. It was tough to be left in the dark so frequently.

Upon the investigators learning that I had taken a copy of the computer files, you would have thought it Christmas morning for a pair of five-year-old children receiving new bicycles. They were simply ecstatic, at least as happy as their solemn faces would allow. They were even happier to learn that once we left the office, neither Laura nor I ever opened the files, therefore preserving their integrity. I expressed my concern over what I had done, and they said not to give it a second thought, that I had complete immunity. They fully understood my reasoning for copying the files, which had been that I feared I may have needed the records to demonstrate my innocence as the case progressed and to preserve potential evidence. Additionally, I had claimed "whistle blower status," which changed everything. They later told us that in fact the files had been helpful in doing just that for both Laura and me; they had been helpful to verify for the government our lack of involvement in any nefarious activities and had provided a wealth of information.

It was interesting how relationships with federal investigators worked. This was the deal – you told them everything they wanted to know, answering each question, which usually led to another dozen or so subsequent questions. In return, they didn't tell you anything. That was standard procedure, no veering off the path, no extraneous conversation, no small talk, all business.

However, in the course of our meetings I did ultimately learn many, many disturbing details, mostly revealed through the questions being asked. Both Paul and Greg carefully recorded Laura's and my responses on yellow legal pads. After a couple of meetings, having watched them take notes for hours, I asked them, "Why don't you guys use laptop computers?" They told me that only their hand-written notes would be admissible in court. Each page of their notes had official signatures of those present. I asked if the case would end up being prosecuted and they said most assuredly yes, it would.

This statement confirmed that in fact what Laura had discovered was indeed something which was criminal and likely to cause Slava to be arrested. Until that point, I didn't really believe anything would happen, just as nothing had happened with the Missouri State Licensure or with the Council on Accreditation.

Their line of questioning was bringing about in me a nagging fear that I might be in danger. Or that Laura might be in danger. When I expressed my fear for both Laura and I, we were told the prosecutor's office had "some concern" for us as well. We were told to vary our daily routines, not to walk my dog, Miles, at the same time each day. The investigators told us they had already spoken with the local police and explained to the police that I was a witness in a serious federal investigation. I was told that my house was placed on a special list which meant that it was more closely monitored by the police and any calls from our residence to the police were to be given top priority. They told me our alarm system was not only now connected to the security company, but also to the police. With my permission, a wire "trap" was placed on my home phone. My level of fear only increased, this information did nothing to assuage the fears that were taking root in my head. We were told that the US federal government was working closely with Interpol. I wasn't even really sure what that was, having only heard it discussed on television shows. So, I looked it up, learning that it stood for The

International Police Organization and it provided a legal mechanism for intercountry police cooperation. The knowledge that police, not only in the US, but in other countries, were investigating Slava was almost more than I could comprehend. One of the investigators said they just wanted to get Slava off the street as quickly as possible. Laura and I did not know what to make of that statement.

I was given the private cell and home phone number of Jeff Jensen, the federal prosecutor in charge of the case. I had already had several phone conversations with him during this time. He wanted me to be able to reach him at any time. We were assured that Laura was in little danger as her knowledge was strictly limited to the financial aspects of the domestic office, she had never been present at foreign meetings, and they believed she had had no direct contact with any suspects they had already identified in the case, other than Slava of course. But they still asked her to be prudent about her surroundings and her daily routines.

I was suddenly very frightened, always watching over my shoulder, becoming afraid of whatever may be lurking somewhere in the dark. Laura insisted on knowing what was going on, almost reprimanding Paul and Greg for what they were putting me through. I asked if Slava was aware that I was cooperating with the authorities and was told, yes, they had visited with him already and he was aware. I began to cry, processing all of their admonitions about how to live my life and this knowledge about Slava made me begin to wonder if Slava would actually hurt me. I had never seen him really violent, other than the time he threw his motorcycle helmet at me, but I had seen him in a state of rage on many occasions. One of the investigators told me that an FBI officer met with Slava and that Slava had been told, "It would be in your best interest if nothing happened to Brenda."

I wanted to scream – "How is that supposed to make me feel better!!" They had basically warned another person not to hurt me! I was now officially terrified one-hundred percent of the time.

It was after this interaction that Laura really took on the investigators.

She was very angry. She told them that we kept giving them information without getting anything in return. She was furious that I was being forced to live a terrified existence. She said that we weren't going to continue to cooperate unless they told us where this was all going. After several seconds, Paul said that the federal government was preparing a large federal and international case against Slava and there would be a number of charges, ranging from money laundering to embezzlement, along with several others. We were told that we would be major witnesses in the case. Once more I began to cry, and we had to stop for the day. I simply couldn't process anything else that day.

When leaving my home and driving to nearly anywhere in the city, I had to drive right past the old Small World office. I found myself going totally out of the way to avoid driving past the building. It elicited such intense angst for me and made me want to stop my car in the middle of the street and just sob. Just saying Slava's name made me weak with grief.

CHAPTER 90

NEVER-ENDING INTERVIEWS

PRIOR TO THIS EVENT, I had never met nor even had a conversation with a federal investigator. They came across as stoic people, not demonstrating much emotion. I imagined that was instilled in them during their government training. They were always professional, courteous, and efficient.

During the months that we met, Laura and I looked at more than a hundred pictures and were asked if we recognized the people in photographs. Sometimes it was evident that the pictures were taken with telephoto lenses. Laura rarely recognized anyone. Often, I did not know the name of the person whose picture I was seeing, but occasionally I could identify the person immediately. Then I would be questioned as to the information I had about that person. Almost always I knew very little. I knew that this person was a driver, or that person was a foreign country coordinator, another person was a director of a local adoption center, or that person was someone's spouse. I successfully identified some of the government officials with whom we had worked in Russia. I could tell them what city a person worked in and what they did for us, as far as I knew. Sometimes they would show me a picture and I would recognize the person but couldn't recall a name. They would sometimes give me a couple of names to choose from to see if I could pick the right name. It seemed that whenever we played this game, I could almost always recognize the name upon hearing it. But the exercise was unnerving, to say the least.

I lived in a constant state of anxiety for nearly a year, worried about both mine and my family's safety. I became jumpy and nervous. Going to work was the best thing for me, giving me something else upon which to focus. My super power of compartmentalizing events in my brain allowed me to function exceedingly well at work, being quite successful. I would walk into my office and shut off that other part of my life. The evenings and weekends were the worst. I became afraid of the dark, wrestling branches, or whistling wind. I rarely went out at night by myself, never to a mall or a gas station. I kept the house alarm on all the time, setting it the second I walked into the house. I had difficulty concentrating or following movies or conversations. I had been an avid reader my whole life, regularly reading a book a week – during that year, I was unable to complete a single one.

One night, around 10:30 PM, I looked out my window at the street in front of my house, an activity that regularly consumed me before going to bed. Across the street and down one house sat an older model, generic, dark-colored sedan. The car was pointed toward our house, so the driver was on the side closest to me. However, it was quite dark, with no moon that night, and I was unable to see anything except that the person sitting in the driver's seat was smoking a cigarette. I lived on a small cul-de-sac and the only regular traffic came from my four neighbors. It wasn't a street upon which people just stopped to have a smoke break. I felt terror well up within me. The interviews with the federal investigators had become more frightening as their questions developed a more sinister sense to them. I stood peeking out the window from behind the curtains for a long time. I found our binoculars to see if

I could read the license plate and the car did not have one on the front, as is the law in Missouri. My legs grew weary from standing for so long. Eventually, the car drove away, and I went to bed, never sleeping that night. I should have called the investigators or the police, I had all their numbers. But I didn't, I think in retrospect because I just wasn't able to think straight. Fear truly inhibits one's reasoning abilities.

Marcia insisted I seek counseling, which I did, earning me a diagnosis of mild PTSD. I explained to my therapist that frequently I felt like I wasn't really participating in the drama but watching it from above as an interested observer. It was easier to manage my emotions if I didn't actually touch them. After a time, I learned to juggle the jumbled emotions, sort and categorize them, and eventually put most of them safely on the shelf.

The federal investigators continued with their inquiries, asking Laura and me about numerous meetings that had been held, giving us dates and times. They wanted to know if one of us was there and if we were, did we recall what was discussed. I explained to them that although I may have been present at some of the meetings in Russia, they were all conducted in Russian and it was rare that Slava translated the subject matter for me. This had been a point of annoyance at the time, but I had begun to feel that it was probably a good thing I knew so little. It seemed to shorten some of the questioning about people and events. Poor Laura spent hours going through finances, looking at hundreds of checks, and being asked questions about expenses, receipts, invoices, etc. Frequently we were quizzed about the purpose of expenses and more often than not, we had no explanation for them. Many of them we had not seen previously.

That's why it was noteworthy the day the investigators were funny. I am not convinced that they meant to be, but the way the question was presented was humorous. On this day we were doing the incredibly tedious job of looking at copies of checks, and trying to provide details or verify a signature. However, frequently neither Laura nor I could provide any information. They began asking us about our main foreign country coordinator, Maria. Sadly, Maria had developed pancreatic cancer and died a couple of years previously. Paul casually asked us if we could recall when Maria had died. I was not completely certain but said I believed it was in in April or May of 2006. Greg looked at a document in front of him and slid it over to Laura and me. As he was sliding a copy of a check across the table Paul asked, "Well, was she still dead in October?" The check indeed was from her account and was signed with Maria's name, but she obviously had not signed it. I was staring at Slava's writing; I sighed, "Oh God."

Laura started to laugh. Not because it was funny that Slava had forged Maria's signature, but because of the way the question had been posed. It was obvious that Maria had not signed the check because she was dead, so I was not quite certain why they asked us the question. Perhaps the purpose was to elicit in me the exact reaction I had given. Perhaps they wanted me to see their reality which was that Slava was not the hero I had wanted and needed to believe he was. I did confirm for the investigators that I believed Maria's name was in Slava's handwriting. If Slava had been doing this, what else was he doing?

One other time we were given a tiny crumb of information. Laura asked about a check and the investigator said that there were many checks, in many different accounts, signed by people in which they were interested. I asked a question about the many different accounts. Paul said, well, we have been following the money. He said, "That is always the key, following the money." He said they had followed accounts into several foreign countries, including Russia, Ukraine, and off shore accounts in the Caribbean. The problem was that it was time consuming to get the foreign governments to cooperate in allowing the US federal prosecutor access to foreign financial information. I wanted to know much more, but as always, they were very tight lipped.

One time, we were questioned about a large amount of money that Slava had paid to some attorneys in Florida. I had never heard of them and neither Laura nor I knew of a reason why Small World would have been making payments to attorneys in Florida. These things were done prior to Laura serving as the agency accountant and it seemed prior to EEAG's establishment. Their questions seemed to be taking on a more ominous tone. There were a number of questions about checks written to people of whom I had never heard, in places that had no connection to Small World to my knowledge.

They asked us a lot of questions about Slava's other businesses. Slava had owned an import business at one time, but neither Laura nor I knew anything about it, other than its name. They asked us a lot of questions about Slava's restaurant, the health club, the nightclub, and the spa. They asked us a lot of questions about people who had been employed at Slava's businesses. But there were very few details we had about most people, events, or issues. I was able to answer some questions about cities which we had all visited, I could name places and people, but substantive information had just not been made available to me by Slava.

We were questioned about relationships Slava had with other business people in the community. They asked about current and previous Small World employees, but never interviewed any of them with whom I was in contact. We were asked if we had any information about the ownership of the health club. I knew none of the details. They asked us about trips that Slava had taken with some of the people from the health club and if we were aware that Small World had paid the expenses. I often knew that he vacationed with some of these people and suspected that Small World paid many of the expenses. I told Paul and Greg that I had shared my concern with the accountant and she had said the expenditures were legal. Most of these activities occurred prior to Laura's involvement as the accountant, which had been the beginning of my being included in the broader scope of the financial aspects of the organization. Previous bookkeepers had been reluctant to share much with me. I knew that Slava could be a male chauvinist and I thought he simply believed that this was his territory and he had instructed the bookkeepers to keep me at arms-length. Also, up until the last couple of years, I was incredibly busy running the adoption, fundraising, and humanitarian aspects of Small World and I had been content leaving the management of finances to Slava. He had begun Small World with his own money and I had never had a reason to doubt anything he ever told me until our last year together.

During the year our interviews were being conducted, Slava kept Small World open. He had sued the board and they eventually settled the lawsuit and returned the control of the money to him. The board president called me and said that as the result of individual suits, the cost of continuing in a legal battle with Slava was something none of the board was prepared to financially weather. Slava was a smart man and knew exactly what to do to regain control of the agency. I was told that non-disclosures were signed and that there really was no more information to be shared with me.

For me, having spent so much of my time, emotion, and energy with the federal investigators, I was deeply disappointed to learn this. Yet, I understood that a protracted legal battle was not worth the huge cost for the board members. They had already given so much of their time and energy to the organization.

Paul told me that they believed Slava had established the business from inception with criminal intentions. I asked what had brought them to this conclusion. He explained that the banking documentation they uncovered gave them that indication. He also said a criminal profiler in their department had done an analysis of Slava and this had been stated in a section of that profile. Having heard this from the investigators and learning that Slava was going to continue to take advantage of people by resuming management of Small World made me despondent. I didn't want any of my families to be hurt. But, I knew in the end there would be families who would most likely be hurt, lose money, and/or have bad experiences.

An additional painful experience for me was the almost complete desertion I felt from the previous Small World board of directors. I had helped each of them to adopt their children and had worked hard to build and maintain the agency. I had led countless humanitarian trips to build playgrounds, and many times some of them joined us. I had a long history with and a great affection for the members of the board of directors and had shared much of my own life with them. Yet in the end, except for my dear friend Phil and his wife Jeni, not one of the board members reached out to me or called me to make sure I was okay. They had to know how devastated I had been. But they never picked up the phone or sent an e-mail. I had to reach out to the board president regarding business issues a couple of times, but other than that, there was no communication from them. I had even developed social relationships with a couple of them, and even from them, I heard not a peep. They dismissed me as easily as you would a stray dog. I had cared deeply for Slava, only to learn that he cared so little for me. Now, again, I was struggling with having cared so much for this group of people only to learn that I really hadn't mattered to them. Phil, Jeni, and their children continue to be dear friends of Laura's and my family.

CHAPTER 91

THE INDICTMENT

EVENTUALLY THE FACE-TO-FACE MEETINGS WITH the federal investigators became less frequent. More of our communications during those final two months were phone conversations where Laura or I would be asked to clarify something. In early August of 2009, during one of my final conversations with the lead investigator, I asked him if he could share the status of the case. I needed to move on with my life, but always looming over me was this impending testimony that would have to be given against a person whom I had at one time dearly loved. I was hopeful that my involvement could in some manner be minimized. It had seemed to me that I had not been able to provide much information that would seemingly implicate Slava in anything. The investigator told me that most of what I had done was confirm what they already knew or at least suspected, but that I would need to remain a key witness in the case. My heart sank.

Laura and I were told that prior to my contacting the federal prosecutor, Slava had already been under investigation by the FBI for several years. I asked what the topic of that investigation had been and they said they could not discuss it with me. I began to accept that there were more concerns than just Slava's establishment of a bank account and passing it off as a business. I had so many unanswered questions about what had been going on with Slava over the previous fifteen years. The investigators told us that the biggest thing Laura and I had been able to do was to "connect the dots for them." The investigator promised to let Laura and I know when Slava was actually arrested.

I asked if there was a time frame for the case. Paul said a grand jury had already been convened and had voted to indict Slava. They were holding off on the arrest, pending receipt of some additional information. I knew there was no reason to ask what they were waiting for; my question would never be answered by them. It was expected that the federal prosecutor's office would officially arrest Slava in the coming weeks, most likely sometime in late September or early October 2009. I asked if Slava knew what lay ahead and if I should be afraid. Paul stated that yes, Slava was aware, but he did not believe I needed to be concerned stating, "Slava has a lot of other things to worry about that are bigger than you."

The investigator added that Laura and I would be confirming the financial information they had amassed and we would be the human faces of the hundreds of documents which would be presented to a jury. Paul explained that juries have trouble relating to cases where all the proof is rooted in documents. I asked if Slava would go to prison and he responded, "Most likely for a long time." This just brought more anguish to me. Slava, the vibrant, life of the party, going to prison – it was just unimaginable.

Ultimately, we were told that most of the information that would be used against Slava was obtained by investigators through alternate means such as the FBI and officials in foreign countries. They frequently mentioned that we were helpful to confirm what they had already figured out or had already discovered. The investigator confirmed to me that a large collaborative investigation had taken place in both Russia and Belarus and hundreds of people had been interviewed. We were told that the US government had worked closely with Interpol on this case and that hundreds of government investigators, both in the US and abroad, had been involved in the case. It seemed to have been a massive investigation.

As I had done many times before, I tried to put this latest information on that shelf in my brain. I had been good at doing this with so many other things most of my life, I didn't understand why this news was so difficult to put on that shelf. I seemed plagued by thoughts of Slava and his future. I was endlessly sad that the man I thought I knew may not have existed at all. I sometimes found myself wishing there was some way in which I could comfort that tender side of him that I had known so well. I had needed to cling to the belief that Slava had not been a truly corrupt person. He had loved his daughter, cried at sad movies, and had seemed loyal to his friends. He had been generous with my family many times through the years. Together we had saved 1800 orphans, and I believed that had been meaningful to him. I needed to believe that. He had also formed friendships with some of our clients, those were real. How could this possibly be the same person?

At times during the interviews when I was growing weary of cooperating and continuing to provide information that was sure to hurt Slava, the investigators would tell me things like, "Slava cherry picked you for this because you had the experience, but also he saw a weakness in you because of your personal adoption story."

One time, one of them told me that I had not meant anything to Slava. I had wanted to scream at him, "How do you know? You weren't present when we were toasting adoptive families, or peeing in a field together in Belarus, or sharing a queen bed in Moscow! You weren't there when he came to my rescue after my knee surgery or when he came to the hospital to see Laura. You weren't there!"

But I had been. Laura had been. We had our own truth.

Our interviews seemed to be over, and I waited for the phone call telling me Slava had been arrested. I needed to know what was happening.

CHAPTER 92

IMPOSSIBLE!

THE WEEKS AFTER MY LAST conversation with the Federal Investigator dragged on. Then, in the span of a few seconds, my world again fell off its axis in an irreversible way. I was driving to work on a bright and sunny day, September 15, 2009. I had not even thought about Slava at all that day, which was slowly becoming more and more common. My cell phone rang, and a Russian friend blurted out, "Slava's dead!" I whispered no, how, when, what happened? She explained to me that Slava had been found in his apartment, apparently having injected himself with the same drug that killed Michael Jackson. I kept asking questions, but she had no answers. My friend said she would call me when she learned more. The bottom line was that Slava had committed suicide just days before being formerly charged with a number of crimes. According to the US Attorney's office and the federal investigators, Paul and Greg, Slava was to be charged with money laundering, embezzlement, and fraud, at a minimum. These were only the charges, and now Slava would never have the opportunity to defend himself.

I immediately called Laura, who was just as shocked as me. Although the news brought me to tears for what I had believed and hoped to be good and pure about Slava, Laura was much more thick-skinned about it. Laura had been angry with Slava for a long time and that was how she chose to deal with the immense pain we had experienced during the past year. She was quite simply too angry to be anything but finished with him.

I also called Paul, having him on speed dial in my cell phone, to find out why he hadn't called me, and learned shockingly that the federal authorities had not yet learned about it. He was in utter disbelief, to say the least. He said he would call me later that day after he was able to gather more information. As I thought about it throughout the day, I realized that for these two men, with whom I had spent many hours and who had poured their hearts into this case for nearly a whole year, all of their work might now become useless.

Over the next few days, I learned that Slava's daughter was the one who found him. I was horrified by this, what a ghastly event for a daughter. Regardless of what Slava had done, he hadn't deserved to die. He needed to pay for his crime, but not in that way. Internally, I was further conflicted and confused. Slava's death meant the end of a scary time for me and the end of my involvement in what was sure to be an ugly and painful court process. But how could I feel relieved to be free of these things at the cost of someone's life, especially someone whom I had loved like a brother. There could be no winner here.

In the days that followed, I learned some of the details surrounding Slava's death. The police found an IV pole, presumably from his surgery center, in his bedroom. I heard about his funeral and knew that he had been cremated and that his ashes would be returned to Russia. He had always loved Russia so much and I was comforted by the knowledge that he would be returned to his homeland.

Paul called me back. He said that the investigation was over, and I was now free to speak with whomever I wished. My "protection" had been removed, the phone trap was removed from my phone, and the local police had been instructed to "stand down." He shared his disappointment because they had spent nearly a year on the case and felt that they had put together a successful prosecution. I asked what the final charges would have been, and Paul stated the focus would have been the crimes that were the easiest to prove, things to do with finance; fraud, tax evasion, and embezzlement. I asked him about Svetlana. He said that they believed she knew very little and there was no point in pursuing charges against her. He said she wouldn't be able to help them reach the people they were trying to reach, adding that the scope of the investigation had been aimed at discovering the people with whom Slava had been working. He didn't elaborate on who this was. He thanked me for all my help and for the first time was much more human with me. He said that he wanted me to be aware that by our living in the same city, there was always the potential that we might someday run into one another, and if that ever happened he wouldn't be able to acknowledge me. He was sorry, but those were the rules by which he had to live, and he wanted to make sure I understood. He asked that I share that information with Laura. We had spent what seemed like hundreds of hours together and it seemed strange to simply say goodbye. But, after such a long and painful year, we did just that. I said, "Goodbye, Paul," as I gently pushed the button on my cell phone, feeling totally empty inside.

I tried to move forward and find joy in my life. I knew that regardless of the outcome, I had done the right thing. I was finally free to speak with whomever I wished. There was a freedom in that, but I wasn't sure I ever really wanted to talk about this part of my life again. I put all the notes from the past year in a drawer, closed it, and walked away. I had new chapters of life ready to be written.

I began to hear from old clients and friends. Those who had sought me out, but to whom I had been unable to speak, were called back. Old connections were revitalized, which helped with my pain, and I knew these relationships would be necessary to help me heal. Yet still, there were no calls from any of the board members, except of course Phil. I did sometime later have a conversation with a board member who apologized for not taking action sooner after hearing about what Slava had done. I understood that they had been in a difficult legal position, but when it had all been over, why hadn't they called?

I experienced some surprises from former clients over the next few months. Once, while walking in a shopping area of town, I encountered a former client with his adopted son. He looked coldly at me and stated I should be ashamed of what I did. I assumed he meant my having turned Slava in. But for me, there had been no choice; it was the moral thing to do. I hoped he wasn't holding me responsible for Slava's death, believing that to be a totally irrational conclusion. He said he loved Slava and that Slava had helped him get his son and none of the rest should have mattered. I just shook my head and walked away. He was blind, and he didn't know any facts. He only knew that he loved his son and that Slava had played a pivotal role and like he said, nothing else mattered. I truly understood. I suspected there were other parents out there who felt the same.

I encountered another adoptive dad who simply stated that he never would have cooperated with the authorities. I could only assume he felt this way because of his gratitude toward Slava for his two children. I didn't argue my case. I had done what my conscience led me to do.

I had long discussions about these reactions with Marcia. She believed that for some clients, knowing what Slava had done in some way tarnished the sparkling vision of their dream adoption. She felt that perhaps emotionally they could not accept the truth about Slava and this was their way of protecting themselves.

It was interesting that some people, who had been clients turned friends, never contacted me. Some friends from whom I felt certain I would hear, remained silent. I had experienced such loss that sometimes it didn't feel that I could take anymore. I had to put this event and most of the people who had been important to my life "on that shelf in my head." I desperately needed this part of my life to be over.

PART 3

CHAPTER 93

THE FBI OPENS IT ALL
BACK UP FOR ME

ABOUT TWO WEEKS AFTER SLAVA'S death, I received a telephone call from Tom, who identified himself as an FBI agent. He explained that he was assigned simultaneously to the local FBI office as well as to the local police department. He asked if I would answer some questions about Slava. I replied that Slava was dead and I had nothing else to say. I was moving on with my life and was tired of having investigators in my dining room. I told him I did not want to meet with him, but he continued to press me. I finally told him, "Fine, if you want to speak with me, here is my attorney's name and phone number and you can talk with him. Let him hear what you have to say, I am not interested."

But, a week later my attorney, David, called me and said, "Brenda, I know you don't want to talk to the FBI agent, but I have heard him out and believe you should meet with him. He agreed to meet with you in my office and I will be right there with you. It will be okay." I respected and admired David, who had also become my friend, and I knew David would protect me and would do his best to shield me from further pain. I had kept him informed about the investigation, so he knew the details of the situation. I agreed to meet.

The day of the meeting I arrived first, and shortly afterward Tom walked into David's conference room. He was tall, muscular, had brown hair, and seemed like a pleasant person. He handed each of us his business card with the embossed, and impressive, FBI logo on it. I would add this new card to my collection, I thought, realizing it was an odd collection for an average American to possess. Once more, I found myself rubbing my fingers across the raised lettering throughout that first interview.

As soon as we sat down, I wanted to know why they were still interested in Slava since he had passed away. Tom said they were investigating some of Slava's associates. I reiterated, as I had to the federal prosecutors, that I didn't really know anything about them. I was probably not the most cooperative interviewee that he had ever worked with, being hesitant to jump back into the nightmare. Sitting in David's conference room, I mostly just wanted to concentrate on the carved wooden ducks sitting in the middle of the table.

Tom explained that the federal prosecutor's case had centered primarily on issues to do with the IRS and the fiscal workings of Small World; fraud, tax evasion, and other crimes related to finance. He said the FBI investigation was centered on criminal issues not related to finance. He told me that the FBI had been investigating Slava for several years and that they already knew a lot about him and his activities. I was stunned to hear again that Slava had been under investigation by the FBI, not wanting to believe him. I was also amazed that two totally separate investigations had been taking place with Slava at the center of each.

Tom began by asking me questions about how well I knew Slava. I told him that eighteen months earlier I would have said I knew Slava extremely well. But now, I was not sure what was real versus what was just the perception that had been forced upon me.

He asked me to describe Slava and his personality. I told him Slava had been a bit of a hedonist, could be quite volatile, but also exceedingly kind. He had been a very complicated person. His first questions were about the visa invitations I had produced for Russians to visit the US. I explained that it was always at Slava's direction and I had no knowledge of the people being invited to our country, other than those that were Small World staff. I explained the process, as I had to Paul and Greg, of Slava giving me a name and instruction and I simply created a letter on Small World letterhead, addressed to the American Embassy in Russia, Belarus, or Ukraine, that "blank" person was being invited by our organization to visit the US. Again, I explained that if I asked about the person, usually Slava told me that we were inviting an official's daughter, for example, to visit the US to improve the relationship with an official in a town from where we were facilitating adoptions. In fact, I could only remember inviting three categories of people: foreign officials, children of those officials, or people who worked directly with our clients and who were invited to attend events like our annual picnics.

Tom continued to ask me a lot of questions about Slava's activities, but I didn't really feel like I was being helpful. I just didn't know anything. Paul and Greg's questions had seemed more businesslike and often felt free of emotion. Tom's questions were more highly charged and frankly, more disturbing. Or, perhaps they just felt that way because I was so emotional after Slava's death.

During one of our conversations I mentioned one of the ladies who had drowned in Slava's pool. I can't recall the topic of the conversation or why this came up. Tom had been looking down at a paper and David had been taking some notes, when both of their heads jerked up staring at me wide eyed, simultaneously asking, "What?" I then said that actually, two people had drowned in Slava's swimming pool.

Both were staring at me as Tom gently placed his pen on the table, and in a calm and measured voice, asked, "Brenda, how many other people do you know that have had just one person drown in their pool?"

I immediately saw where he was going and answered, "Well, none."

He paused and then added, "Well, didn't you think it was pretty odd that you know someone who had TWO people drown in their pool in the relatively short time you knew them?"

I had to agree with, "Well, I guess yes, now that you put it that way." I explained I had chalked it up to the fact that all of the Russians I knew seemed to drink a great deal and I had never really thought too much about it.

Tom then asked me if I ever made the arrangements for or had any knowledge of the young people returning to Russia. I said I never had any knowledge about them after creating the visa invitations for Slava. I never knew when they arrived, or when they left. Tom asked me if I had ever met any of the visitors, other than staff. I replied that I didn't recall ever having met any of them, other than some of the officials, or having any knowledge of them after their arrival in the US.

I wanted to know why he was asking about these invitations, hoping he would be more forthcoming with information than the federal investigators had been. Amazingly, he was considerably more informative than Paul and Greg had been. Tom explained that they could find no record of many of the girls after their arrival in the US. He said that many of them hadn't returned to Russia or hadn't been found in the US. I had been aware that some Russians came to the US and never returned when their visas expired, just like immigrants from other countries. I suggested perhaps the girls just married or changed their names to remain in the US. This was to me a more palatable explanation for the missing women than any other scenario I could imagine, or what I feared he was insinuating.

Tom assured me that after exhaustive national and international searches over several years, many of the girls had not been located. He eventually told me that human trafficking was most likely to have been added to the charges the FBI would have levied against Slava. This was extremely shocking to me and I couldn't even fathom what had happened to the young women brought to the US. I couldn't believe that Tom was telling me Small World had been responsible for sponsoring young women, enabling them to obtain visas to enter the US, and then once here there was no indication of what happened to them. I wanted to know more about the investigation, but Tom refused to share. This was a hard conversation to process because my world with Slava had centered on saving children, and this seemed to be the opposite.

As I tried to process what this information meant, my head was spinning with potential explanations for the missing women and girls, some in their early teens. Unfortunately, I couldn't create an accounting of his statements that made sense to me. The nefarious scenarios running through my head did not in any way match up with the man I knew and trusted. After our meeting, I called David to review that conversation, wanting to make sure of what I had heard. I had wanted David to tell me I had been dreaming and no such conversation had taken place. But, David had been truthful and reiterated what Tom had said. This information would only be allowed to live on the most secret shelf in my brain. Other than the writing of this story, this information never gets pulled from my brain's lock box.

It was thankfully time to end for the day and I agreed to meet with Tom again in David's office.

CHAPTER 94

TOO MANY DEATHS

ONE EVENING ABOUT THREE DAYS later, Tom called me at home and asked me if I were sure that two people had drowned in Slava's pool. I said I only knew what Slava told me, which was two people drowned in his pool over the years, further telling him that my staff had also been aware of this. I did share that Marcia and I had gone to the wake for the nanny, who had been the first to drown. I wanted to know why he was asking. He explained that they could only find police reports for one drowning victim and again asked me if I were sure. I reiterated that I only knew what Slava had told me and had no other firsthand knowledge.

The next time we met, the first thing I did was to ask about the deaths in Slava's pool. Tom stated they had canvassed Slava's neighborhood and everyone, but one family, agreed that there had been two drownings in Slava's pool. Yet, there seemed to be no record of a second incident in any of several local police departments with which he spoke. He explained that he had been unable to find the second drowning victim listed on any coroners list anywhere. There seemed to be no good explanation for the discrepancy. I knew that not only was I certain, but Laura, Marcia, and Maureen had also given the same response of "two" when questioned about the number of drownings in Slava's pool. Regardless of whatever spin the FBI wanted to put on this information, I needed to believe they had been unfortunate accidents.

That led to Tom questioning me about other deaths related to Slava. The first I could recall was Slava's handyman, who had been found hanging from a tree one morning many years, maybe twelve or thirteen, before. But I had no information and was unable to even recall his name.

I then shared the little information I had about the husband of one of our foreign country coordinators in one of our Russian cities, who had been found floating in a river in Russia, having been shot in the head. I explained that Slava had told me the coordinator's husband may have been involved in some kind of criminal activity. He asked if I had ever met him and I said yes, he had seemed like a lovely person. But again, I repeated that I had no first-hand knowledge about anything related to any of the deaths, only knowing what Slava told me.

I described the story of the Russian government official from one of the towns in which we had a program who lost her husband after his car was purposefully forced off the road outside of Moscow. Again, I had no additional information. But, I did recall that Slava told me the official and her husband had been wealthy and once again, Slava mentioned criminal activity, in fact this time calling it organized crime. Tom asked me how Slava had known the car had been purposefully run from the road – I had no explanation.

The last one of which I knew was Slava's former daughter-in-law who had been found dead in a New York City hotel, her death reportedly resulting from a drug overdose. Tom pressed me for more information and I explained that I was not sure when Slava's son and Olga divorced and knew nothing about their relationship. He asked a lot of questions about Olga and how well I had known her. Since she had been Alex's nanny, I had been able to describe her quite well. She had been a sweet, young woman when I had known her.

Both my attorney and the FBI agent just stared at me. They had odd, incredulous looks on their faces. They almost simultaneously asked me how I could not think something odd when one man's life was touched by at least six tragic and/or unusual deaths, some of which were purported to be murder. I replied that since the deaths occurred over a period of about twelve or thirteen years, and I had such scary experiences in Russia personally, I chalked them up to the violence, alcoholism, and drug abuse of the Russian culture. But to myself, I was thinking, *How had I not made any connections, why had I not questioned the oddity of so many deaths?* But I knew the answer, I had been loyal to Slava and I believed most everything he told me.

I tried to explain to both Tom and David that Slava was extremely charismatic and his explanations were always plausible. He usually readily dismissed most events as unimportant. It had not been hard for me to follow his lead and I spent little time thinking about these events after they happened. But I have to say that even to my ears, my explanation sounded weak. I felt naïve, gullible, and suddenly not very smart.

But now, years later, and being able to give myself some compassion, I realize that as a child, I had been conditioned to do what I was told and to avoid asking too many questions, it was a safer way to live. I had been raised in the perfect atmosphere, which enabled someone such as Slava to manipulate me. When faced with an aggressive person in a position of power, questioning him was a challenge difficult for me to manage.

CHAPTER 95

PLANNING AHEAD

THE MEETING CONTINUED WITH TOM asking me pointed questions about Slava's behaviors, his habits, and his beliefs. He asked me, "Did Slava tend to plan things ahead of time, was he meticulous about things, and did he prepare for events?" as well as other questions along this line. I replied that Slava was capricious by nature and such a poor planner that once when leaving for a trip to Russia, he had to stop at the bank to get money and then stop by the Fed Ex office at the airport to get his visa, which had arrived late because he requested it too late for it to be delivered to his home! I shared the story about our not having a place to sleep when we arrived in Moscow because Slava hadn't thought to make a hotel reservation. I used to laugh at him as we would be on the phone while he was packing for his trip to Russia and the plane would be leaving in less than three hours. That was my Slava, and these were typical behaviors. He certainly did not plan things ahead of time, at least not the Slava I knew. I always had to qualify my statements that way now.

I took a few minutes to silently think about the pride I had previously felt in my keen ability to assess other people, a skill I began cultivating as a young child. I realized that I had not been able to gauge Slava accurately at all. How could I have been so wrong in my judgment of him?

Tom spent a lot of time asking me general questions about the way Slava did things, things that happened on our trips, etc. He next asked, "So, what would you say if I told you Slava left eight suicide letters and they were dated weeks before his death?"

I was still processing the information that Slava had left so many notes and hadn't even begun to process the timeline when David burst out, "You don't think he killed himself, do you?"

Tom then told David that the vial of Propofol found in Slava's apartment had no lot numbers on the bottle. It was impossible to trace; legally, it did not exist. He added that was a classic means of terminating people in organized crime.

I burst into tears and was totally unable to cooperate any further. I had just spent a year being afraid of Slava and being involved in an excruciating investigation, which I thought was horrific enough. Now here was an FBI agent talking to me about organized crime! It was impossible for me to process all this information. I had loved Slava. He might have been unethical and committed fraud and embezzlement, but did his activities include a foray into organized crime? I would not believe that.

As I sat there crying, Tom asked David if they could speak in the next room. I immediately straightened up; I wouldn't be involved in any more secrets. I wasn't going to allow it! Had Paul and Greg known this? Why had no one ever told me what was really going on? I stepped over to the wall, put my ear against it, and could hear everything Tom and David were saying to one another. Tom said to David, "You *need* to get her to cooperate; we think she might know more than she thinks she knows."

David then asked, "Where is all of this going?"

"We think Slava was a leader in organized crime in St. Louis and we are investigating his contacts," Tom responded. "We are trying to identify the people with whom he was working." I was more stunned by this than when I learned the truth about EEAG, my knees felt as if they would buckle and my head was spinning.

I stood there with my head leaning against the wall, wanting to scream, "I don't know anything, leave me alone!"

Suddenly, I realized I was faced with admitting I had listened through the wall and I could run, screaming out the door in terror, or pretend I hadn't heard a thing. I was scared enough that I wanted to know everything I could, and my mother's voice in my head prevented me from admitting I had been rude and had eavesdropped, something of which she would have greatly disapproved.

I quickly sat down and waited to see what would come next. In a few minutes, they reentered the conference room, and sitting back down, David took my now trembling hand and told me everything would be okay, but that it was very important that I just answer a few more questions. I agreed to do so because now I wanted to know things from Tom as well!

Tom took a small stack of papers out of his briefcase. He said that he had copies of the typed suicide letters which had been written utilizing a Russian keyboard and signed by Slava, and that he also had translated copies. David began asking questions about the letters. I sat there in silence trying to pay attention, needing to process what I had just heard. It was unfathomable to me that Slava would have taken the time to write eight letters. They all looked to be at least one or two pages long. That was not something the Slava I knew would have done! *He would have called me and made me write them,* I thought.

Tom then asked if he could read me a few small sections to get my opinion about them. I asked if any of the passages he wanted to share were about me. He replied that, although Slava had referred to me in one of the letters, he wanted to discuss something else. I immediately asked about the letter that referenced me and learned that Slava had written something in a letter to the woman who took my place at the agency. I wanted to know what was written and asked if I could read it. Tom replied that it probably was not a good idea because what Slava said about me was very nasty. I pressed Tom, and David asked if he could look at it. Tom handed a copy of the translated suicide letter, referencing me, to David, who read it and quickly returned it to Tom. David turned to me and said, "No, Brenda you can't read this, I just can't let those sick, ugly words into your head." I trusted David and that was good enough for me.

I told the agent that I was uncomfortable with all of this and that I believed that on some level Slava really did care about me. I said I didn't want to answer any more questions. He replied in a chilly voice, "Brenda, our profilers deemed Slava a sociopath. We believe that from the beginning, Slava chose you because he felt he could manipulate you as the result of your belief in what you have frequently referred to as your 'mission.' He never, ever really cared about you."

I was so confused, perhaps he was right. I was suddenly more tired and heartsick than I had been in months. Hadn't Paul said almost the same thing? I had feared this for a long time and should probably have known when Slava was calling me stupid or other equally nasty names through the years. I should have paid more attention when he was screaming at me or humiliating me in front of others. Maybe I did not matter to him. But deep in my heart, I could not accept this.

Tom continued and read brief excerpts from some of the letters. He asked me if the words written sounded like Slava. After fifteen years of working with him, traveling with him numerous times internationally, fighting with him, and making some wonderful memories with him, I could honestly say that what was written did not sound like anything like words Slava would have said. He simply didn't talk that way. The grammar was too good and not at all how Slava spoke. I shared with Tom that over the years, Slava regularly called me to ask how to phrase something he wanted to say properly in English. I had done the writing for some of his businesses and I knew his English language skill set. Slava did not have the command of the English language which would have been necessary to write the words he read to me.

He then asked me if I would find it in character for Slava to plan his suicide a month ahead and to have penned eight typewritten letters to people. To me, that behavior did not mesh with the "fly-by-the-seat-of-your-pants" Slava that I knew. But, then again, I told the agent, I am not sure I really knew Slava at all.

I recognized Tom was insinuating that it was likely that Slava had not written those letters and that someone else had. I was nearly hysterical at the implication that Slava was involved in something so untoward that he had been murdered, and the letters had been written by someone else. Whoever had written them had written nasty things about *me!* That realization was more than I could bear. The voice in my head kept saying, "The bad people wrote about *me!*" Repeatedly, those words kept ringing inside my head.

With tears in my eyes, I asked Tom if he had any other things he wanted to ask or share with me. I desperately needed to escape from that room, feeling light headed and battling nausea. I was emotionally exhausted. He expressed his apologies, but they needed to find out what else I might possibly know. He asked me several more questions about Slava and people of whom I had never heard. He asked me about events for which I had no knowledge. Some of his questions were similar to what I had been asked by the federal investigators. I told him I had looked at pictures, documents, and checks for the feds for months and suggested that he speak to them. I told him I knew they had taken good notes. Tom told me he had already met with them, several times.

I asked how this would all end, how would I ever know what happened in the investigation. He told me, "I'm sorry, you will never know. Someday you may hear about a big arrest, but you will never know for sure if it had a connection to all of this."

I asked if he were certain that Slava had not committed suicide and he said they were positive. I don't recall my next question, but until the day I die, I will recall his next sentence. "Well, is it suicide if you have a gun to your head and have been handed a deadly drug?" That picture was not something I was happy to have in my head, and not one easily shelved, but I was the one who had pressed the issue.

I wanted to know if the truth about his death would be released to the public and Tom replied, "Probably not, there was no reason to do so." But, he never told me I couldn't share what David and I had just learned.

I remember feeling extraordinarily beaten down. I asked if I had reason to be afraid. Tom said, "No, you don't have any information that is worth much to anyone anymore, and if someone working with Slava thought you did, you would already be dead." I had heard so many shocking things over the past eighteen months, there just didn't seem to be any shock neurons left in my brain. I was just empty as I sat there staring at him, having no words left to say, completely numb all over.

CHAPTER 96

THIS IS THE END

Our interview finally concluded, and I had given them all the information I had. There didn't seem to be any more questions left to ask and I certainly had nothing left to offer. David asked Tom to contact him if they had any additional questions. I was grateful, yet again, for David's protection of me. We got up to leave and I looked at Tom and asked, "I was never as afraid as I should have been, was I?"

He answered, "No, probably not."

I asked, "Why didn't anyone tell me?"

His last response, "I guess they didn't want you to run." I could hardly believe the cavalier way in which he spoke those words. David and I just stared at him.

Recovering from the shock of Tom's words, I hugged David, shook hands with Tom, and left the room. It was the last time I ever spoke with anyone in any official capacity about Slava.

As I walked down the hall after leaving David's office, I realized there would never be answers to many of the questions that had been raised for me during the past eighteen months. God had given me some answers, but many others would forever remain a mystery. Were the federal investigators and the FBI correct, had Slava begun Small World with illegal intentions from the very beginning? Had he and Svetlana really been robbed in St. Petersburg or was he just setting up the groundwork for the creation of EEAG? What was the real story with the deaths of the people in Russia, or those here in the US? Who had written those eight letters? At the end of his life, had Slava been sorry for it all?

CHAPTER 97

FROM "DREAMS" – A JOURNAL TO CELEBRATE ANDREI

As I worked to process everything that had happened, I feared the negative emotions surrounding Slava would drown out the memory of the noble work we had accomplished. This journal entry reminded me that the wonders of our mission won't ever be forgotten.

This is an excerpt from the journal of Small World adoptive dad, Mike Hogan, written for his son on the day of his adoption. It so touched me and painted such a poignant picture of an adopting parent's perspective, it had to be included. It demonstrates the magnitude of the life-changing work Small World did. Mike recently confirmed to me that he will be sharing the gift of this journal with Andrei on his twenty-first birthday.

Tuesday, March 24, 1998

From the lobby of a spa whose English name means "Oak Grove," in a small city named "Iron Water" near Pyatigorsk. ("Five Mountains"), Russia.

Oh Andrei—

You are one beautiful boy. So small, but so cheerful. I cried when I first saw and held you. You came so naturally into your Mother's and my arms. So alert. So interested. So apparently happy to be held & touched & kissed. You are frail & lack full strength in your little legs. But, from the strength in your little fingers as you squeezed one of my own, I know that you will be a strong boy. With love & care & enough to eat – and with the help & encouragement of your brother and sisters – you'll be everything you could hope to be in no time at all.

You're one of three very lucky babies delivered to three very lucky & joy-filled sets of parents today in Pyatigorsk. If we could package & share the feelings emanating in the head doctor's office earlier this morning, there would be no more wars, no more hunger, no more orphans. It was one of the most poignant & powerful moments in my life - every bit as moving as the day on which I married and the times I helped in the births of your new siblings. We worked so hard & traveled so far to find you, Andrei, and it was worth every second & every inch. As I looked into the faces of the _____ and the _____ (the other adoptive parents), I saw my & your Mom's joy reflected back as if from a mirror. How can someone so small generate so much warmth & passion?

Later this morning, we stood before a judge in the 3rd floor courtroom in the city's court. He tried to be stern & official – and succeeded throughout questioning us – but he smiled when he congratulated us upon being approved to adopt. Though I don't recall his exact words when he met with all three sets of parents after our formal court proceedings, I do remember the intent of his remarks. He asked us to tell you that you were Russian & to encourage you to be proud that you are. He wished you well in your new life & told us he hoped we would be very good parents to you. And, though he said that Russia was going through hard times now, he was optimistic that it would enjoy better times to come. He hoped we'd bring you back to visit someday, to see your home city & better understand your roots. I pass these words along so that you'll remember them, too.

It's been snowing lightly since last night and your home city of Pyatigorsk is covered with two inches or so of snow. The clouds hang low, obscuring all but the lowest reaches of the surrounding mountains from which the city takes its name. People are walking, bundled in fur hats and warm coats against the cold, along and across the streets of the city. Old yellow & red trolleys slide noiselessly along train tracks, picking up & dropping off passengers. A few adults stop from time to time to make & throw snowballs compressed from perfect snow. Though our morning was hectic, it took place in a quiet & serene little mountain city. We have more – far more – in your new country, Andrei. But in things that count & that cross boundaries universally, they have a great deal here as well.

I hope you generate the same inquisitiveness about other places, peoples & cultures that I have, Andrei. I hope that I, as your Dad, can help to open your mind to how much exists beyond what you can see, just as my parents and your Mom's parents did for us. What a gift that is, Andrei. Without it, we might never have had the courage to search for you. With it, we have found you. You're a beautiful son, Andrei. God, you are a beautiful son.

Love,
Dad

P.S. – As a way of thanking him for approving your adoption, we presented the judge with an inscribed gavel. It read: "Justice – Wisdom – Compassion. Andrei Hogan & Family." I hope he fully understands the power in those words. I hope he continues to practice them. The world gets better, day by day, through the actions of each of us as individuals. One person's actions can & often do bring out the best in those around them. Enough individuals, acting nobly, can yield great & powerful results. Collectively, at our best, we can be awesome. But it takes an individual's actions – leadership – to get us going. Promise me you'll think about and act on these words when you're older. Not everyone can build a bridge, Andrei, but we can all build something. Get strong to be strong, Andrei, so that others can draw strength from your example. Pick your own paths, Andrei, but remember that others may follow you. Pick well, Andrei. Pick justly. Pick wisely. Pick compassionately.

CHAPTER 98

THE AFTERMATH OR MAYBE A NEW BEGINNING

I KEEP THE BUSINESS CARDS of the federal investigators, the federal prosecutor, the postal inspector, and the FBI agent in a dresser drawer in my bedroom. On those days when I really can't believe this actually all happened, I pull out their cards and run my fingers over the raised government insignias and smile. I had once believed, I had trusted and been loyal, only to be shattered, but I had survived.

In the end, what do we really know? I am certain I can neither villainize, nor canonize Slava. Many unanswered questions remain. I believe he was a very complicated man with perhaps his own set of internal demons. He made poor decisions, but together we had saved 1800 children and I shall never lose sight of that. How could such a person be as unscrupulous as both the FBI and the federal investigators believed? There were a lot of allegations against Slava, but nothing had been axiomatic to me through our years together. Now, only God can judge him and his motivations. Whatever the impetus behind his creation of Small World, he had been essential to our success in making the world a better place for the children and families of Small World Adoption Foundation of Missouri. I would never believe he had simply been a Machiavellian individual intent on inflicting harm.

Laura and I witnessed the good in Slava many, many times and we knew it was real. We also chose to believe that Slava did really care about both of us, regardless of what anyone said. I had loved him like a brother and no matter what, I would never believe that we had meant nothing to Slava. In spite of it all, Laura and I both chose to forgive him.

But I also had to examine my own culpability in what occurred. If I had paid closer attention, listened to the whispers of others, or asked more questions, would I have seen the signs? Did my history enable me to see only what I wanted, a man and his wife to whom I mattered and in whom I could believe? It will be an unanswered question for all time – should I have known or was I even able to?

In this world, nothing is ever what it appears and who really knows what is in the mind and heart of another human being. That view belongs only to God. Laura and I refuse to lead cynical lives. We refuse to doubt the motives of everyone we meet and wait inevitably for their evil side to appear.

What did we do when it was all over? I was able to finally overcome my fear of being watched or followed or being in danger. I decided to honor my burning need to empower others to find their way out of the darkness and write this book. Laura and I went on to live full lives, to do the best we could every day, finding peace and happiness, caring for and loving our families, and continuing to work to make the world a better place.

And we will always, always remember our dear friend Slava.

PART 4

CHAPTER 99

EPILOGUE

LAURA WAS ABLE TO WALK away from Small World and continue down a successful life path as the owner of her own accounting firm. Ryan went on to be a successful financial planner. Alex graduated from high school and got a job. I believe I have the three most special children in the world and adore each one. I also have two outstanding step-children, Jessica and Taylor. Most importantly, they are all happy.

After leaving Small World, I searched for a job. I desperately hoped to get one that would allow me to continue helping children. I interviewed for a job with Dr. Michael Meehan, Associate Director of Epworth Children and Family Services. A few days after the interview, I met with one of the partners of the consortium for which I would hopefully work, Kevin Drollinger, who would ultimately offer me the position with Michael's recommendation. I felt I had to be honest and disclose my involvement in the federal investigation, which had the potential to eventually land in the newspaper. Of course, at that time Slava was still alive and my involvement in the investigation was in its infancy. I shared an abbreviated version of the story with Kevin.

Fortunately for me, Kevin had, early in his career, had a co-worker who had been involved in nefarious activity and he had been interviewed by the FBI. He could relate to my story. The most fortuitous thing for me was that Kevin was friends with Catherine Hanaway, the Eastern Region Federal Prosecutor at the time, whom he called after I left his office. According to Kevin, Catherine confirmed the account I had shared and encouraged him to hire me.

I was offered the position of CEO for a consortium, which handled foster care and adoption cases for three non-profit agencies, Epworth Children and Family Services, Family Resource Center (now known as FamilyForward), and Youth in Need. I recognized my good fortune in quickly obtaining another position at which I could fully utilize my skills and passion. Through these three amazing organizations, I discovered what truly committed non-profit organizations can achieve in ethical, honorable, and law-abiding ways. Thank you, Michael, Kevin, and Catherine, you were instrumental in helping me to land on my feet and maybe even saving my life. I am unsure I would have survived the loss of my beloved Small World without another place on which I could focus my attention. I still feel blessed every day I get to do this work.

After I began my new position, I recognized that I would need help. I was ultimately able to bring both Marcia and Maureen on at the new company. We remained together until Marcia's retirement but are still close friends.

Five years after I left Small World, the licensing authority for Missouri contacted me and asked if one of my companies would accept the closed Small World files which Svetlana had stacked in a bedroom of her apartment. Federal law mandates the files be stored in a locked facility. Svetlana told the state that she did not have the means to store the files and had been storing them in her apartment for a few years.

There was no action the state could take other than to try to find a "home" for the files. So, knowing my familiarity with the files, I was asked if one of the partners in my company would accept the files. The

CEO for Family Resource Center graciously agreed. The 1500 or so files were transported to my office and Maureen scanned the official adoption documents into a special file on the agency's server. Doing it during breaks from her usual responsibilities, it took Maureen over four years to scan and save the documents.

As I was concluding the writing of this book, my good friend David Korum suggested that I reach out to the federal investigators, the FBI agent, and the federal prosecutor. I was unable to locate the first three, but the former assistant federal prosecutor, Jeff Jensen, who would have prosecuted the financial case against Slava had he lived, spoke briefly with me. Jeff had recently been appointed by the President of the United States to the position of US Attorney for the Eastern Region of the United States, the same position formerly occupied by Catherine Hanaway. Impressively, Jeff remembered the case and explained that the federal government considered me to be a victim under the Victim's Rights Legislation and connected me with Kimberly Sanders, the Victim Witness Coordinator for the federal prosecutor's office in St. Louis. David, Laura, and I met with her at the Federal building in downtown St. Louis. After explaining my rights as a victim and providing answers to procedural questions, Kimberly recommended that I file "Freedom of Information Act" (FOIA) requests to the agencies involved in the investigations of Slava and Small World. She could not have been more helpful to us in guiding us down the path for information but also in confirming our experience. Maybe my questions could be answered, and the nightmare would truly be over.

THE FIRST FOIA RESPONSE

Amazingly, just before this book went to publication, I received the first response to one of our many FOIA requests. The FBI sent my attorney David, who filed all the requests, a CD containing information on multiple investigations regarding Slava. David gave the CD to me.

I was hopeful that I was holding in my hands further proof of what Laura had discovered so many years before. I had been accused publicly of being a disgruntled ex-employee in a local newspaper reader-response posting after an article about Slava was published. Disgruntled? No. Heart-broken, absolutely.

The investigations covered in the pages I received had begun years before the Small World case in which I was involved. Because the FBI can only send a limited amount of material at a time, I was informed I had to submit an additional request for the remainder of the investigations involving Slava from approximately 2002 to his death in 2009. We submitted the request but expect it will be several months before receipt of the remaining reports. So, with an anxious heart, I face more waiting and wondering what I will find.

Nearly every page of the documentation I received, other than the initial investigation into Slava when he first immigrated to the US, was stamped "Classified" or "Secret." The bolded words classified, or secret, also had a large X through the words, signifying the pages had been properly redacted for release, thus no longer considered classified or secret. Each page also contained a stamp stating the redacted information may be declassified in 2035.

The first page of the file was a darkened silhouette of a person I believe to be Slava. Since the original photograph was copied onto the CD, it was impossible to truly identify the person. However, the photo depicted a person with dark, curly hair, I could make out a stethoscope hanging from around his neck, and it was the leading document in an FBI file about Slava. I made the assumption that this was a photo of Slava. I held that picture, of such degraded quality, and now years after it had been taken I began to sob, my heart breaking once again over the person I had loved.

I moved past the picture to examine the rest of the documents. Going forward, all statements in italics depict wording copied exactly as they appeared in the file I received from the FBI.

It was interesting seeing the way the FBI system treated Slava as an immigrant from Russia in the 1980s. Perhaps they still follow the same process with immigrants, but I can only address what I viewed in this particular file. From what I read, after Slava entered the US in 1981, it appears he became a target of what seemed to be a routine investigation. According to the documentation in the file, *"The FBI case was opened on referral from Immigration and Naturalization Service (INS), who advised subject had lived in a priority country."* In some places in the reports, Russia is also referred to as *a category country.* Slava is the "subject" throughout the reports.

Although heavily redacted, it appears all of Slava's family members were identified and underwent full FBI vetting. The FBI's review of the interview between INS and Slava gave the following information. *"Reason for leaving USSR: 'I don't agree with the political system in the USSR.'"* (Slava's recorded response.) The case was subsequently closed with the FBI having no concerns about Slava's entry into the US. It was surreal to be reading about Slava's life in this way and to read the exact words he spoke so many years ago.

In 1995, there is further documentation which lists three businesses owned by Slava, as well as Small World. Two of the businesses I never heard him mention. There are pages that disclose the value of the home he purchased, the taxes he paid, and even a description of the house. In this group of reports, there is a line that states, *"Specific Info Desired."* Someone, presumably an FBI agent, had hand written next to the inquiry, *"Residences & Business Locations, Any information on other family members in particular."* One un-redacted quote in the reports states, *"A computer check of the subject's residence, revealed the following information: Several individuals listed this address as their destination on their I-94s."* All names are redacted. The INS form I-94 is the visa allowing foreigners to enter the US. The FBI was clearly interested in the visitors Slava had invited from foreign countries.

There were several pages discussing the circumstances and locations of some of the people Slava had sponsored to come to the US. Some of the investigation centered more on the visitors than Slava. I had done visa invitations for hundreds of visitors but had always used our office address and our agency name as the sponsoring entity. It was clear, after reviewing the FBI documents, that Slava had completed a number of visa invitations on his own, utilizing either his home address or the address of his surgical center as the sponsoring address. Some of this investigation was also looking into Slava's import business.

As I was going through page after page of mostly meaningless, nearly totally, redacted documents, my heart skipped a beat when I turned to the page that was an official "FBI Investigative Request Form" for information related to Small World Adoption Foundation. The form requested information: *1) Who is associated with specific telephone numbers, 2) Determine address of business, 3) Determine ownership of property, 4) Determine financial background, and 5) Determine Corporate business info.* This form was followed once again by pages of redacted information. I hardly slept that first night after reviewing those pages. I so desperately wanted to understand what it all meant, but recognized that those answers wouldn't be available until 2035. I can't succinctly summarize my emotions as I read through the pages and pages of FBI reports. It was a combination of many things; confusion, loss, grief, anger, disappointment, but more than anything else it was once again profound and overwhelming sadness.

I came across a report dated June 27, 1995, depicting the FBI's attempts to contact Slava to interview him, *"Several attempts to contact subject have in the past proved negative."* The report further explained that Slava had finally agreed to be interviewed, but the meeting would need to wait until he returned from a trip he was making to Atlanta. Slava knew he was being investigated! Yet he never said a word about it to me. He shared so much with me, it was nearly impossible to believe that he kept this secret. On January 30, 1996, a form closed this investigation. For what had the FBI been searching?

Suddenly, I remembered sometime in the first couple of years I was working with Slava, one of our clients came into the office with quite a story. The client stated she had been at a St. Louis Cardinal's baseball game and two FBI agents sitting behind her were whispering to one another about Small World and Slava. I totally brushed off her comments and made some excuse in my head for what she had overheard. I can't explain my failure to listen and really hear her words, other than my complete blind faith in Slava.

The next time the FBI stepped back into Slava's life was on August 24, 1999. A report described a process of adding Slava to an existing investigation. The report states that the title of the document was being *"changed" to reflect the addition of subjects* _____ *and Viacheslav Platonov*. The form approves expenditures for an agent from a redacted city to come to St. Louis for the investigation. A subsequent page states, *in view of the success that Source has experienced in St. Louis, it is proposed that Source again visit St. Louis for the purpose of meeting with* _____ *to discuss details of (redacted area).*

Tears came to my eyes as I read the next pages. *On* _____ *a confidential Source who is in a position to testify, was contacted by the reporting Agent immediately following a meeting with* _____. *This meeting was consensually monitored and recorded by the reporting Agent utilizing a closed-circuit television. It should be noted that the language utilized during this meeting was Russian. The confidential Source provided the following information concerning the content of Source's conversation with* _____. (Redacted area.) How could these conversations have been about activities of the same person I worked with and spoke with every day? It also became evident to me that at least one of the FBI agents spoke fluent Russian.

"Source indicated that… (redacted space)… advised that Slava Platonov ran an adoption agency and that he was 'moving kids from Russia.'" This statement was followed by several pages of references to recorded telephone conversations.

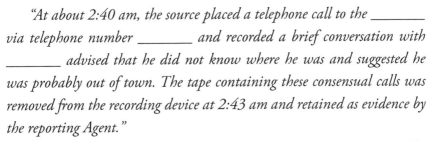

"At about 2:40 am, the source placed a telephone call to the _____ via telephone number _____ and recorded a brief conversation with _____ advised that he did not know where he was and suggested he was probably out of town. The tape containing these consensual calls was removed from the recording device at 2:43 am and retained as evidence by the reporting Agent."

The shock of what I read continued the assault on my already terribly bruised, battered, and sad soul. Documentation dated January 13, 2000, announced a Priority Investigation was opened by the Organized Crime Section – Eurasian Unit! Here it was in black and white. A reference was made to "organized crime," which had first been mentioned to me by the FBI agent, Tom, following Slava's death.

"Sometime after this exchange with _____ Source was approached by Viacheslav Platonov. Platonov greeted Source and suggested that Source try a particular fish dish which was being prepared that evening, Source ordered this dish and Platonov left the Source shortly thereafter. (Redacted area) At this point, Source left Zhivago's Restaurant."

"It should be noted that Source was contacted at a predesignated location shortly after leaving Zhivago's Restaurant and a fresh cassette tape was placed in the recording device on the Source's person." The Source then went to a restaurant called Le Haim, after which the report contained large redacted sections.

Since this information was provided to me through a FOIA request regarding investigations into Slava, it was clear that this information was about him. The next staggering tidbit I read was: *"Details: On January 13, 2000, St. Louis SAC (redacted name) approved a (redacted space) directed at the criminal activities of suspected Russian mafia members living in the St. Louis metropolitan area. The (redacted space) will focus on Medicare fraud, drug trafficking, Immigration, and Naturalization Service, fraud and prostitution. This (redacted space) will work in concert with a (redacted space) operating in Houston that also is targeting Russian mafia members.*" I learned from my attorney, David, that SAC is an FBI term for Special Agent in Charge.

The information, though sketchy and incomplete, supported what the FBI agent had said to David and me in October of 2009, the FBI had believed Slava had a role in organized crime. At times, what I read so overwhelmed me I had to stop reading and go walk the dog or pour myself a glass of wine.

Following this stunning information were several pages, again primarily redacted, of a conversation between Slava and an FBI agent who was wearing a recording device. It is not clear from the information provided if Slava knew he was speaking with an FBI agent or not.

"At approximately 10:00 PM, Viacheslav Platonov, herein after referred as "Slava," came to (…large area of redaction…)."

"Slava said he didn't do that and that he was a doctor. He advised he had a practice in St. Louis and he was making money by working as a doctor. Slava said the restaurant was just for fun and he was not making any money on it. Slava said his restaurant was a very clean operation, everything was according to law, and that everybody was paying taxes." (redacted area)

"Slava said he knew a lot of people in Russia, Ukraine, Moscow, St. Petersburg, and in south of Russia."

(redacted area)

"Slava advised he didn't do business in Russia, because a lot of people lost their money. Slava recalled 'black Tuesday,' the day the Russian currency crashed. Slava said that he and his friends lost all of their profit and barely got out. Slava advised he and his friends were buying some product in Poland and moving it to Russia and they were doing very good. Slava conveyed he had a pension fund, which was invested in the stock market, and his practice was very secure, and he was a man of very small desires, and not after big money." (redacted area)

"Slava said he had lot of friends, high-level people in Russia, including the Prime Minister (Vladimir Putin), also the Prime Minister's right-hand man who was a good friend of Slava and with whom Slava attended school.

Slava also said he knew the mayor of St. Petersburg and mayor's wife." (large redacted area)

"Slava said a restaurant business was for someone with a lot of cash, because you can clear it through the books very fast. Slava said he doesn't have the cash, but if someone had a lot of cash and wanted to launder to become legit, then the restaurant business was very good for that. Slava said if someone owns a restaurant, people assume that is was used for laundering money."

The next section was comprised of pages of redacted comments from a confidential source.

In April of 2000, there is a report, again nearly completely redacted, which discusses trips and interviews with subjects in San Antonio, Texas. This is followed by several more pages of conversations between a confidential source and someone in Zhivago's restaurant. The confidential source was asked to identify some photographs of people. Some of the descriptions of phone calls were at odd times, such as 4:30 in the morning.

It was evident that at least one of the confidential sources was a Russian speaking person because one of the reports is described as a rough translation of the source's words. It further became clear to me that a Russian person, in whom I am sure Slava had placed his trust, had turned into an FBI informant.

The next set of reports began in September of 2000.

"On (redacted space) a confidential Source, who is not in a position to testify, provided the following information to the reporting agent: Source visited Zhivago's Restaurant on Saturday evening, (redacted space). Source learned through conversation with the bartender that Slava Platonov was returning from Frankfort, Germany late that evening. Platonov has a new partner in the restaurant which the bartender pointed out to the Source. The bartender did not identify this individual by name. Source described this individual as being a white male in his late 40s, have short blond hair. Source further described this individual as barrel chested and being heavy."

"Source visited the club and advised that there were a lot of unusual activity and people in the club."

The club being referred to here is the Enigma Lounge, located on the bottom floor of the building, right below Zhivago's.

Following a few more redacted pages regarding conversations taking place at Zhivago's, the following was revealed. *"On (redacted space) Source, who is not in a position to testify, provided the following information: Source advised that (redacted space) assisted Russian emigres with (redacted space) assisted other illegal aliens by (redacted space)."*

"Source identified (redacted space) Last Name Unknown (LNU) as an individual who sold heroin, cocaine, and ecstasy to young adults in Creve Coeur, Maryland Heights, Chesterfield, and Manchester, MO. Source advised that (redacted space) LNU either owned or managed a (redacted space) located at the (redacted space) Creve Coeur, Missouri. (redacted space) and (redacted space) also sell ecstasy tablets in the same areas."

"Source stated that (large redacted space) Platonov's (redacted space) LNU, is an illegal alien who (redacted space). (redacted space) plans on residing in United States when her visa expires."

"Source advised that (redacted space) is a prostitute and is approximately (redacted space) prostituted from (redacted space) conducting out-service calls."

"Source identified the Enigma Night Club as a club where ecstasy is sold on Thursday, Friday, and Saturday nights. The club managed by an unidentified (redacted space) also known as (redacted space)." This is followed by several more pages of redacted conversation with or about Slava.

"Source reviewed a number of driver's license photographs and identified the photograph of (redacted space). Source advised at this point that (redacted space) had (redacted space) the previous evening at Zhivago's Restaurant. Source identified the driver's license photograph of Slava Platonov and also identified a driver's license photograph of (redacted space)."

In subsequent pages, a confidential source provided to the FBI a number of business cards collected throughout an evening at Zhivago's and Enigma.

It is clear that the confidential sources referred to in the FOIA documents were a number of different people. Sometimes a report would say the "source can testify" and other times the source would be labeled "not able to testify," some of the reports required translation, others not. Why were some able to testify and others not?

In a document dated April 19, 2001, *"Platonov told Source that the Spa of Eden earns $3,000 to $4,000 per week in proceeds. Source advised that Platonov sells imported Russian diamonds to a jewelry store, believed to be near the intersection of MO Highway 141 and Manchester Road."* He never mentioned anything to me about this! I had been involved in helping him with other business –but never anything to do with diamonds.

A report dated April 20, 2001, *"A confidential Source, who is in a position to testify, provided the following information to the reporting agent: Source visited Zhivago's Restaurant the previous Friday evening and had a conversation with (redacted space) advised Source that it is common belief among the employees at Zhivago's that (redacted space) was approached by INS agents and IRS agents to provide information regarding Slava Platonov. Slava Platonov is looking for (redacted space) and wants to talk to him."*

"Source learned this from (redacted space) moved out of his apartment."

"Source reports Slava Platonov appears to have a new "right hand" man who is from the Ukraine and runs the night club in the basement of Zhivago's Restaurant. This individual is also active in finding children in the Ukraine for adoption in the United States and first worked as a cab driver."

This was the meager bit of information that could be gleaned from over 150 pages of agents' reports I received from the FBI through our FOIA request. Although disappointing because so much of it was redacted, it is easy to see that something nefarious was going on and I had been completely blind to all of it. I dined regularly at Zhivago's and had visited the lounge downstairs. I never had any indication that there was anything illegal going on.

The restaurant did close, but would that have been the end of the investigation? I now have many more unanswered questions than I had before.

However, this small amount of documentation I received from the FBI confirms what David and I were told so many years ago in our final meeting with the FBI in his office. I hadn't wanted to believe it, but now it had been laid out in black and white – there was no escaping the truth, Slava had been involved in illegal activities, and most likely those activities were tied into organized crime. I eagerly await the remaining FOIA documents.

I began to question myself. If Slava had been doing something illegal at Zhivago's and Enigma, what was the truth about Small World? I had learned firsthand that good and evil don't always operate independently, sometimes they are as intertwined as the threads of a sweater.

The End

This was never just a story, it was my life, and I realized that I had been an ordinary person who was placed in extraordinary circumstances. I didn't begin working on this book for several years after walking away from Small World. When I left, I suspected that the adoption program in Russia, which had been unstable for the past year, was headed for complete and permanent closure. That did happen, as I anticipated, in a little less than two years. I hadn't wanted to write anything that might endanger the possibility of more orphaned Russian children finding their ways to loving homes in America. Small World remained open for about eighteen months after I left, and I hadn't been able to write about it while it remained in business. It had been my baby, with Slava, and I needed it to be as deceased as he before I began telling its story. Additionally, I needed both of my parents to be either deceased or infirm to the point of an inability to comprehend my words, before publishing my book. I was never looking for vengeance and never wanted to hurt either of them.

I felt writing my story would be a cathartic exercise that would help me finally put these chapters of my life to rest, and I learned a lot as I put my thoughts and feelings into words. I needed to understand motivations and to put the experience into a perspective that made sense to me. I learned that many of the actions, and more importantly my failure to have a clear vision, to take action or take a stand, stemmed from the trauma of the first eighteen years of my life. My abusive childhood made me a perfect victim for someone seeking another to manipulate and my need for acceptance perhaps prevented me from seeing things clearly. This realization moved me to share my story with others to remind people of the damage done to children by abuse, failing to build a positive self-esteem in them, failing to protect and love them, and failing to make them feel valuable.

I overcame those childhood horrors, but I could have just as easily gone down a destructive path. We have to do better as a society for the children whom God has graciously given us. When you put my book down, go hug your children, or call them and remind them that you love them, and always cherish them for the wondrous gifts they are. It is the responsibility of every adult to report incidences of abuse and/or neglect to the authorities. Confidential reports may be made by phoning: 1-800-4-A-Child (1-800-422-4453)

And, I want to empower those who have suffered at the hands of another. People suffer traumatic life experiences, huge disappointments and challenges, and even events that totally shatter them, but it is up to the survivors to choose what to do about those experiences. We owe it to ourselves and to those that love us to forgive others, move forward, and make the most of life. When you have the choice to choose the light, take it. Life is too short to allow bitterness to occupy even one tiny cell in our brains. I believe we should all be grateful for what we have, be kind to others, give of ourselves, and be thankful to God.

I still have many questions remaining. Perhaps one day I will find more answers in the remaining FOIA responses.

People have asked me if I would have changed any aspect of my life. The answer is no. My childhood experiences gave me the internal fortitude to fight a foreign country for my own child, then enabled me to play a primary role in the rescue of 1800 Eastern European orphans, and finally to move on to positively impact thousands of American youth in foster care. I have been blessed to be able to truly make a difference in the lives of children and families and I believe I helped to make the world a better place. I could have received no greater gift than the opportunities that have been bestowed upon me.

ACKNOWLEDGEMENTS

THERE ARE MANY PEOPLE TO whom I owe much. The support for this daunting endeavor was unbelievable. The first person to whom I owe bushels of thanks is my daughter, Laura, who was the true hero in this story. Laura's husband, Kris, gave me writing advice. My son, Ryan, and daughter-in-law, Rachel, cheered for me and inspired me and never let me quit, even when I really wanted to! Without my son, Alex, most likely none of this would have happened, and I am eternally grateful for and to him.

Laura's Godmother and my dear friend, Anne Aycock, first planted the seeds for this book 30 years ago and then convinced me I could write it. She was the first one to read the truly raw version and gave input. She deserves my deepest gratitude for always believing in me.

I am thankful to my three dear friends, Marcia Levin, Maureen Franklyn, and Tanya Duchild, who worked with me, cried with me, and propped me up when I needed it. Marcia was one of my amazingly honest and forthright proof readers, being the consummate fact checker. I would never have made it through many of the things described in this book without both Marcia and Maureen. They became members of my family, my best friends and sisters in the truest sense of the word, "loving aunties" to all three of my children, and true Godsends in my life.

Thanks also to other dear friends, proof readers, and fact checkers; Tina Dalpiaz, Dave Gilles, Kim Groneck, Michael McLaughlin, Art Henn, Kelly Trainor, and Donna Ward. Meghan Beverage was my final and fabulous editor, and this book wouldn't be what it is without her tremendous talent and expeditious efforts!

Jim and Lois, my former in-laws, hold a special place in my heart for not only believing in me regarding this book, but believing in me since I was nineteen years old. You showed me what it was like to be truly loved and helped me to be a wonderful parent myself. I owe you so much! Thank you.

I am thankful to my attorney and dear friend, David Korum, who spent hours with me in FBI interviews, oversaw the submission of the FOIA requests, and who provided me guidance when I didn't know who I could trust or what to do next.

Thanks to Small World clients/friends Tracy Stamper and Tom Barkman. Tom, a professional photographer, provided some of the photographs for the book taken during his travels to Russia when he and Tracy adopted their son.

I am filled with gratitude to Denise, Jayne, and Becca, who joined me in Hungary when we were working so hard to free the *Szeged 28* – love you guys, it all started with us!

There were many other friends who gave me help, supported me, and truly inspired me throughout this process and I have to thank a few of them; thanks to Dave, Cathy, Michael, and Tana Gilles; Ken, Kelly, Dennis, Anna, and Leeza Trainor; Phil, Jeni, Maddy, Duncan, Bryn, and Grant Corbin; Bob, Michelle, Alex, Josh, Matt, Gracie, Becca, Jon, Zach, and T.J. Ritter; my (normal) Pokeno buddies; Tonya, Pam, Mary, Maureen, Laura, and Kim; and the many other wonderful people, too many to name. Extra thanks to Phil for also providing some of the pictures.

Thanks to Small World clients Mike and Martha Hogan and their family for allowing me to share the beautiful page from their journal for Andrei!

United States Attorney Jeff Jensen deserves a shout out for the support he gave me during the Small World investigation and then later connecting me to the Victim's Rights Counselor, Kimberly Sanders, who assisted us with the FOIA requests. Also, thanks to Kimberly!

Thanks to my husband, Mark, for standing next to me while I worked hard to finish this book.

Lastly, my most heartfelt thanks go to the 1800 Small World children and their parents, who allowed me to play a role in their lives. It was an extraordinary opportunity, and one for which I am most grateful. Many of you came into my life for only a moment. Some of you have stayed forever. Regardless, blessings and love to all of you.